Confronting Power
The Practice of Policy Advocacy

CONFRONTING POWER
THE PRACTICE OF POLICY ADVOCACY

JEFF UNSICKER

Kumarian Press

An Imprint of Stylus Publishing

Sterling, Virginia

Published by Stylus Publishing, LLC
22883 Quicksilver Drive
Sterling, Virginia 20166-2102

Design by Pro Production Graphic Services
Copyedit by Rose Marye Boudreaux
Proofread by Beth Richards
Index by Robert Swanson
The text of this book is set in 11/13 Adobe Garamond

Library of Congress Cataloging-in-Publication Data
Unsicker, Jeff, 1950–
    Confronting power : the practice of policy advocacy / Jeff Unsicker. — 1st ed.
        p. cm.
    Includes bibliographical references and index.
    ISBN 978-1-56549-533-3 (cloth : alk. paper) — ISBN 978-1-56549-534-0
    (pbk. : alk. paper) — ISBN 978-1-56549-535-7 (library networkable e-edition) —
    ISBN 978-1-56549-536-4 (consumer e-edition)
    1. Social policy—Citizen participation. 2. Social planning—Citizen participation.
3. Political planning—Citizen participation. 4. Social advocacy. 5. Social change.
I. Title.
    HN18.3.U57   2012
    303.3—dc23
                                                                        2012008419
13-digit ISBN: 978-1-56549-533-3 (cloth)
13-digit ISBN: 978-1-56549-534-0 (paper)
13-digit ISBN: 978-1-56549-535-7 (library networkable e-edition)
13-digit ISBN: 978-1-56549-536-4 (consumer e-edition)

Printed in the United States of America

∞ All first editions printed on acid-free paper that meets the American National Standards Institute Z39-48 Standard.

Bulk Purchases

Quantity discounts are available for use in workshops and for staff development.

Call 1-800-232-0223

First Edition, 2013

    10 9 8 7 6 5 4 3 2 1

For Ruth Ann and our sons, Neill and Michael

Contents

Acknowledgments

Countless others contributed to the ideas contained in this book and to the effort to produce it. I have had the privilege to work with and learn from many advocates, far too many to list here. However, several deserve special mention. My first introduction to policy advocacy was as a young staff member with the Community Congress of San Diego, California, where I was mentored by Anne Dosher and John Wedemeyer. Through several partnerships between the SIT Graduate Institute and the Advocacy Institute (AI) in Washington, DC, I had the good fortune to work closely with David Cohen and his colleagues at AI; David is a role model and inspiration to many of us. I have learned a great deal from reading and annually rereading the work of Jim Shultz, Lisa VeneKlasen, and Valerie Miller, excellent advocates as well as the authors of the primary texts that I have used in my policy advocacy courses at SIT. Their impact on my thinking is evident throughout this book.

My multiyear involvement in the advocacy movement to close and replace the Vermont Yankee Nuclear Power Plant has provided an opportunity to learn with those who have been leading the fight for decades, of whom Deb Katz, director of the Citizens Awareness Network, deserves special mention, and with a group of young, talented advocates such as James Moore of the Vermont Public Interest Group. We all owe a great debt to our important allies in the Vermont legislature, especially representative Sarah Edwards, senator Jeanette White, and former senator and now governor Peter Shumlin.

The case study of BRAC advocacy unit in Bangladesh was made possible by long-term collaboration and friendships that grew out of a joint program in Nongovernmental Leadership and Management. Particularly important have been close friend and colleague Samdani Fakir, Salehuddin Ahmed, and Sheepa Hafiza. I am grateful for all the support I received from Mojibul Huq and many other members of Sheepa's unit. The case studies of Oxfam America's Climate Change Campaign were made possible by Kent Genzler, who was director of Oxfam America's Learning, Evaluation, and Accountability Department, and the close collaboration with Gabrielle Watson—the campaign's "embedded evaluator." I learned a great deal through interviews with dozens of Oxfam staff, including members of the campaign team led by Vicky Rateau, and others in the Policy and Campaigns Division led by Paul O'Brien. The case study of Kids Are Priority One Coalition is based on class sessions that Kim Friedman has led on multiple occasions; along with the students, I have learned a lot from her about the role of message framing.

The consultancies with BRAC and Oxfam were feasible because of my sabbatical leave from SIT. Adam Weinberg, former provost and now president of SIT and World Learning, ensured the approval and funding. My faculty and staff colleagues in the SIT Graduate Institute are a constant source of learning and inspiration. I have learned much about policy analysis from Nikoi Kote-Nikoi as we developed SIT's concentration in Policy Analysis and Advocacy and many times cotaught one of its courses. I also learned much from my faculty colleagues who were part of the team that designed and facilitated Leadership for Social Justice Institutes for the Ford Foundation International Fellowship Program, and with whom I coauthored a resource book on the topic: Aqeel Tirmizi, Maliha Khan, Marla Solomon, and Ken Williams.

Without a doubt, my greatest debt is to the SIT students who have been in my courses and did professional practicum placements in the field of policy advocacy. I have learned a lot from their experiences from around the world, and am always inspired by their deep commitment to just and sustainable social change. Most of the content in the book has emerged through my efforts to synthesize our different experiences and the relevant literature so they develop the analytical skills of highly effective advocates. I am deeply proud of how so many are using those skills as citizens, staff, and managers of community programs and, in many cases, as full-time advocates. Sixteen of those former students volunteered to read and provide input on various chapters of the book. They are Becca Young, Chad Simmons, Christine Meissner, Dinah Frey, Dylan Kreis, Erin Peot, Genet Hunegnaw, Jessy Needham, Kendra Pierre-Louis, Kimberly Calkins, Laura Raymond, Mandy Park, Marni

Salmon, Megan Fletcher, Tony Baker, and Will Fenton. The case study of the Tambogrande Defense Front in Peru is based on the capstone paper of yet another former student, Rosa Maria Olortegui, who also served as a teaching assistant during her second year of studies. Susal Stebbins-Collins, another student and former teaching assistant, who is also a very experienced advocate, read most of the book in often rough draft form and provided numerous insights and editorial comments.

As the manuscript was being transformed into a book, Kumarian Press publisher Jim Lance, production editor Alexandra Hartnett, and content editor Rose Marye Boudreaux were immensely helpful.

To all of them and to so many who go unnamed, thank you so very much.

PART ONE

1

Introduction

IN PERU, THE CITIZENS OF TAMBOGRANDE FORM A "DEFENSE FRONT" TO BLOCK A multinational corporation from digging an open pit mine in the middle of their town.

In Bangladesh, one of the world's largest development nongovernmental organizations (NGOs) builds capacity to influence policy makers and government officials regarding the needs and rights of the rural poor, migrant workers, and other vulnerable groups.

In Ghana, a policy think tank researches the impact of HIV/AIDS on the country's economy, and working with allies within NGOs and civil society, the media, various international donors, and government agencies persuades policy makers to create a national commission to combat the spread of the disease.

In the United States, citizen associations, public interest groups, and environmental organizations in Vermont organize to replace a forty-year-old nuclear power plant with safe and green alternatives, while other Vermont organizations convince the state legislature to increase funding for early childhood education.

The US affiliate of a global NGO helps convince members of the US House of Representatives to expand funding for poor countries that are most affected by rising sea levels, droughts, floods, and other consequences of climate change.

These citizens, associations, organizations, networks, and coalitions are practicing policy advocacy, one method for social change committed to the needs and rights of people and the planet. It focuses on different problems and issues in different parts of the world, applied at multiple levels from local to global.

I have been involved in policy advocacy campaigns and initiatives for nearly four decades (including the campaign to replace Vermont's nuclear power reactor [see Case B in chapter 3, pages 51–57]). During many of those years I have also been involved in the systematization and sharing of knowledge about policy advocacy. My first experience was from 1974 to 1980 as the primary facilitator for sessions on policy advocacy during a year-long leadership education program for staff of community-based human service and social action organizations in San Diego, California. Most recently, as a professor of sustainable development at the SIT Graduate Institute in Vermont, I have regularly taught a course on policy advocacy for experienced and aspiring social justice professionals from the United States and around the world.

This book is an effort to share what I have been learning with a broader audience. It provides resources—general concepts and specific case examples—which are useful for two targeted audiences:

- advocates who are engaged in planning, conducting, evaluating, and learning from their own campaigns and initiatives; and
- students who wish to understand and become (more) deeply involved in policy advocacy work.

Defining *Policy Advocacy*

While there are many appropriate definitions, I use the following definition:

> *Policy advocacy is the process by which people, NGOs, other civil society organizations, networks, and coalitions seek to enhance social and economic justice, environmental sustainability, and peace by influencing policies, policy implementation, and policy-making processes of governments, corporations, and other powerful institutions.*

This is a value-laden and somewhat dense definition. In this chapter I briefly discuss the definition's components as an initial introduction to policy advocacy.

But first it is helpful to point out that other terms are often used for *policy advocacy*. For example, many Europeans refer to it as "campaigning" or "policy influencing," and the term *public interest lobbying* is used by many in the United States for what I am calling policy advocacy. No term is more correct than another. Effective advocates need to be able to differentiate an activity from the words used to describe it, as well as to clarify the language they are using. To that end, in this book, *campaign* is used in a more limited sense to describe a focused advocacy initiative rather than the entire field of practice. *Lobbying* is used to describe only the element of an advocacy initiative that involves direct communication with policy makers. Moreover, while *advocacy* is very often used to describe actions that are outside my definition, in this book it is simply used as a shortened version of *policy advocacy.*[1]

With that understanding, we return to the definition and the meaning of its terminology. The following highlights one element of the definition: the advocates.

> Policy advocacy is the process by which **people, NGOs, other civil society organizations, networks, and coalitions** seek to attain political, economic, cultural, and environmental rights by influencing policies, policy implementation, and policy-making processes of governments, corporations, and other powerful institutions.

Who the advocates are will vary depending on who is affected by a policy, if and how those people are organized, and if yet others are committed to working with or for them. In some situations, where advocacy focuses on the policies of institutions that are relatively small and accessible (for example, a local government body), one individual or a small loosely organized group can successfully influence policy. However, in most situations, successful advocacy requires one or more formal organizations, often working together through networks and coalitions.

There is great variety in the types of organizations involved in advocacy, ranging from those formed and controlled by people affected by a policy to outside organizations with useful technical knowledge and skills. Some of those organizations are solely committed to policy advocacy; others also provide services or carry out other functions. Indeed, many problems can only be solved through a combination of policy advocacy and other activities, such as health services or consumer education.

Some organizations have many staff dedicated to this work, often with specializations in different aspects of advocacy (research, organizing, media, lobbying, etc.). Other organizations have no designated staff for advocacy and rely totally on board members, executives, program managers, and professional staff to do advocacy alongside their other duties. Still other organizations have no staff and rely completely on citizen volunteers.

The following highlights the *purpose* of policy advocacy.

> *Policy advocacy is the process by which individuals, NGOs, other civil society organizations, networks, and coalitions seek to build **social and economic justice, environmental sustainability, and peace** by influencing policies, policy implementation, and policy-making processes of governments, corporations, and other powerful institutions.*

The purpose is what advocates seek to build, protect, and expand. One could choose other terms to describe that purpose, for example, "political, economic, cultural, and environmental rights." But whatever words are chosen, it is important to recognize that advocacy begins with the advocates' vision of a better world. Efforts to realize that vision can focus on one or a combination of many different issues, such as halting construction of an open pit mine in the middle of a small town or passing legislation that will provide aid to regions most affected by global warming. What they have in common is a commitment to challenge the power of self-interested elites in order to protect and enhance the interests of the general public—especially those parts of the public that have been socially, politically, and economically marginalized—and of nature.[2]

The following highlights what are often referred to as the targets of policy advocacy—the *powerful institutions* that advocates must influence to achieve their purpose.

> *Policy advocacy is the process by which individuals, NGOs, other civil society organizations, networks, and coalitions seek to attain political, economic, cultural, and environmental rights by influencing policies, policy implementation, and policy-making processes of **governments, corporations, and other powerful institutions**.*

Frequently, decisions and actions by those institutions work against the public good. Yet the institutions also have the power to enable progress.

Advocacy often focuses on governments, including multigovernmental organizations such as the World Bank and corporations, since they are typically the world's most powerful institutions. However, many other institutions can be the focus of advocacy. For example, a college or university has significant power over the lives of its students and often influences the community where it is located. Even the executive board of a progressive citizens' association or trade union might become the focus of advocacy if it were to misuse its power and become unresponsive to its membership.

The following highlights what advocates seek to influence.

> *Policy advocacy is the process by which individuals, NGOs, other civil society organizations, networks, and coalitions seek to attain political, economic, cultural, and environmental rights by influencing **policies, policy implementation, and policy-making processes** of governments, corporations, and other powerful institutions.*

A policy, for our purposes, is any decision that guides the behavior of an institution of power.[3] Advocacy influences those institutions by influencing the *policies* those institutions enact. It also does so by influencing *policy implementation,* since too often policies are enacted that guarantee rights or are in the interest of the public and marginalized groups but then are not enforced or ever put into practice—at least not fully and effectively.

Moreover, advocacy efforts can sometimes influence powerful institutions through influencing their policies on *policy making,* that is, the decisions about what structures, systems, rules, and practices will guide the process by which institutions enact and implement policies. Policy advocates seek to ensure that those affected by an institution's policies may have a meaningful role in the policy-making process. This type of advocacy often focuses on policies related to public access to information, transparency, and active participation.

Since policies guide the behavior of various types of powerful institutions, they take many forms, which include constitutions, government laws and proclamations, and corporate guidelines. Budgets of governments (from national to local) and other powerful institutions are among the most powerful policies; they establish how and from whom resources will be secured, as well as how and in whose interests the funds will be spent. The judicial branch of government may make policies through precedent-setting decisions in court cases. Corporations make many policy decisions that have an impact on the public—what to sell, where to invest, whether and how to intervene in elections and policy making, and so forth. Financial aid eligibility requirements of colleges or universities are policies that strongly affect students and the institution. So too are the membership admission criteria for a citizens' association or trade union. What all these policies have in common is that they are decisions made by institutions that have a significant impact on the lives of others or on the environment.

The following highlights the fact that advocacy is a process of influencing policies.

> Policy advocacy is the **process** by which individuals, NGOs, other civil society organizations, networks, and coalitions seek to attain political, economic, cultural, and environmental rights by **influencing** policies, policy implementation, and policy-making processes of governments, corporations, and other powerful institutions.

As such, it can take many forms. While often associated with confrontation—for example, grassroots mobilization, boycotts, and street protests—in many situations advocacy involves more collaborative methods, such as educating political officials and forming partnerships with public institutions. Frequently, advocacy strategies employ a combination of confrontation and collaboration, either by design or because different advocacy groups choose to pursue different approaches, possibly at the risk of tensions among them. Whenever possible, the advocacy process should involve methods for raising political consciousness among the public or marginalized groups and building their capacity to be engaged in advocacy strategies. However, in every case, the process must include specific methods for *influencing* the person, people, or structures that will make a policy decision. The influence may be direct (for example, lobbying, letters, and petitions) or indirect (for example, media coverage and public opinion polls). The choices advocates make depend on multiple factors, including the historical moment, the distribution of power in society, the policy-making institutions, the specific policy issues, and the current political space for participation in policy making.

Chapters and Cases

Having offered a definition of *policy advocacy*, we now move to chapter 2, which focuses on conceptual maps and introduces four different ways to understand various elements of an advocacy campaign or initiative.

The fourth map, Advocacy Circles, is one that I developed through my teaching. It is discussed more thoroughly in chapter 3 and chapter 4. Preceding each of those chapters is a case study that grounds the conceptual framework in relation to the practice or experience of a specific advocacy campaign or initiative.

The next chapters, which constitute Part Two, go into more depth regarding aspects of policy advocacy that correspond to four circles in my conceptual map (advocates, policy, politics, and strategy) and to two related topics (advocacy communications and advocacy evaluation and learning). Each of those chapters has a corresponding case study. Each case is introduced prior to its chapter and poses a learning exercise. The remainder of the case follows the chapter and offers an opportunity to compare the reader's notes with what actually occurred.

The chapters are neither academic reviews of the relevant literature nor are they how-to guides; there are already many good resources of each. Rather, the topic of each chapter is covered by relying on one or a small number of readings I use in my courses. A number of those readings are chapters from two very useful books that I have used as course texts for the past five years: *The Democracy Owner's Manual* by Jim Shultz and *A New Weave of Power, People and Politics* by Lisa VeneKlasen with Valerie Miller.[4]

I also draw heavily on another very useful resource: *Advocacy for Social Justice* by David Cohen, Rosa de la Vega, and Gabrielle Watson.[5] I have known David Cohen for many years and had the privilege of working closely with him for five years on a series of leadership for social justice institutes. They were cosponsored by SIT and the Advocacy Institute in Washington, DC, which David Cohen cofounded as a way to share what he had learned through his work as a national leader in public interest advocacy. His experience and wisdom are why many of us consider him the "dean of advocacy." Thus it is fitting to close this introduction with some of his advice:

> There is value in getting started. Nothing teaches more than experience, whether it is new skills being learned or confidence built to overcome the risks inherent in social change. When getting started, people must avoid getting paralyzed by the need for comprehensive, systemic change. One rarely goes from "what is" to "what should be" in a single leap. . . . Rather they are realized through a long-term incremental process that keeps sight of a larger vision. Small changes and ongoing activities are vital.[6]

Notes

1. *Advocacy* is used to describe a wide range of efforts to promote a position or cause, which may or may not include promoting change in policy. For example, *advocacy* is commonly used to describe the arguments made by an individual in the context of a discussion or debate that has nothing to do with policy change. Thus, *policy advocacy* as used here is only one type of advocacy. On the other hand, advocacy is closely associated with professionals who advocate on someone else's behalf. Lawyers, who are advocates in many countries, represent clients in matters of law, including in courtrooms, where they are incapable of representing themselves. In the social welfare professions in the United States and other countries, advocates (or *client* advocates) represent individuals who do not know how to access services they are entitled to under existing policies and programs.

2. The focus on *rights* is one way that policy advocacy, as defined in this book, excludes efforts by the elite or their representatives to influence public policy. The elite do use many of the same advocacy methods (media, lobbying, etc). But, to support those methods, the elite almost always have far greater access to financial and other resources than do advocates, especially those advocates who are from or working for the poor and marginalized groups in society. However, the primary difference is regarding goals: this book focuses on advocacy for the public interest, on efforts to gain and protect political, economic, sociocultural, and environmental rights; it does not include efforts by the elite to protect or expand their own self-interests.

3. Less formal organizations and even individuals can formulate policies defined this broadly (for example, "It is my policy to get up by 6:30 a.m. every morning."), but advocacy is focused on those institutions that have an impact on a significant number of others.

4. Jim Shultz, *The Democracy Owner's Manual: A Practical Guide to Changing the World* (New Brunswick, NJ: Rutgers University Press, 2002); Lisa Vene-Klasen with Valerie Miller, *A New Weave of Power, People and Politics: The Action Guide for Advocacy and Citizen Participation* (Warwickshire, UK: Practical Action Publishers, 2007).

5. David Cohen, Rosa de la Vega, and Gabrielle Watson, *Advocacy for Social Justice: A Global Action and Reflection Guide* (Bloomfield, CT: Kumarian Press, 2001).

6. David Cohen, *Advocacy for Social Justice,* 4.

2

Conceptual Maps

A GOOD CONCEPTUAL MAP OR FRAMEWORK HELPS SIMPLIFY AND FIND ORDER WITHIN
the complex web of people, institutions, ideas, and power that shape
policy advocacy efforts. Thus, if well used, a map can be an invaluable
tool for planning, implementing, evaluating, and learning from an
advocacy campaign or initiative.

However, it is important to be mindful that, in the language of the
noted linguist and philosopher Alfred Korzybski, "the map is not the
territory."[1] Language is not the same as the reality it is used to describe.
The complex reality or territory of advocacy work is not the same as any
one conceptual map.

Therefore highly effective advocates have several conceptual maps
that allow them to simplify or find order in different aspects of their
work. In this way, they are similar to someone who might have different maps of the city where that person lives. One of the maps shows the
streets and bus lines, another is topographical, another highlights famous tourist spots (pulled out when hosting out-of-town visitors), and
yet another is a hand-drawn map given to new friends when invited over.
While of course there is only one physical reality of the city—the intersections, hills, museums, homes, and so forth are there no matter which
map is used—each map illuminates some dimension of that reality in a
way that helps with life in the city.

For this reason, when teaching policy advocacy, I introduce a number of conceptual maps. Each illuminates certain dimensions of the complex, real world of advocacy campaigns and initiatives. Each also omits
or obscures some dimensions. As long as one knows when and how to

use each one (a topographical map is generally not the best choice when trying to find a bus stop or museum), they become essential tools for observing, thinking about, and doing advocacy.

In fact, I argue that the ability to use multiple maps or frameworks is one of the key competencies that distinguishes a well-educated advocate from someone who is limited to a single framework learned in a training workshop or from a manual or any other single source.

This chapter presents a brief overview of four different maps. The first three were developed by other experienced advocates who have done extensive work in reflection, synthesis, and capacity building with organizations and movements engaged in advocacy and social change.[2] The fourth is a map I have developed. The maps are then compared and contrasted with a focus on how each might be used for analysis and action. In chapters 3 and 4, the advocacy circles map is discussed in more detail and it is then used as a framework for the remainder of the book.

Advocacy's Road Map

The first map is from the *Democracy Owner's Manual* by Jim Shultz.[3] It grew out of his extensive experience as an advocate, consultant, and trainer with public interest organizations and coalitions in the United States. Shultz is the founder of the Democracy Center, now based in Cochabamba, Bolivia.[4]

Like most conceptual maps of advocacy, including most of those in manuals and tool kits used by advocacy groups, Shultz's road map (see figure 2.1) is linear in that it depicts the process as a sequential series of steps or phases.

Objectives, according to Shultz, are the advocates' answer to the question, What do we want? Good objectives emerge through a process that is "half policy analysis, half political intuition." They are "dramatic and compelling," "small enough to achieve something of value in a reasonable time," and "lay the groundwork for future advocacy."[5]

Figure 2.1 Advocacy's road map

Objectives → Target Audiences → Messages → Messengers → Taking Action

Source: Jim Shultz, *The Democracy Owner's Manual: A Practical Guide to Changing the World* (New Brunswick, NJ: Rutgers University Press, 2002), 71–81.

Target audiences are defined by answering the question, Who do we need to move? They include the person or people who will make the decision to implement (or not implement) the change the advocates want; Shultz refers to them as the "primary targets." Other audiences include all the actors who might influence the primary target(s), for example, their key allies and supporters, opponents, media, various community and political organizations; Shultz refers to them as the "secondary targets."[6]

Messages are the answer to the question, What do your target audiences need to hear? They become the "campaign's mantra, repeated over and over again every chance [the advocates] get."[7]

Messengers are people identified by asking, From whom do they need to hear it? In effective advocacy, there is often "a mix of messengers, people who can give their points a combination of human sympathy, expert credibility, and political clout."[8]

Taking Action is the final step in Shultz's road map. "With your objectives, your targets, your messages, and your messengers clear, it is time to settle on the concrete actions that will make you heard and get the powers involved to move. . . . These range from gentle to in-your-face, from lobbying to media work to protest. Which one to pick depends on the situation, but as a rule it's best to take those actions that involve the least work and the least confrontation but still get the job done."[9]

Advocacy Process and Strategy Development

The second map is from *The Advocacy Sourcebook* by Jane Covey and Valerie Miller and draws primarily on their experiences in the Global South.[10] Published in 1997 by the former Institute for Development Research, it was one of the first comprehensive resources in the field.

As do many others, this map depicts a sequence of steps, this one consisting of nine, that are part of a cyclical process (see figure 2.2).

Societal vision, according to Covey and Miller, is the advocates' "long-term vision of the ideal society" and is important for establishing overall goals for social change.[11]

Macro analysis requires the advocates to research and understand the "macro forces and power relations that will be affecting their advocacy."[12] One example is mapping the relative strength and power of civil society, the state, and the market.

Problem analysis begins with needs assessments, participatory research, participatory rapid appraisals, and similar methods. "By involving

Figure 2.2 Advocacy process and strategy development

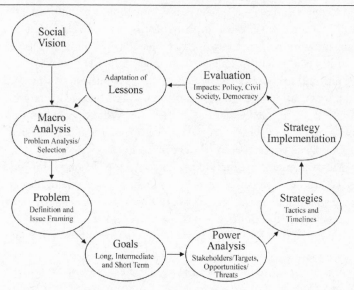

Source: Jane Covey and Valerie Miller, *Advocacy Sourcebook: Frameworks for Planning, Action and Reflection* (Boston: Institute for Development Research, 1997), 84. Copyright 2002 by World Education. Reprinted with permission.

the people closest to the problems in their identification and ongoing analysis and solution, advocacy helps strengthen grassroots capacities to participate effectively and hold officials accountable over time."[13] Once identified, problems are analyzed with regard to consequences, causes, and solutions, and then prioritized. The priority problems are then defined for internal clarity and framed in terms of an issue that is compelling, urgent, and inclusive for an external audience.

Goal setting then focuses on four levels. Covey and Miller offer a set of questions to use in setting those goals:

1. "What are the *transformational* goals we want to accomplish—goals aimed at transforming the inequitable structures and power relationships of society related to the problem or issue?
2. What specific actions, decisions and changes do we want in the *long-term*? What will best address the basic cause of our problem and how will we be able to maintain our gains if successful?"
3. What are our *intermediate* goals? What constitutes victory?
4. "What *short-term or partial* victories can we win as steps toward our longer-term and transformational goals?"[14]

Power analysis focuses on identifying and analyzing "the relative power of the different individuals and groups who are concerned about our specific problem and the related policy solution being proposed to address it."[15] It is similar to but is one level more specific than macro analysis. The *Advocacy Sourcebook* contains a series of tools, including Opportunities and Threats Analysis and Stakeholder Analysis and Target Identification, that can be used together or separately for this purpose.

Strategies emerge from goal setting and power analysis. They involve a sequence of tactics or activities designed to influence different advocacy targets—those who have the power to make decisions and those who have the power to influence them—as well as undermine the opposition. They are developed in the context of "the current political environment and political moment," and should "involve, strengthen and mobilize . . . constituents and allies so their power and energy can grow and be sustained."[16]

Implementation involves carrying out the tactics or activities.

Evaluation of advocacy impact involves three dimensions or levels. "At the policy level, success is winning a desired policy, program or behavioral change. At the level of civil society, success is strengthening grassroots groups and NGOs so they can build more democratic relations of power in society and hold public and private sector institutions accountable. At the level of democracy, success is increased political space for NGOs and popular organizations to operate without repression."[17]

Lessons from the advocacy efforts close the circle by feeding into future macroanalysis, problem analysis, goal setting, power analysis, strategies, implementation, and evaluation.

Advocacy Planning Moments

The third map is from *A New Weave of Power, People and Politics* by Lisa VeneKlasen with Valerie Miller.[18] It draws primarily on experiences in the Global South, especially with grassroots women's organizing. Lisa is director of Just Associates, with offices in Washington, DC, Central America, south Asia, and southern Africa that support social movements.[19] Valerie is one of the organization's associates.

Most other authors who present sequential maps (including Shultz and Covey and Miller) are careful to note that the actual process does not always follow the steps, stages, or phases in their frameworks. VeneKlasen and Miller chose the term *planning moments* rather than *steps* to emphasize this point: that advocacy often involves "two steps forward, one step backward"[20] and very often from side to side.[21] In the chapter "The Basics of Planning for People-Centered Advocacy," the authors summarize ten moments as shown in figure 2.3.

Personal and organizational assessment, or what VeneKlasen and Miller also describe as looking inward, engages the advocates, as individuals and organizations, in self-analysis. The assessment involves clarifying an organization's "vision, mission and strategies" and "developing a long-term political vision to guide advocacy."[22]

Contextual analysis or understanding the big picture focuses on political context, from local to global. It also examines the nature of power that marginalizes some groups in the political process.

Problem identification and analysis involves defining and prioritizing problems that will be the focus of advocacy, and doing so in a way that builds the organizations' constituencies.

Choosing and framing the advocacy issue involves exploring possible solutions in ways that "slice a big problem into manageable advocacy issues." Framing the issues is focused on describing the advocates' cause to achieve "wider public appeal."[23]

Long-term advocacy goals are the "political, economic and social changes the advocacy efforts seek to accomplish," and short-term advocacy goals are "the desired outcomes for the specific advocacy solution."[24]

Power mapping identifies "targets, allies, opponents and constituents. It examines stakeholder interests, positions and conflicts. It reveals hidden mechanisms of power that affect marginalized groups' participation as well as important allies within decision-making structures."[25]

Policy and situational research involve "gathering information about the policies, laws, programs, and budgets shaping [the advocates'] issue, and about its causes and the people it affects."[26]

Figure 2.3 Advocacy planning moments

1. Personal and organizational assessment
2. Contextual analysis
3. Problem identification and analysis
4. Choosing and framing the advocacy issue
5. Long-term and short-term advocacy goals
6. Power mapping
7. Policy and situational research
8. Advocacy objectives
9. Activities, actions, tactics and implementation
10. Measuring progress and adjusting action

Source: Lisa VeneKlasen with Valerie Miller, *A New Weave of Power, People and Politics: The Action Guide for Advocacy and Citizen Participation* (Warwickshire, UK: Practical Action, 2007), 83–85.

Advocacy objectives incorporate information about power and policies to "spell out the desired changes in policy and decision-making structures, as well as how [the advocates] will use political space and strengthen citizen engagement. Finally, they indicate how the advocacy will ultimately improve people's lives."[27]

Activities, actions, tactics, and implementation are the means to achieve the objectives, while recognizing that "the nature of the political environment, opponents and targets will inform [the advocates'] media, outreach, lobbying and negotiation tactics."[28]

Measuring progress and adjusting action means that "ongoing evaluation helps ensure that the advocacy responds to the political opportunities and follows organizational priorities [and] allows groups to adjust their actions to changing situations."[29]

Advocacy Circles

While I find the preceding three maps and a range of others to be very useful tools, in the process of teaching advocacy, I felt the need to develop a relatively simple way to visualize the dynamic, iterative dimensions of the reality or territory of advocacy. My students began to refer to it as "Jeff's advocacy circles" because the core elements are represented by five intersecting circles (see figure 2.4).

Advocates, the smallest circle, represents a group of people, a formal organization, network, or coalition of people and organizations seeking to influence policy makers on one or more policy issues. To be effective, advocates must have or develop the capacity to

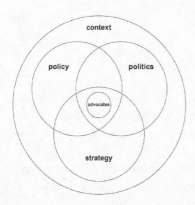

Figure 2.4 Advocacy circles

- analyze and act in accordance with the larger context;
- carry out policy research and analysis;
- identify, analyze, and navigate a political system composed of numerous different actors;
- develop and carry out various strategies and tactics for influencing policy makers; and
- monitor, evaluate, and learn from all of the above.

The advocates circle appears in the center, at the nexus of the other circles, because the advocates' work is shaped by and involves efforts related to all the others.

Context is the largest circle, encompassing all the others, and represents the much larger political-economic-cultural context in which the advocacy occurs, which is the product of multiple and overlapping historical dynamics, sometimes including the outcomes from the work of previous advocates.

The three other circles—policy, politics, and strategy—represent different arenas advocates work in. Sometimes I simply call these circles the what, who, and how of advocacy. In contrast to a map that includes steps or stages, the overlapping circles suggest there is ongoing activity in each arena, and those activities continually interact and influence those in the other arenas.

In the policy arena, the advocates and various other actors carry out research or less formal forms of information gathering to define a problem or set of problems, their causes, and one or more policy goals that are designed to (partially) address the causes and solve the problems.[30]

In the politics arena, there are formal and informal systems that make or change and implement policies, as well as numerous actors who are engaged with those systems. The main actors are the policy makers who need to be influenced, the advocates' allies and opponents, the media, and the general public.

In the strategy arena, the advocates plan and carry out activities they believe will help them influence targets and thus achieve their policy goals. This includes (a) analyzing the political systems and actors, including themselves, and (b) combining that knowledge with their policy goals to formulate intermediate and short-term objectives for specific strategies and tactics (amount of media coverage, number of letters to a policy maker, etc.) and for outcomes.

Monitoring, evaluation, and learning are key functions that are not represented by a separate circle because they are integrated in each of the others. One can distinguish three different foci of monitoring and evaluation:

- Process monitoring and evaluation focus on what advocates do (or fail to do) in relation to those strategic or tactical objectives and/or to best practices in the field.
- Outcome monitoring and evaluation focus on whether there were changes in policy related to the advocates' goals or intermediate objectives. Other possible outcomes include changes in the capacity of civil society to sustain advocacy and affect change in the future, and changes in governance or the relevant policy-making processes that create more political space for meaningful participation by civil society.
- Impact evaluation focuses on whether a policy change, if enacted and implemented, actually solves the problem it was supposed to solve.

Learning consists of knowledge and insights that guide adjustments to advocacy work in the middle of a campaign and when planning future campaigns. Effective advocates take time to clarify and share their learning, often in the form of lessons.

The Four Maps in Perspective

There are significant differences between the four maps. They certainly look different, and they have different numbers of steps or moments or circles or arenas.

Moreover, as noted previously, the maps were developed in different contexts. Though Shultz in fact wrote most of the *Democracy Owner's Manual* while living in Bolivia, it is a synthesis of knowledge and insights he gained through advocacy work in the United States and especially in California. The authors of the *Advocacy Sourcebook* and *A New Weave* are specifically focused on the Global South, and the latter has an even greater focus on citizen-centered advocacy by grassroots social movements of marginalized communities. The advocacy circles grew out of a graduate course, and like this book, seek to provide a general model that is relevant to the Global South and North and from the grassroots to transnational networks.

Because of their different origins, as well as the nature of language, the maps use different terms to describe the same territory, or use the same term to describe different aspects of advocacy. Some of this can be attributed to the classically confusing language of *goals* (or, in some cases, long-term, interim, or medium-term, and short-term goals) versus *objectives*.

On the other hand, a key term like *strategy* is used in different ways, either to describe the whole process of advocacy (that is, all the steps) or only the part that involves planning and taking specific actions, or some combination of the two.[31]

That said, the most important differences in the maps are largely the degree to which any one element of advocacy is highlighted in relation to the others. For example, as shown in table 2.1, the policy circle in my map corresponds with one step in the Shultz's road map (step 1: setting the objective), two steps in Covey and Miller's Advocacy Process map (steps 3 and 4: problem and goal setting) and four moments in VeneKlasen and Miller's Advocacy Planning Moments map (moments 3, 4, 5, and 7: problem analysis, issue framing, setting goals, and setting objectives; though part of what is included in the latter two moments could also be what is included in the strategy circle).[32]

While there are one or more steps in Covey and Miller's Advocacy Process map and one or more moments in VeneKlasen and Miller's map that correspond to each of the advocacy circles, the road map does not have steps that correspond to three of the circles: advocates, context, and evaluation and learning.

Table 2.1 Comparing the four maps

Unsicker	Shultz	Covey and Miller	VeneKlasen and Miller
Advocacy Circles	Advocacy's Road Map	Advocacy Process and Strategy Development	Advocacy Planning Moments
• Advocates		• Societal vision	• Personal and organizational assessment
• Context		• Macro analysis	• Contextual analysis
• Policy	• Objectives	• Problem • Goal setting	• Problem identification and analysis • Long-term and short-term advocacy goals • Choosing and framing the advocacy issue • Advocacy objectives
• Politics	• Target audiences	• Power analysis	• Power mapping
• Strategy	• Message • Messenger • Taking action	• Strategies • Implementation	• Activities, actions, tactics, and implementation
• Monitoring, evaluation, and learning		• Evaluation • Lessons	• Measuring progress and adjusting action

Of course, as an experienced advocate and analyst, Shultz is more than aware of these aspects. Part 1 of the *Democracy Owner's Manual*, which consists of five chapters on the "key debates that democracies decide," provides an extensive analysis of the context of advocacy. Moreover, in another framework, Shultz discusses "nine key questions" that are grouped into two sets. One set, focused on "looking outward," includes the five questions that correspond to the five steps of the road map. The second set, "looking inward," contains four additional questions, two of which directly correspond with the advocates circle and another with the learning and evaluation.[33]

So, ultimately, which map is best? That of course depends on the situation and need. How will you use it? Do you need a street map or topographical map?

In my experience, Shultz's road map is most useful for a relatively straightforward advocacy campaign, especially at the local or subnational level. A group of people who are relatively unfamiliar with advocacy can quickly grasp the sequence of steps, especially through answering the very clear questions associated with each.

For more complex campaigns that are either longer or focused on a larger policy target, the other maps are likely to be more useful.

In some of those cases, especially at the planning stage, there can be advantages to working with a series of sequential steps, such as those provided by Covey and Miller.

In other cases, it may be more helpful to focus first on one of Vene-Klasen and Miller's specific moments and then move to others based on the nature and process of the campaign. This may be especially useful at the point of building community awareness prior to even considering an advocacy campaign, or at another point when those in an ongoing campaign need to stop and reflect on a specific aspect of their work.

One advantage of the advocacy circles is they are simple and highly visual, and thus for many it is easier to keep all the moving parts in mind. The intersections of the circles emphasize the point that all the authors cited here make: that advocacy is not a linear process but rather iterative, in which one part of the process is constantly informing one or more of the others. For this reason, it is helpful for dissecting an ongoing campaign from basic short-term campaigns to more complex longer-term ones with larger policy targets.

Effective advocates would do well to have all four of these maps, and others as well, in their conceptual toolbox. The rest of this book provides the information and understanding needed to include and effectively use the advocacy circles map.

To begin that process, the following chapter provides a more thorough discussion of the circles map, beginning with a short case study of an actual campaign: "A Small Town in Peru Battles a Multinational Mining Corporation."

Notes

1. The phrase first appeared in his book, *Science and Sanity: An Introduction to Non-Aristotelian Systems and General Semantics* (Lancaster, PA: International Non-Aristotelian Library Publishing, 1933). His point—that an abstraction derived from something, or a reaction to it, is not the thing itself—goes well beyond my use of it here and indeed has had a significant influence on many prominent thinkers of the twentieth century, such as anthropologist and cyberneticist Gregory Bateson. I first read the quote in Bateson's "Form, Substance and Difference" in *Steps Toward an Ecology of Mind* (Chicago: University of Chicago Press, 1972).

2. While this chapter focuses only on maps included in the three books, it should be noted that all the authors provide knowledge and analysis that far exceed the focus of this chapter. In very complementary ways, each provides a comprehensive, insightful, and useful introduction to advocacy. In addition, Jim Shultz's *The Democracy Owner's Manual: A Practical Guide to Changing the World* (New Brunswick, NJ: Rutgers University Press, 2002) and Lisa VeneKlasen with Valerie Miller's *A New Weave of Power, Politics and People: The Action Guide for Advocacy and Citizen Participation* (Warwickshire, UK: Practical Action Publishers, 2007) provide in-depth discussions of contextual issues. One of Shultz's contributions is a thorough overview of policy issues that governments must address and alternative policy choices (from the appropriate role of government to taxes, budgets, regulating the market, protecting the public, and so forth), which is a minicourse in civics. VeneKlasen's *A New Weave* includes a more general but very strong discussion of power and empowerment. Both offer significant how-to guidance for the different aspects of advocacy, and *A New Weave* also contains workshop designs, forms, and other practical materials.

3. Shultz, *Democracy Owner's Manual.* Shultz's summary of the road map is chapter 5, which is also available on the website of the Democracy Center: http://democracyctr.org/wp/wp-content/uploads/2011/10/Strategy-chapter-DOM.pdf.

4. See http://democracycenter.org.

5. Shultz, *Democracy Owner's Manual,* 72–73.

6. Shultz, *Democracy Owner's Manual,* 76.

7. Shultz, *Democracy Owner's Manual,* 76.

8. Shultz, *Democracy Owner's Manual,* 77.

9. Shultz, *Democracy Owner's Manual,* 77.

10. Jane Covey and Valerie Miller, *Advocacy Sourcebook: Frameworks for Planning, Action and Reflection* (Boston: Institute for Development Research, 1997). Note: The Institute for Development Research (IDR) merged with World Education in 2002. The *Sourcebook* and other publications by IDR can be ordered through http://www.worlded.org/docs/Publications/idr/idr_pubs.htm.

11. Covey and Miller, *Advocacy Sourcebook,* 65.

12. Covey and Miller, *Advocacy Sourcebook,* 65.

13. Covey and Miller, *Advocacy Sourcebook,* 65.

14. Covey and Miller, *Advocacy Sourcebook,* 72.

15. Covey and Miller, *Advocacy Sourcebook,* 73.

16. Covey and Miller, *Advocacy Sourcebook,* 79.

17. Covey and Miller, *Advocacy Sourcebook,* 102.

18. VeneKlasen with Miller, *New Weave,* 83–85.

19. See http://www.jass.org.

20. VeneKlasen and Miller, *New Weave,* 83.

21. VeneKlasen and Miller, *New Weave,* 83.

22. VeneKlasen and Miller, *New Weave,* 84.

23. VeneKlasen and Miller, *New Weave,* 84.

24. VeneKlasen and Miller, *New Weave,* 84.

25. VeneKlasen and Miller, *New Weave,* 84.

26. VeneKlasen and Miller, *New Weave,* 84.

27. VeneKlasen and Miller, *New Weave,* 84.

28. VeneKlasen and Miller, *New Weave,* 84–85.

29. VeneKlasen and Miller, *New Weave,* 85.

30. Problems are complex in reality and conceptually. Chapter 1 notes that the purpose of advocacy is to realize a vision of social and economic justice, environmental sustainability and peace, or simply a better world. In its most basic sense, a problem is a condition that is inconsistent with that vision, for example, poverty, racism, toxic pollution, armed conflict, and so forth. Advocacy can address those aspects of a problem that are linked to (a) the existence of a policy that is causing a problem or at least creating barriers to its resolution, or (b) the absence of a policy needed to solve the problem or at least enable communities and organizations to do so..

31. Shultz uses *strategy* to describe all five steps of the road map (in fact, the map is discussed in the chapter "Developing a Strategy"). Covey and Miller use the word to describe only the sixth (planning) and seventh (implementation) steps in their map. VeneKlasen and Miller use strategy differently in different parts of their book. In their overview of the ten moments, they use strategy only in the description of the ninth moment: actions, tactics, and implementation. However, in a subsequent chapter, "Mapping Advocacy Strategies," they include the process of setting goals and objectives as part of strategy. In my map, the term is used to describe one of the three arenas that interact with each other. Strategy consists of the often ongoing processes of translating policy change goals (policy

arena) into objectives and framed messages, and choosing and implementing actions to influence policy makers (political arena).

32. Some aspects of moment 5 and moment 7 correspond with the policy circle, but other aspects more closely correspond with the strategy circle.

33. The document is available through the Democracy Center's website: http://democracyctr.org/wp/wp-content/uploads/2011/10/Advocacy-Strategy .pdf.

In it, the two questions that correspond to the advocates circle are described as follows:

- "Resources: What have we got? An effective advocacy effort takes careful stock of the advocacy resources that are already there to be built on. This includes past advocacy work that is related, alliances already in place, staff and other people's capacity, information, and political intelligence. In short, you don't start from scratch, you start from building on what you've got.
- Gaps: What do we need to develop? After taking stock of the advocacy resources you have, the next step is to identify the advocacy resources you need that aren't there yet. This means looking at alliances that need to be built, and capacities such as outreach, media, and research which are crucial to any effort."

Another question corresponds to the evaluation and learning circle:

- "Evaluation: How do we tell if it's working? As with any long journey, the course needs to be checked along the way. Strategy needs to be evaluated by revisiting each of the preceding questions (i.e., are we targeting the right audiences, are we reaching them, etc.?) It is important to be able to make midcourse corrections and discard those elements of a strategy that don't work once they are actually put into practice."

A fourth question makes additional points related to the strategy circle:

- "First efforts: How do we begin? What would be an effective way to move the strategy forward? What are some potential short-term goals or projects that would bring the right people together, symbolize the larger work ahead, and create something achievable that lays the groundwork for the next step?"

CASE A

A Small Town in Peru Battles a Multinational Mining Corporation

Rosa Maria Olortegui, coauthor

On November 22, 1999, the citizens of Tambogrande, a small town in an agriculturally rich valley in northern Peru famous for lemons, mangos, and other food products, awoke to startling news.[1] A multinational mining company was preparing to dig an open pit mine to extract gold, zinc, and copper deposits located underneath their town. The Manhattan Minerals Corporation, based in Canada, had received the concession from the central government of Peruvian president Alberto Fujimori, and the mayor of Tambogrande had signed off on it. Representatives of the corporation and government argued that the mine would be good for the town. It would create jobs; modern housing would be built for the eight thousand residents who would be displaced; and funding would become available for local development initiatives.

But many Tambograndinos, led by Godofredo García Baca, an agricultural engineer, rejected those arguments. They claimed that the mines would divert water, pollute the environment, damage agriculture, and radically disrupt their way of life. An organized resistance was soon established in the form of the Tambogrande Defense Front, whose members represented a broad cross section of farmers and other citizens. The town's parish priest connected them with the Catholic archdiocese in Piura, the regional capital. Through its networks, advocacy-oriented national and international nongovernmental organizations (NGOs) were contacted. A number of those organizations formed the Tambogrande Technical Support Committee to work with and for the Defense Front. While the local advocates were solely focused on stopping the mine, the focus of the Peruvian and international NGOs included larger goals of expanding human rights, changing mining laws, and increasing political participation in relation to the Peruvian government and multilateral agencies.

Officials of the Manhattan corporation tried different methods to gain the Tambograndinos' support. According to many of the advocates, these included hiding information, lying, paying off some residents to form a support organization, bribing a local newspaper to provide positive coverage of the mining plans, and labeling their opponents as terrorists.

In response, the front's first task was to become better informed about the laws and the facts related to the mine. With help from Technical Support Committee members, they learned that the central government, which is supposed to regulate industry and protect citizens, had a conflict of interest because it was a 25 percent shareholder in the project. They also learned that the corporation had been allowed to begin construction without completing the legally required environmental impact assessment (EIA).

In July 2000, when Manhattan released a "baseline study" that supported the corporation's claims that there would be no environmental damage, the advocates sought an independent review. Oxfam America, which was one member of the Technical Support Committee, identified and paid for a Canadian mining expert to do the analysis. His report concluded that Manhattan's document did not meet international standards. Moreover, he determined that toxic contamination of water, soil, and air were likely, and that no further drilling should be allowed without a complete EIA.

However, central government officials refused to meet with the front's representatives and hear their legal and technical arguments. Then, in November 2000, Fujimori fled the country to escape charges of corruption and human rights abuses, and the government was in a state of flux. In this context, the front organized a mass protest. For two days in February 2001, marchers blocked access to the mining facilities. Some marchers became violent and damaged offices and burned down several of the model homes that Manhattan was proposing for the displaced families. The corporation filed lawsuits against the front's leaders. A month later, García Baca was murdered, an act that most advocates believe was in retaliation for his opposition to the mine.

The leaders of the front and the Technical Support Committee condemned all the violence and held meetings to gain a consensus among all factions, including those who would have preferred to retaliate, for a new approach. They began circulating a petition to demonstrate public opposition to the mine, ultimately gathering over twenty-eight thousand signatures. In the face of such strong opposition, the mayor rescinded his approval for the mines. A proposal was developed for a formal referendum, a "municipal consultation," to officially vote for or against Manhattan's concession. Peru's new president, Alejandro Toledo, had made campaign promises to protect the rights of the Tambograndinos, but he now argued that the problem was mostly a matter of a misunderstanding. He sent a government ombudsman to meet representatives of the front and its supporters and negotiate a way they could participate in the completion and evaluation of the long overdue EIA. The advocates wanted more, including a new law that would guarantee communities the right to make their own decisions about their development. After a first meeting, the advocates decided they did not trust the government and moved forward with the plans for the municipal consultation. The government rejected the referendum on the basis that it had "no legal framework." However, with funding and international observers from Rights and Democracy, an international NGO based in Canada, the vote was taken in July 2002. Over 73 percent of the nearly thirty-seven thousand registered voters turned out, with 98.6 percent voting no to the mines.

While the central government continued to reject the outcome of the municipal consultation, the advocates' new communication strategies ensured that the vote had a powerful impact in the court of public opinion, locally, nationally, and internationally. After the violence of the previous year, the symbols at the front's rallies were changed; clenched fists and similar images were replaced with those of lemons and mangos. In Piura, one local NGO organized public forums, and another used its radio station to educate the public. NGOs in Lima used their media savvy and contacts to get national coverage. They organized traditional street demonstrations (*pasacalles*), dramatizations, wrote original songs, and created colorful posters and bumper stickers that asked, "Can you imagine *ceviche* without lemon?" (Ceviche is one of Peru's favorite national dishes.) The Peruvian and international NGOs publicized the Tambogrande resistance through the Internet. Stories were carried in the international press. Thus the vote was literally heard around the world and even led to similar community-initiated referenda on mining interests in Argentina and Guatemala.

In December 2002, when Manhattan finally produced an EIA, it was incomplete and portions of it were in English only. At about the same time, the corporation's chief executive suggested that the 25 percent share of the mining interests held by the central government should be transferred to the municipal government for investments in local agricultural development. Under public pressure, and likely irritated by the potential loss of its own share in the project, the central government responded in 2003 by demanding that Manhattan submit a complete report, all in Spanish, and by strengthening citizen participation in the regulations regarding the review of EIAs. For Manhattan to be approved, the government required three public hearings in Lima, Piura, and Tambogrande.

Manhattan complied. But the advocates rejected the new report and the hearings. In November, on the night before the first hearing in Lima, advocacy groups held a protest ("Night of the Lemon"), alerting the public to the possibility that the government might approve the EIA even though they believed it had significant flaws. The following morning the government decided that the situation was not safe and canceled the hearing. Fearing an even more volatile situation in Tambogrande, that hearing was also canceled.

When the third and final hearing was to take place in Piura, the front organized busloads and truckloads of Tambograndinos to go and protest. When they negotiated with the police to peacefully enter the university auditorium where the meeting was to be held, the government again decided it was not safe and canceled. Thus, technically, the EIA could not be approved, and the mining could not move forward.

The final blow was a decision by the central government to require Manhattan to immediately meet one of its original contractual obligations: it had to provide evidence of the funds and capacity necessary to process ten thousand tons of minerals per day. When the corporation failed to comply, its concession was officially withdrawn.

Manhattan had lost. The Tambogrande Defense Front, and the church and advocacy NGOs that had supported them, had won.

LEARNING EXERCISE

Identify the actors or activities that correspond to each of the five advocacy circles and the three types of outcomes discussed in chapter 2. Compare your answers to those provided in chapter 3 (see pages 30–49).

1. Advocates
   - Who were they?
2. Context
   - What are the most significant elements that influenced the advocacy campaign?
3. Policy
   - How did the advocates define the problem, and what were their policy goals?
4. Politics
   - Who were the policy makers?
   - Who were the allies?
   - Who was the opposition?
   - Who was on the fence?
5. Strategy
   - What strategies and tactics did the advocates use to achieve their goals?
   - In particular, how did the advocates frame their message?
6. Monitoring, Evaluation, and Learning: What if any outcomes resulted from the advocacy:
   - Policy (Rejected bad policy? Enacted or implemented good policy?)
   - Policy-making processes or governance?
   - Capacity of civil society?

Optional Activities

Repeat the preceding process with the five steps of the road map in the *Democracy Owner's Manual* described in chapter 2: objectives, audiences, message, messengers, and taking action. Did you get different insights about the campaign from the two different maps? If so, what are they?

You can also do the same for the other two maps in chapter 2: the nine steps in the Advocacy Process and Strategy Development in the *Advocacy Sourcebook* and the ten moments in *A New Weave of Power, People and Politics*. Given that each is more complex than the road map, fully using either map requires more information about the actors and experience than is supplied in this brief case study. However, even identifying what information would be needed is a good learning exercise.

Note

1. The data for this case is drawn from Olortegui's "Tambo Grande Vale Mas Que Oro/Tambo Grande Is Worth More Than Gold" (MA capstone paper, School for International Training Graduate Institute, 2006).

3

Advocacy Circles
Basic Elements

CHAPTER 2 BRIEFLY INTRODUCED SEVERAL CONCEPTUAL MAPS, CULMINATING WITH advocacy circles (see figure 2.4). This chapter examines in more detail the map's basic elements and applies them to Case A—the struggle by the citizens of Tambogrande, Peru, to stop the construction of an open pit mine in the center of their town. The first five sections focus on each of the circles: advocates, context, policy, politics, and strategy. The final subsection focuses on evaluation and learning. Chapter 4 examines how these basic elements intersect and overlap in ways that reflect the complex, iterative nature of advocacy.

The Advocates

Who Will Lead and Do the Work?
The advocates (see figure 3.1) are a group of people, a civil society organization, a network, or a coalition of organizations that have a vision for a more just, equitable, and sustainable world and therefore want to bring about change.[1]

This book focuses on advocates who experience or are concerned about problems facing the general public, marginalized groups, or the environment. They are brought together by the realization that policy changes are necessary to solve those problems.

The advocates—whether a group, organization, network, or coalition—may be focused exclusively on policy change. Or the advocates may have a broader mission and set of activities, only one of which is policy change.

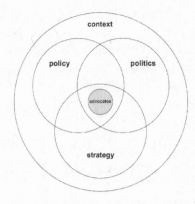

Figure 3.1 Advocates circle

Most often, advocacy related to any specific policy issue involves multiple groups, organizations, networks, or coalitions. For purposes of focusing one's work or study, it is helpful to clarify if one's analytical orientation (unit of analysis) will be an entire network or coalition or if it will be one member—that is, a single group or organization.

If one is working for or studying one of multiple organizations involved in influencing a specific policy, it is helpful to view the process from that organization's perspective, placing it at the center of the conceptual map. The other groups, organizations, networks, and coalitions that are also doing advocacy are understood as other actors in the politics arena. The relationships between the advocates (the organization) and those actors might vary, from having no contact to working together as allies, either as a loose network or as members of a formal coalition.

Another possibility is for the unit of analysis to be a formal coalition of organizations. The coalition, including its members, is placed at the center of the map, and all the other groups, organizations, networks, and coalitions are again understood as other actors in the politics arena.[2]

The effectiveness of advocates is shaped by many factors, including expertise, access to resources, and credibility. One key variable is whether the advocates have a clear constituency that they can mobilize and are accountable to. Some advocates are membership organizations (for example, community associations and labor unions); their members are constituents. In such organizations, members often hold leadership roles, directly representing and speaking on behalf of the organization when doing advocacy. On the other hand, some advocates that are not membership organizations have other ways of building and maintaining a connection with a constituency. Such constituents may have a direct stake in the outcome of the advocacy (for example, a change in food stamp policy for low-income people), but they can also be people who are willing to act because of their moral concerns related to the issue that is the focus of the advocacy (for example, middle-class people who wish to alleviate others' poverty). In the case of a coalition, some but not all members may have clear constituencies, sometimes overlapping, sometimes distinct.

TAMBOGRANDE CASE: ADVOCATES

In view of the preceding discussion about units of analysis, we can understand Case A either by focusing on the Tambogrande Defense Front as the advocates or on the alliance of the front and the Tambogrande Technical Support Committee as the advocates, which includes regional and national Peruvian nongovernmental organizations (NGOs) and at least two international NGOs. Here we view the case from the perspective of the front. The support committee will be understood as the front's primary (but not only) ally; we will return to this when discussing the circle or arena of politics (see page 37).[3]

The case study suggests that the front is a new organization, composed of citizens of Tambogrande (in fact, some organizations from other towns were also members) who came together to defend their town by opposing the mine. It does not appear that they have any other mission or function other than preventing construction of the mine.

The front has a very clear constituency: the citizens of Tambogrande who oppose the mine. They know the local economy, politics, and culture, and their livelihoods would be dramatically affected by the outcome of the advocacy. Other aspects of the front's capacity included some members with more technical knowledge, such as García Baca's knowledge of agronomy engineering, which is the most apparent in the case description.

Context

All policy advocacy campaigns or initiatives exist within a larger context—an immediate political-economic-cultural context embedded in multiple others, and a specific moment or period in time embedded in a longer historical context (see figure 3.2).

Generally, these are realities the advocates have very little or no control over, for example, trends in the global economy or the timing of a key election. But they are realities the advocates always need to work within, and often react to.

While it is impossible to understand or even be aware of the totality of one's context, it is important for advocates to analyze at least the major elements that will most directly shape or constrain their work. A primary element of one campaign's context, for instance, the inequities in the global economy, may be the focus of another campaign; but even that campaign will be shaped and constrained by a yet larger context. When possible, effective advocates take advantage of opportunities or otherwise use those factors to their advantage.

TAMBOGRANDE CASE: CONTEXT

The case study provides only limited information about the many contextual factors that certainly shaped or constrained the front's advocacy. We do know that the campaign took place during a time of turmoil and transition in the central government; the president in power when the advocacy began (Fujimori) fled the country because of corruption charges, and a new president (Toledo) took power. This created various opportunities. The Tambograndinos were able to raise their concerns with Toledo during at least one of his campaign events when he was very likely to pledge support for their

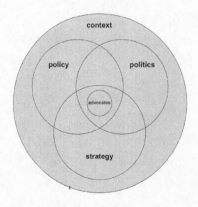

Figure 3.2 Context circle

cause; even an insincere pledge can be used by advocates once a candidate has been elected.

While not stated in the short case description, we can be fairly certain of another key contextual factor: the concession to Manhattan Minerals and Peru's more general policy of encouraging foreign investment were the result of global politics. Beginning in the 1980s and expanding during the decade preceding the concession, a policy of structural adjustment and other prescriptions of the Washington consensus were imposed on nations in the global South by the International Monetary Fund, the World Bank, and major bilateral aid nations such as the United States. In that context, the Peruvian government must have been under significant pressure to provide open access and reduce barriers (such as environmental protection policies) for foreign investors, including transnational mining corporations.

Policy

What is the problem? What are the advocates' goals?

Simply put, the role of policy advocacy is to solve problems that are affecting the lives of the general public, marginalized groups, or the environment.[4] An effective solution requires that the advocates understand what is causing the problems and involves proposals for policy change that address those causes (see figure 3.3).

Not all problems require policy change of course. Staff members of an organization or coalition may conclude that a problem can be solved

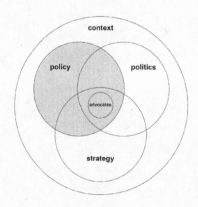

Figure 3.3 Policy circle

by improving or better coordinating existing services, and that no policy changes are necessary to do so.

But many problems do require policy change. Even if a problem might be solved by better or more coordinated services, it is often the case that those changes cannot occur without some changes in policy. For example, for a local health clinic to improve its outreach and prevention work, it may need the municipal government to change its budget (one of the most important policies that institutions make) and provide money to hire enough staff to do that work.

In some cases, the *only* solution to a problem (or at least the necessary next step in a longer-term solution) is policy change.

The problem-cause-solution sequence is not as simple as it may sound. With large and complex problems and multiple causes, careful policy research and analysis may be required if the advocates are to be confident that the policy change they recommend will in fact solve the problem. They do not want to succeed in changing a policy and then find that the new policy is ineffective or even makes the problem worse.

Policy research is also important for generating evidence that can be used to build public support and for convincing policy makers to enact the change that the advocates seek, both of which are key elements of the strategy circle.

If the advocates do not have the capacity (expertise, time, funding, and so forth) to do their own research, they need to identify others who can help collect and analyze existing information from publications and reports or carry out new data collection.

Ultimately, through this research and analysis, the advocates will identify one or more policy change goals. Each goal can be understood in terms of the four categories of policy change in table 3.1.

The first two categories of policy change goals are perhaps the most common focus of advocacy: preventing, removing, or at least lessening the effects of policies that have a negative impact. The reason is simple:

Table 3.1 Four categories of policy change goals

	The policy is or will be *harmful.*	The policy is or will be *helpful.*
It is an *existing* policy.	1. Repeal or amend; if not, block implementation.	4. Protect and ensure implementation.
It is a *proposed* policy.	2. Block enactment.	3. Formulate if necessary; ensure enactment and implementation.

the policies of powerful institutions (governments, corporations, multi-lateral banks, trade organizations, and so forth) are most often dominated by powerful elite groups in society whose visions and concerns are different from and often in opposition to those of the advocates.

If for these reasons or any other a policy has been adopted that is either causing or contributing to a problem of concern to the advocates, they may work to repeal the policy. If not possible, they make seek to amend or reform the policy. Unless and until such a policy is repealed, amended or reformed, the advocates' goal may be to block its implementation (category 1). If the policy is still in the proposal stage, they work to block its enactment (category 2).

The third category of policy change goals represents the most proactive work that advocates do: formulate a new policy that will help achieve their vision or solve a problem and then get it enacted. In other cases, the advocates may support a helpful policy that has been proposed by a like-minded policy maker or other advocacy group. While all four categories of goals require advocates to have a solid policy analysis with evidence, it is especially important for formulating a new policy.

The fourth category of policy goals follows a successful effort to secure adoption of a helpful policy. Whether these policies are the direct result of the advocates' work or have other origins (for example, external pressure to conform to international conventions and treaties that support human rights and the environment[5]), advocacy focuses on protecting these policies from repeal or revision by the same forces that have created harmful policies or would propose a new policy that would undermine a helpful policy.

Even if a helpful policy is enacted and protected, it will not have an effect if it is not fully and effectively implemented. Unfortunately, that is very common. Thus the fourth category of goals also includes a focus on implementation. In fact, some apparently helpful policies may have been supported by the elite to placate or diffuse the concerns of the general public or marginalized groups, all the time with the intention of ensuring that the policy is not implemented. In any case, a great deal of social justice advocacy is focused on ensuring—or forcing—the implementation of helpful policies.

TAMBOGRANDE CASE: POLICY

The Tambogrande Defense Front began as the result of a widely held analysis of the problem: if an open pit mine were built in the mid-

dle of town it would "divert water, pollute the environment, damage agriculture, and radically disrupt [the Tambograndinos'] way
of life" (page 25 in Case A). The cause was not clear at first, other
than that something had allowed the mine to receive a concession
to begin exploration.

With the help of the support committee, members of the front
came to understand that Peru's national government had at least
partially contradictory policies. One policy was generally helpful
in that it required an environmental impact assessment to determine
that there would be no negative impacts on the community, and that
any mine must be approved by the local government. Another more
general policy was harmful because it encouraged foreign investment by mining and other industries by reducing barriers to their
operating in the country.

Thus, to achieve its primary policy goal of preventing the mine's
construction, the front needed to focus on two types of policy goals:
ensure implementation of the helpful policy (category 4) and block
the implementation of the harmful policy (category 1).

The case study reports that at least at the point of the first meeting with President Toledo's representative the front's policy goal
was expanded to include a more general law that would grant not
only Tambogrande but all Peruvian communities the right to decide
whether a mining concession should be awarded. This was also one
of many goals of the support committee. However, it does not appear to have remained a priority goal for the front, nor is there any
indication that the front focused on any of the other policy goals of
the national and international NGOs, such as reforming if not re-
pealing the policies that favored foreign investment and control over
the local economy.

As the process unfolded, the front did not have the resources or
expertise to generate credible evidence that the mine would harm
its community and environment. The external study supported by
Oxfam America proved to be critical for this purpose.

Politics

Who must be influenced? Who will help? Who will oppose?

As stated previously, for advocates to effectively respond to the immediate problems facing a community or the environment, they must
understand if and how those problems are related to the policies (current

or proposed) of powerful institutions. In some cases, they must have the capacity to formulate and promote new policies.

To do so, the advocates must be able to navigate the arena of politics (see figure 3.4). They must know which institutions are relevant to their concerns. They must understand the institutions' policy-making processes. More specifically, they must understand who within each institution makes the decisions and who influences the decision makers. In addition, they must understand the other actors who have a stake in influencing policies, either in opposition to or in support of their policy change goals. And, at all times, the advocates must be highly aware of the type and amount of power wielded by the policy makers, opponents, and allies.

One of the most common failings is when a group or organization identifies a problem and then simply begins educating or mobilizing the community without a clear understanding about the institutions it must influence, how they work, and who else is involved in that process.

Sometimes it is relatively easy to understand the relevant politics. The policy change goal might be achieved by influencing a single institution. Few if any other actors may actively oppose or support the advocates' efforts. To return to a previous example, to improve outreach and prevention services of a local health clinic, the municipal government may be the only relevant institution to approach. There may even be very clearly developed and transparent procedures that specify who has what responsibilities and authority at each stage of the budgeting process, including the options for public participation. There may be general community support for the clinic, and no group or organization will directly oppose the improvements.

However, even in those cases, the reality is usually more complex. For example, it is common for a municipal budget for health services to

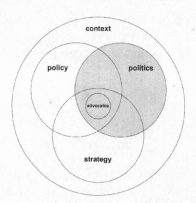

Figure 3.4 Politics circle

depend heavily on funds allocated to it by a state, provincial, or national government. Thus it may be necessary to first, or at least also, influence budget and other policy decisions at that level. Or, while there may be no direct opposition to improving the clinic, it is likely strong forces are opposed to any increase in government spending.

In most cases, the reality is quite complex, and the advocates must spend considerable effort to understand the political arena. Frequently, a number of institutions have policies that have an impact on the problem, not only different levels of government (local, state, national, and even multinational), but also different branches of government, different committees or agencies within those branches, and other powerful institutions such as corporations. In such situations, the relative authority of different institutions may not be clear or may even be contested.

Frequently, even when an institution's official policy-making procedures are formal and clear, the real decisions may be made through informal, nontransparent, and decidedly nonparticipatory processes. This is especially true because in most cases the power elite dominate these processes. Many of the policy makers are themselves from the elite; even when this is not the case, most policy makers have achieved their status through the support of the elite (for example, through contributing to election campaigns, controlling the media, and so forth). The elite influence policy-making processes through methods ranging from using social networks that provide unequal access to policy makers to using their resources to hire lobbyists or bribe officials.

And, frequently, a tangled web of other groups wish to influence policies. Some may oppose the advocates' goals, including those formed by the power elite to advance their own self-interests. Others groups may have goals that are the same as or similar to those of the advocates, but not all may be willing to work together. Still other groups may be competing with the advocates for the attention or resources of policy makers to achieve their own goals. In some cases these groups have a vision and values similar to those of the advocates. For example, if the advocates seek to increase funding for a health clinic, others may be seeking funds for a new youth center, and the municipal budget cannot support both.

Within this context, successful advocates must continuously seek to identify and understand, and to revise as appropriate, three categories of political actors:

- primary target—the institution or institutions that must be influenced to achieve the advocates' policy goals and, as specifically as possible, the person or people in those institutions who have the power to make the relevant policy decisions;

• opponents—influential people, groups, organizations, and coalitions that have a stake in preventing the advocates from achieving their policy goals; and

• allies—influential people, groups, organizations, and coalitions that have a stake in the advocates' successfully achieving their goals.

A more complete set of actors in the political arena, including secondary (or intermediate) targets, fence sitters, and the general public, is discussed in chapter 7.

TAMBOGRANDE CASE: POLITICS

Primary target. To achieve the front's policy change goal of preventing construction of the mine, there were at least three possible targets: the corporation, the town mayor, and the central (national) government.

The corporation's management or board of directors in Canada could have agreed with the front's (or later, the consultant's) assessment of the negative social and environmental impacts that were likely if the mine was built and therefore backed out. Or it could have decided that community opposition, including violence, made the mine a poor investment decision and backed out for that reason. But neither of those occurred, and the corporation acted as the primary opponents.

The mayor was targeted, and as a result of the advocates' pressure, he rescinded his officially required approval of the mine. But, as the advocates likely anticipated, it quickly became evident that the mayor's power was disregarded if he did not agree with the central government.

Thus the central government became the primary target. In the case study, and perhaps among the front's leadership, it was never totally clear who specifically within the government had the formal power (authority) to make the policy changes that the advocates sought, such as full implementation of the laws about environmental protection (including impact reports) and blockage of laws and government decisions that promoted foreign investment by streamlining approvals, and so forth. While the legislative branch had passed the laws, it appears that the president or his ministry of mines and energy was the real decision maker about how the laws would (or would not) be implemented.

Opponents. It is not stated in the case, but in addition to Manhattan Minerals Corporation, we can be relatively certain that other opponents included most foreign corporations with investments in Peru and those members of the Peruvian power elite who benefitted from foreign investment deals. Members of government (elites and some bureaucrats) who would see benefits from the 25 percent investment share or from corporate bribes also had a stake in opposing the front's policy change goals.

Allies. The initial allies were in the Catholic Church, specifically the parish priest and leaders in the regional archdiocese. The front developed a highly effective alliance with the Technical Support Committee, collectively and with individual members. The committee members' national and international networks, including those in the media, became additional allies.

Strategy

How will the advocates achieve their goal?

Strategy consists of the planning and actions the advocates use to seek to (partially) solve problems by influencing policy institutions to accept their policy change goals. It requires the advocates to complete an initial analysis of the context and especially the policy and politics arenas (see figure 3.5). The planning and implementation of a strategy tests those analyses, and in the process they are often deepened or revised.

A strategic plan can be understood as the advocates' answers to a series of questions. What will it take to convince or force a policy maker or group of policy makers to accept the advocates' policy change goal? What will it take to create those conditions? Is there a sequence of activities that are necessary to create those conditions? Is it necessary or helpful to achieve a sequence of policy change objectives to achieve the larger goals?

Advocates may incorporate a myriad of actions into their strategies, from confrontational protests to collaborative joint projects with policy institutions. Effective choices are based on what is most likely to work

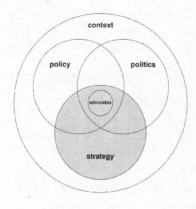

Figure 3.5 Strategy circle

in a specific situation. When possible, effective advocates choose actions that are most likely to achieve their policy change goal with the least expenditure of their limited resources or to create more political space and civil society capacity for future advocacy.

All strategies are based on an understanding of how a specific decision maker or body of decision makers can be influenced. That most often involves some direct contact between advocates and the decision maker. Collaborative joint projects are a form of direct contact; more common are lobbying visits and written communications. The success of collaboration and often lobbying depends on success in building relationships between the advocates and decision makers.

Influencing policy makers may also involve indirect contact. Confrontational protests, designed to demonstrate public opinion or gain media attention, are a form of indirect contact; other forms range from direct contact with the person or people who have the most influence with the decision maker to litigation in the courts.

All strategies involve ensuring, and ideally expanding, the advocates' capacity to influence decision makers. While this can take many forms, the distinct advantage of social justice advocates is their people power, and thus strategies are often heavily invested in public education, organizing and mobilizing constituents, and building coalitions.

Those who plan effective strategies also pay special attention to how those strategies resonate with different audiences, that is, the policy makers, the people with access to policy makers, different segments of the public, constituents, other organizations, and so forth. While attention should be given to the medium of communication, it is especially important to carefully plan how the message is framed.

TAMBOGRANDE CASE: STRATEGY

Within the Peruvian context it is not surprising that the first actions were protests, including burning buildings, targeted at the corporation. However, as the front's strategy evolved and became more sophisticated, it focused on influencing decision makers in the central government.

Direct contacts with government, in the form of meetings with ministry officials and the president's ombudsman, did not achieve the front's goals. On the other hand, by giving officials credible evidence that the corporation's initial impact study did not meet the requirements of the government's own laws, and presenting a petition signed by the vast majority of Tambograndinos, the front likely made it clear that it was a formidable force the government could not simply ignore.

Indirect contacts with the policy makers appear to have been more successful. In particular, the municipal consultation or referendum—in defiance of government warnings that it would not be legal—appears to have been a highly effective means of communicating with and mobilizing citizens across Peru and others outside the country. Public education activities by the front's allies (from radio programs in Piura to street actions in Lima) and growing attention in the mass media, including the Internet, exposed the way the government was handling the situation and produced growing public pressure for change.

Public education and other communications improved with the change in how the front framed its message. Replacing symbols of fists and angry people with lemons and mangos helped to more effectively connect the farmers of Tambogrande with the food, culture, and people across the nation.

The combination of these actions appears to have forced the corporation to attempt buying off the front by proposing that the 25 percent share of the mine go to the town rather than the central government. That action likely led to discord in the alliance between the central government and the corporation. At the same time, the government must have felt pressured by growing public attention to the plight of the Tambograndinos. It is likely the combination of these factors that caused the government to change course and institute more demanding conditions for final approval of the mine.

Once the government changed its conditions, the front's strategy once again employed mass protests (including the possibility of violence) to shut down the hearings, block approval of the corporation's impact study, and achieve its policy goal.

Evaluation and Learning

Evaluation and learning are crucial to effective advocacy both in the midst of a campaign or initiative and after it has been completed.

At the start of a campaign, there are a great many unknowns. The policy issues may be complicated. Aspects of the political processes may be intentionally hidden from public view. The initial strategy might generate unanticipated responses that must be addressed. Thus during such a complex and changing process, the most effective advocates tend to be those who are skilled at monitoring progress, assessing outcomes to date, learning from those observations, and adjusting analyses and strategies midcourse.

At the same time, the advocates are typically overstretched by the demands of the work and relatively limited resources. Thus it is always difficult to systematically monitor, assess, learn, and change.

After a campaign, there may be more time to step back and conduct a more systematic evaluation and learning process (though many advocates may feel compelled to immediately move on to the next campaign). There is also the benefit of hindsight.

Like all evaluations, the focus can be on process, outcomes, or impact. Process evaluation examines how well the campaign was planned and carried out. One of the standards for assessing this is to determine how well an activity was done in relation to best practices, based on the learning that has emerged from previous evaluations. For example, did the communication materials used for constituent education use language and examples that were directly relevant to them?

Outcome evaluation examines the changes the activities have or have not brought about. Some of these changes can be process outcomes. For example, did the constituent education program result in five hundred people writing a letter to the policy maker?

Three types of long-term outcomes are commonly examined. Two of those possible outcomes are always relevant:

- Did the campaign achieve its policy goals? Was there in fact a change in policy?

- Did the campaign strengthen the capacity of the advocates and advocacy networks to continue working for policy change and social justice?

A third outcome is relevant in all but the most open and transparent of political contexts:

- Did the campaign change processes of policy making so that it is more possible for citizens to have a meaningful voice?

In most cases, the third outcome may be a desirable but side benefit of a campaign to change a specific policy. For example, while advocating that the municipal government increase funding for the local health clinic to improve outreach and prevention services, the general procedures for citizen input might be clarified and improved. In some cases, the first and third outcomes are the same; the campaign's policy change goal is to change policies about policy making. For example, the goal may be to make significant changes in the way budgets are formulated and approved by the municipal government without concern for any specific budget decision.

Assessing those outcomes is complicated by several issues, the first of which is tension between the outcomes. It is very common and often essential for a coalition of organizations to form and work toward a policy change. A new coalition, especially the trust and solidarity between different groups, is a good example of the second outcome: strengthened capacity for future advocacy. However, it is not uncommon for policy makers to ask the advocates to compromise and accept only a portion of what they are seeking. If the coalition members cannot agree on what is an acceptable compromise, the options may become: achieve a partial policy victory but harm the coalition, or hold the coalition together but without any change in policy.[6]

Second, when there is a policy change, or a change in the policies on policy making, it is often impossible to identify all the causes of that change. Multiple advocacy organizations and coalitions may be engaged in the struggle. The change may have resulted (partially) from inside efforts by progressive policy makers or their advisers. The change may have been (partially) forced upon the policy makers by stronger policy institutions. For example, a national government policy for improving outreach and prevention by health clinics may have provided an incentive or requirement for increasing municipal government funding. In such cases, attribution of the change to any one advocacy group, coalition, or campaign is not possible. Rather the evaluation might seek to examine and assess the contribution of the advocates within the larger process.

Impact evaluation is more complicated and difficult than outcome evaluation because it examines to what extent the original problem is solved after a policy has changed. Most often a significant lag time occurs between when a policy is changed and when its impact can be seen. One reason for the delay is the time needed to fully implement a new policy, and the implementation process itself may significantly influence the degree of impact. During the lag period, the conditions that caused the problem or were necessary to solve the problem may have changed because of unrelated factors. And other policy or program changes may have been developed and are helping solve the original problem.

Intertwined with process, outcome, and impact evaluation are accountability questions that have to do with costs and outcomes of investing scarce resources (staff and citizen volunteer time, funds, and so forth). Which investment alternatives have the greatest impact? An advocacy campaign versus other interventions or programs (for example, more health services)? One advocacy campaign versus a different campaign? Strengthening one part of an advocacy campaign (for example, more staff for media relations) versus another part (for example, more staff for lobbying policy makers)? The questions are most often asked by supporters (organizational leadership, donors, and so forth), but they are of equal concern to those directly engaged in advocacy work. The obvious difficulty is trying to answer such questions when, as already noted, they require measurements of outcomes and impact that are nearly impossible.

Since the complicated, difficult nature of evaluating advocacy means that assessments will always be imprecise, it becomes all the more important to focus on evaluation for the purpose of learning. It may be impossible for advocates to specifically attribute an outcome to their efforts or prove that the ultimate impact of their work will be equal to or greater than investments in other interventions. But it is possible to improve the effectiveness of advocacy through asking process, outcome, and impact evaluation questions, and drawing lessons that can be applied immediately in a campaign or in future campaigns.

Of course, individual advocates are constantly drawing lessons. But the effectiveness and contributions of such learning are significantly increased if done systematically and shared by individuals and teams. One way to draw lessons is to compare and contrast a current advocacy experience with previous experiences, one's own and those of others. Case studies are one source of information about others' experiences.

Another way to draw lessons is to examine a current experience through the lens of concepts in the literature about advocacy, including discussions of best practices. Does the experience confirm and possibly deepen or expand a point made in the literature? Or does it challenge a point and suggest a new one?

One way to capture the lessons is in the form of general recommendations or advice that would be helpful to other advocates in planning, implementing, or evaluating a campaign. (More challenging, but possible, are recommendations or advice based on meta-learning, that is, lessons about drawing lessons from a campaign that can guide other advocates' learning.)

Doing case study research is a means to describe a campaign and then focus on the evaluation and learning dimensions. The primary questions are: How effective was the campaign? What lessons can be learned from the experience?

TAMBOGRANDE CASE: EVALUATION AND LEARNING

The front appears to have been relatively effective in terms of process evaluation, even though it is unlikely its members would have thought about it in those terms. At several points, the advocates re-evaluated the situation, learned, and changed strategies, taking into account responses from policy makers, changing conditions, and new opportunities, as well as the tragic loss of their leader.

Some of the advocates' actions reflect generally understood best practices in advocacy. For example, when the front reframed its message and symbolism, it connected to deeply held values common among most Peruvians and demonstrated a personal connection between the lives of the rural Tambograndinos and the citizens in urban areas. Likewise, the alliances the front built with national and international NGOs appear to have been based on its terms (when to take risks, when to compromise or accept an external offer, and so forth) and not, as is too often the case, on those of the larger better funded and more professional organizations. (If so, it is likely the NGOs in the alliance also deserve credit.)

Process outcomes, for example, the size of its protests, number of signatures on its petition, the turnout for and the results of the referendum, and so forth, indicate that the front achieved many organizing objectives.

In terms of policy change outcomes, the front fully succeeded in its primary goal: the mine will not be built. In terms of governance change outcomes, at one point the front demanded a new law that would guarantee local communities the right to make decisions about their own development; it did not achieve that goal. On the other hand, by forcing the government to establish a procedure that required the foreign corporation to submit a full report, all in Spanish, that would be reviewed during public hearings, it may have set a precedent that would make other government decisions, at least concerning extractive industries, more transparent and participatory. (On the other hand, the fact that protests prevented the hearings from taking place may have limited if not eliminated the precedent-setting quality of this outcome.)

In terms of capacity-building outcomes, the emergence of the front itself represents a positive outcome. The members must have gained greater confidence in their rights and ability to influence policy decisions. It is likely that a number of the members have developed significant leadership and advocacy strategy skills. While the Technical Support Committee likely disbanded after the victory, the personal and organizational networks that were established will likely continue and be drawn upon if and when a new need arises for collaboration. One can expect that the mining concession to Manhattan Minerals will not be the last attempt to extract the minerals from under Tambogrande.

It does not appear, however, that the front joined any national network or coalition of community or grassroots-level organizations that was being affected by external development, or if one did not exist, that the campaign helped develop one. The solidarity and mutual learning made possible through a coalition is likely necessary if towns are to continue fighting off new concessions, much less get a law passed that guarantees their right to determine their own development. If each local community relies on the national and international NGOs to support them, it is unlikely that the balance of power between the community groups and the larger NGOs will consistently give decision-making priority to the groups that represent those who would be most affected by external development.

The evaluation of impact outcomes is less of an issue in an advocacy campaign that is focused on blocking a policy (for example, permission to construct a mine) rather than one that creates a new policy (for example, the development of a new irrigation system for local farmers). However, in this case, the external impact assessment report could be used to estimate the benefits, which are equal to the amount of damage that would have been caused if the mine had been constructed. The possibility of placing a monetary value on some of those benefits would make it feasible to at least partially evaluate investment outcomes, although it is very unlikely that the front would be concerned with such a number.

In terms of learning, numerous lessons can be drawn from this evaluation. One might be that advocacy campaigns should operate within and fully use their cultural context. The front's approach to reframing its communication is an obvious example, as is the effective use of traditional street demonstrations (*pasacalles*) by its allies in Lima. But Peruvian political culture includes the protests that shut down major highways and in some cases destroy property; in the final stages of the campaign at least, the threat of potentially violent protest was instrumental in the victory.

Notes

1. As noted in chapter 1, a single person might be the advocate for change in the policies of an institution that is relatively small and accessible, such as a school or a village government; but even in those situations success usually requires the advocates to be at least a group of people if not a more formal association or organization. For that reason, the book only uses *advocates* (plural).

2. From the point of view of studying advocacy, yet another possibility is to consider the informal networks of multiple organizations and coalitions engaged in advocacy on a common issue as the unit of analysis. However, from the perspective of someone involved in an advocacy process, such networks are usually too diffuse to prove useful.

3. Note, however, that viewing the case from the perspective of one of the national or international NGOs or the support committee as a whole raises at least some significant differences in terms of policy goals, political analyses, and strategic options. An important issue that runs through all the elements of the case is the degree to which the members of the support committee were unable to dominate the Defense Front, given the inherent differences in resources, access to knowledge, and other sources of power imbalance.

4. A problem is a situation or condition that one or more groups of people find unacceptable and that reflects the groups' values and vision of what is right

and desirable. Thus not everyone in a society will agree that a given situation or condition is a problem.

5. Of course, human-rights-oriented policies are themselves the result of advocacy by various actors.

6. On the other hand, if the coalition remains intact, it is often possible to continue working toward the original policy change goals.

CASE B

Vermonters Advocate to
Close a Nuclear Power Reactor

The Vermont Yankee Nuclear Power Plant began operation in 1972 with a forty-year license from the US Nuclear Regulatory Commission (NRC).[1] Organizations and networks of citizens, professionals, and others concerned about the dangers of nuclear power opposed the plant's construction and ever since have sought to shut it down.

The owners of the plant and other proponents of nuclear power argued that it is "safe, clean, and reliable" (see www.safecleanreliable.com). Opponents argued that the risk of a radioactive release because of equipment failure, an operator's mistake, or a terrorist attack, which could result in massive illness, death, and long-term environmental destruction, is simply too great. To support their position, they pointed to Three Mile Island and Chernobyl. In response to those who suggested that such problems were in the past, the advocates brought up a near disaster at the Davis-Besse Nuclear Power Station in Ohio and to the radioactive tritium that was leaking into groundwater around reactors in California, Connecticut, Illinois, Massachusetts, and New York. With regard to Vermont Yankee, the advocates listed fires, lost radioactive fuel rods, cracks in the steam dryers, and stuck valves that caused an emergency shutdown. They also said it is absurd to generate tons of highly radioactive waste, dangerous for thousands of years, with no viable system for disposal, and that the real costs of nuclear power are hidden by massive government subsidies to the industry.

Advocacy efforts became especially vigorous after 2001, catalyzed by a proposal from the multinational Louisiana-based Entergy Corporation (see www.entergy.com) to buy the plant from Vermont's public utility companies, and then after it was purchased, to increase the power output (referred to as an uprate) of the aging plant by 20 percent, to store the reactor's excess radioactive waste on its grounds, and to seek a new twenty-year license to operate after 2012.

The New England Coalition (NEC), based in Brattleboro, was the longest-standing member of the local advocacy network, having been formed in the 1960s to stop the construction of Vermont Yankee and other nuclear power plants in the region.[2] NEC's senior adviser helped convince the governor of Maine to request an "independent safety assessment" of the Maine Yankee Nuclear Power Plant and then helped ensure a public review of the many problems that were uncovered, ultimately causing the plant's owners to decide to shut it down in 1997.

The Citizens Awareness Network (CAN; www.nukebusters.org) was formed by Massachusetts residents in response to a near-catastrophic accident that occurred in 1992 at the Yankee Rowe Nuclear Power Plant in western Massachusetts. CAN's advocacy was instrumental in the process that resulted in the owners' shutting down the plant. CAN then expanded and formed chapters in five states, including Vermont.

Nuclear Free Vermont by 2012 (NFV) was formed by a group of citizens in Brattleboro and surrounding Windham County towns. Its initial focus was to raise awareness and demonstrate public opposition to the reactor by getting a nonbinding resolution on the 2002 agendas of many local town meetings (which are a uniquely New England form of direct democracy in which decisions about town and local schools matters are made at an annual gathering open to all town residents).

Joined by yet other organizations, including statewide and regional nonprofit organizations such as the Vermont Public Interest Research Group (VPIRG; www.vpirg.org) and by many unaffiliated but well-informed and highly active citizens, NEC, CAN, and NFV were at the forefront of the revitalized efforts to close Vermont Yankee and replace it with a combination of increased efficiency and renewable and other safe sources.

Despite their advocacy, efforts to block the sale to Entergy, to stop approval of the 20 percent uprate, and to slow down the approval of on-site radioactive waste storage in dry casks all failed. On the other hand, the efforts, which ranged from legal challenges to mobilizing large numbers of speakers and protestors at many different public hearings, resulted in various safety and economic concessions by the corporation and its regulators that would have been unlikely had there been no contestation. One of those concessions was charging below-market rates on electricity sold within Vermont (which amounted to about one-third of the state's power).[3]

Parallel to these efforts, NFV focused on the inadequacy of the emergency evacuation plan for responding to a radiological release at Vermont Yankee. And it continued to use town meeting votes to demonstrate public opposition to Vermont Yankee. Its 2002 resolution calling for an immediate shutdown and transition to alternative energy sources met with only limited success because many voters questioned the feasibility of that demand. So NFV reassessed its strategy. The following year it put a resolution on the ballots of fifteen Windham County towns that called for the plant to be closed when its license expires in 2012 and for the state to plan for renewable alternatives. Despite the fact that the Entergy Corporation spent over US$240,000 (compared to US$4,000 raised by NFV) to defeat the initiative, it passed by overwhelming margins in eleven of the towns and lost by only a handful of votes in Brattleboro, the largest town. The following year NFV put another resolution on the ballot only in Brattleboro that simply called for planning to replace Vermont Yankee's nuclear energy by 2012 and added a call for state support to help with training and other support for the plant's employees. The latter element effectively blocked Entergy's ability to publicly oppose the resolution, and it passed with a 73 percent majority. In 2005 NFV used the town meeting day ballot in Brattleboro to focus on the inadequacy of the evacuation plan with a resolution that called for Entergy to pay for major improvements in warning, staffing, and testing; it passed by an 84 percent majority.

CAN continued to use various grassroots education and direct action tactics, including supporting civil disobedience by various affinity groups at Vermont Yankee's corporate headquarters, as well as to advocate for intervention by the governments in the neighboring states of Massachusetts and New Hampshire, which would be as or more affected (depending on wind direction) by a radiological release.[4]

By the end of 2005 the primary focus for advocacy shifted to whether Entergy will be allowed to continue the reactor's operation after 2012. By law, that requires the approval of the NRC and the Vermont Public Service Board (PSB). The NRC is responsible for assessing safety and related issues, while the PSB's jurisdiction is basically limited to whether the extension will be in the economic interest of the state's rate payers (i.e., businesses and home owners).

However, most advocates held out little hope that either of those bodies would rule against continued operation. They knew that the processes the NRC used to rule on the uprate and on-site waste storage were strongly biased in favor of the industry. They pointed out that the NRC had not only approved the recent applications for Vermont Yankee, but that it also had approved every one of the dozens of other applications for nuclear power plant uprates, on-site storage, and, most importantly, permission to operate after the initial licenses have expired. The advocates also pointed out that NRC policy requires the assumption that there will be adequate storage for nuclear waste, even though few political realists believed that the long-planned solution, a storage facility at Yucca Mountain in Nevada, would open at any time in the near future, if ever, and noted that NRC policy explicitly prevented consideration of a possible terrorist attack on a nuclear facility when considering applications for new licenses.[5]

Even against these odds, the NEC continued to hire lawyers and technical experts to intervene in the NRC and PSB proceedings. While CAN and

NFV began to search for an alternative approach, they appreciated NEC's efforts as a way of raising public awareness, slowing down the process, and at times using the discovery procedures in legal cases to secure information that would otherwise not be available to advocates.

Two other bodies could also close Vermont Yankee. By law, a nuclear plant could also be closed by the Federal Emergency Management Agency if there is not a viable evacuation plan. But again experience at other power plants (for example, Indian Point near New York City, where a governor-commissioned study clearly demonstrated the inadequacy of that plan) suggests that there was almost no chance of succeeding on that front. Thus NFV's efforts regarding the Vermont Yankee evacuation plan were primarily focused on strengthening public awareness and opposition to the plant, as well as on forcing improvements that will decrease the level of disaster in the event of a radiological release.

The other body with the power to close the reactor was the Entergy Corporation itself. In fact it could do so at any time the financial costs (and possibly corporate reputation costs) outweighed the benefits. But efforts to require an independent safety assessment similar to the one done at Maine Yankee, which might identify the need for expensive repairs, had been ignored or deflected by a popular Republican governor, his energy agency, and the NRC. And other efforts, such as requiring significant increases in the costs of the evacuation plan, were unlikely to make enough difference.

Thus, as advocacy organizations developed their strategies for blocking operation after 2012, some of them focused on the possibility of the Vermont legislature, the most democratic and transparent of all the possible targets, making a decision on whether the plant could continue operation after the license period. It was also the most liberal target because Democrats held the majority in the house and senate.

However, the legislature's right to make this decision was debatable, even though it had voted to approve the original construction of the reactor. Moreover, even where there was a fairly clear legal basis for the legislature to approve or deny Entergy's proposal for on-site storage of radioactive waste that exceeded its current capacity, their decision had outraged the Vermont Yankee advocacy networks.

The advocates had sought to delay the storage decision until thorough studies had been conducted related to such issues as the environment, public health, and economic risks. But in the final days of its 2005 session, the legislature suspended normal rules and voted to approve a "compromise" worked out behind closed doors with Entergy Corporation officials that approved enough on-site storage to continue operation through 2012 in exchange for payments to a renewable energy fund.

The legislative leadership argued that this was the best possible deal it could negotiate, since most Vermonters outside of Windham County were unaware of the safety issues and very interested in receiving the benefits of below-market electricity rates. However, when two of those leaders tried to explain their actions during a meeting in Brattleboro, the advocates organized a protest that received wide coverage in the media.

Soon thereafter the leader most identified with what the advocates considered a betrayal of their position, Peter Welch, Vermont senate president pro tem and a liberal Democrat, announced he would seek the Democratic Party's nomination for the November 2006 election to the state's one seat in the US House of Representatives. The seat became vacant when congressman Bernie Sanders decided to seek election to the US Senate. In January, Sanders, a very popular and extremely progressive independent, planned a campaign kickoff rally in Brattleboro and invited Welch and other Democrats to share the stage.

A group of advocates called a meeting to plan yet another protest against Welch at the rally. However, members of NFV argued for a different approach. Since nearly every advocate strongly supported Sanders, and since a protest might negatively affect his campaign, the advocates' proposal was to ask Sanders's staff to speak with Welch and arrange for him to meet with them about Vermont Yankee legislation during his final session as Vermont senate president. The other advocacy groups agreed with the proposal, and Welch agreed to meet with them.

Working with advocates, a local state senator had introduced a bill that would give the legislature the power to decide whether the reactor would be allowed to operate after 2012. (The bill stated that the PSB could not issue the required certificate of public good unless and until the general assembly determined by vote that continued operation was in the best interest of the state.)

To regain support for his US House campaign in Windham County, Welch made a commitment to make it a "must pass" bill in his final term in the Vermont legislature. Throughout the session, a group of advocates from different organizations in Windham County met regularly, often with four of their local legislators who shared common values and goals, to plan ways to support the bill and to hold the senate president to his word. Smaller groups made multiple trips to the state capitol for meetings with the senate president, and with his help, the speaker of the house and the chairs and key members of relevant committees.

The Windham County advocates also networked with VPIRG, the Conservation Law Foundation, and Vermonters for a Clean Environment to support the bill's passage. Each of those organizations has staff who work on a daily basis with legislators on environmental issues, and thus they provided the Windham County advocates with important insider information and lobbying capacity.

The advocates planned the message carefully. It was not a decision about supporting or opposing the Vermont Yankee reactor and certainly not about supporting or opposing nuclear power in general. Instead, in their literature and meetings with legislators the advocates spoke about good governance and the responsibility of the legislature for due diligence on what everyone could agree was a critical issue facing the future of the state. They said that such decisions should be made in Vermont by Vermonters, and not in Washington, DC (by the NRC) or in Louisiana (at Entergy headquarters).

They also worked with supportive legislators to amend the bill so that it mandated studies of the economic, health, and environmental issues related to extended operation and public engagement through hearings and other processes. The senate president closely followed these developments and worked with the leadership and Democratic caucus in both chambers to ensure its passage. In the end, with no hope of defeating the bill (but with the belief that they ultimately would win the mandated vote on Vermont Yankee's future), the Republican leadership decided to support it as a good governance bill, and in May 2006 it passed by a nearly unanimous vote.[6] The governor signed the bill, and it became law as Vermont General Assembly Act 160.[7]

In June the network of local and statewide advocacy groups made the decision to continue as a more formal coalition called Safe Power Vermont and work even more collaboratively on the second phase of their legislative strategy: ensuring that when the mandated vote did occur, most likely in 2008, the decision would be to not approve extended operation. That phase is the subject of Case F.

LEARNING EXERCISE

Using the questions at the end of Case A, quickly map this case by identifying the content of the five circles and the three types of outcomes.

Next, focus on the overlaps or intersections among the three arenas, policy, politics, and strategy, by identifying ways a development in one arena influenced one or both of the other arenas. Compare your analysis to that offered in chapter 4.

Optional: Use another map or two, either the nine steps in the *Sourcebook*'s Strategy Framework or the *New Weave*'s ten moments.[8] Identify any additional insights gained by comparing these maps.

Note: Case F will invite you to think about how the advocates' goals and strategies needed to evolve once Act 160 had passed and the new challenge was to convince the legislature to vote against allowing the Vermont Yankee reactor to continue operation after March 2012.

Notes

1. Vernon is located on the Connecticut River in the southeasternmost corner of Windham County, Vermont. The largest town in the county, Brattleboro, is about

seven miles to the north. The Massachusetts border is five miles to the south, and New Hampshire is immediately across the river.

2. Known until recently as the New England Coalition on Nuclear Pollution, the NEC is in fact not an organizational coalition but rather a board-directed nonprofit with individual members (see www.necnp.org).

3. Hydropower from Canada provides another third of the power (that company's contract expires in 2015). About one-sixth comes from small renewables, including biomass, wind, hydro, landfill and farm methane, and the final one-sixth is from the general market (primarily fossil fuel plants in other states). For the advocates, the below-market rate for Vermont Yankee power is a double-edged sword in that it has made it more difficult to close the plant.

4. CAN often argues that citizens in these states suffer from "radiation without representation."

5. US senator Harry Reid, of Nevada, now Senate Majority Leader, is one of the leaders among those who oppose the facility. In 2010, he did not mince words on the matter (which no longer appear) on his website: "The proposed Yucca Mountain nuclear waste dump is never going to open. Since I was elected to Congress in 1982, I have been fighting against Yucca Mountain because it threatens the health and safety of Nevadans and people across the United States. The science is incomplete, unsound, yet clearly demonstrates that Yucca Mountain is not a safe site for isolating nuclear waste. The tide is turning on Yucca Mountain, and it is time we look at viable alternatives and realistic approaches to long term nuclear waste storage. My highest priority is to ensure the health and safety of Nevadans and I will continue to fight against bringing spent nuclear fuel to Nevada."

6. Another or perhaps the primary reason for the Republicans' support may have been to reduce the credit the senate president could claim for having achieved a hard-fought victory and thus the degree to which he could regain support in Windham County.

7. An Act Relating to a Certificate of Public Good for Extending the Operating License of a Nuclear Power Plant, 2006 Vt. Acts & Resolves No. 160, http://www .leg.state.vt.us/jfo/envy/ACT160.pdf.

8. Jane Covey and Valerie Miller, *Advocacy Sourcebook: Frameworks for Planning, Action and Reflection* (Boston: Institute for Development Research, 1997); Lisa VeneKlasen with Valerie Miller, *A New Weave of Power, Politics and People: The Action Guide for Advocacy and Citizen Participation* (Warwickshire, UK: Practical Action Publishers, 2007).

4

Advocacy Circles
Intersections

CHAPTER 3 DESCRIBES THE BASIC ELEMENTS OF EACH OF THE FIVE ADVOCACY CIRCLES. However, one of the main points of this conceptual map is the significant overlaps among the circles. This chapter discusses the intersections among the policy, politics, and strategy circles.

In cases when an advocacy process is focused on a relatively short-term, local issue and involves only a handful of advocates, the dynamics of these intersections may be less obvious. In such cases the processes of policy analysis, political analysis, and strategic analysis are often simultaneous, and the impacts of one on the others are seamless. On the other hand, when advocacy is long term and dealing with larger social issues, the interactions become more important to understand. When a team of advocates is responsible for different elements of the campaign, the intersections can also be a source of tension if not consciously addressed.

Case B, which focuses on a critical first stage of the campaign to replace the Vermont Yankee nuclear reactor with other safe sources of energy, is used to illustrate these points. As background for the specific discussions of (a) the intersections of policy and politics and (b) the intersections between that policy/politics dynamic and strategy, a brief overview of the advocates and context circles is provided in the following section.

CLOSE VERMONT YANKEE CASE: ADVOCATES AND CONTEXT

Advocates. The case is written from the perspective of an informal network of three organizations whose primary focus is closing

58

nuclear reactors, and most immediately Vermont Yankee. The network's members are the New England Coalition (NEC), Citizens Awareness Network (CAN), and Nuclear Free Vermont (NFV). While NEC and CAN had a few mostly part-time and underpaid staff, all three had been formed through grassroots action, and volunteers who live in the vicinity of the reactor did most of the work.[1]

Context. While the campaign focuses on closing one nuclear reactor, it takes place within a much larger, decades-long struggle over whether nuclear power should be used to generate energy in the United States (parallel struggles occur in other countries and among them in the United Nations). More specifically, it takes place at a moment when many nuclear reactors are being privatized, purchased from public utility companies by several very large private corporations.

Intersections of Policy and Politics

The policy arena of advocacy (see figure 4.1) involves identifying a problem or set of problems the advocates are dedicated to changing, analyzing the causes, and proposing a solution. The solution may be partially or exclusively focused on changing policy. The necessary change becomes the policy goal.

The political arena of advocacy involves identifying and understanding the institutions of power (governments, corporations, and so forth) whose policies must change to solve the problem.

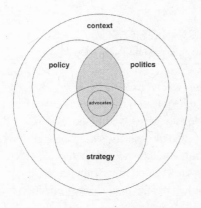

Figure 4.1 Intersections of policy and politics

While those two processes may appear to be sequential and simple enough, the intersections between them are usually iterative, multiple and often complex. It is rarely possible to first formulate a policy solution or goal and then identify the policy institution it fits.

Problems Caused by a Political Institution's Policies

The second step in policy analysis after problem identification is to understand what is causing the problem or problems. Frequently the cause, at least partially, is the fact that a powerful institution has either established a harmful policy or failed to enact or implement a helpful policy. In some cases a cause is an institution's policies about policy making, that is, about access to information, citizen participation, and so forth. For these reasons, policy analysis is often interconnected with understanding the policy arena.

Changes in Policy Analysis in Response to Changes in Targets

It is also common for advocates to expand or refocus their policy research as they explore different policy institutions that might allow them to achieve their solution. As they go through the iterative process between policy analysis and political systems analysis, advocates focus on the powers and limitations of each policy institution and thus the specific policy evidence and arguments that are needed to influence each.

In the same process, advocates encounter policy research and analysis that have been generated by staff of the policy institution or other political actors, especially opponents. Frequently this requires the advocates to do further research and analysis that takes their arguments into consideration, if not directly counters their arguments.

CLOSE VERMONT YANKEE CASE: INTERSECTIONS OF POLICY AND POLITICS

Policy. The initial problem analysis focused on the high risk of a radioactive release affecting the people and the environment of the region. Other concerns include radioactive waste, the lack of a viable emergency evacuation plan, and the real costs of nuclear energy. The cause is a combination of national and state policies that support and permit reactors to operate, the policy-making processes that increasingly limit external participation in policy decisions, and the institution's failure to effectively implement the portions of those policies that could lead to the decision to close Vermont Yankee. For those reasons, the simple policy solution—close the reactor—was in fact very complex and highly connected to the arena of politics.

Politics. The primary targets at the outset of the case were the US Nuclear Regulatory Commission (NRC) and the Vermont Public Service Board (PSB). The case focuses on retargeting the advocacy to focus on the Vermont state legislature. The advocates' allies included organizations that were equally involved in the latter process, such as the Vermont Public Interest Research Group (VPIRG), several nuclear energy experts who had become critical of the industry, and a handful of progressive legislators. The advocates' primary opponent was the Entergy Corporation, which owns the reactor, and its allies included various large business interests and the politicians they influence (if not control). At the time, the most important of those politicians were US president George W. Bush, vice president Dick Cheney, their strongly pro-corporate, pro-nuclear team in the Executive Branch, and Vermont's Republican governor Jim Douglas and his Department of Public Service.

Thus, at the intersection of policy and politics, the advocates' initial efforts focused on two policy institutions and a series of policy decisions: Vermont's sale of the reactor to Entergy, then the corporation's request to uprate the previous power production by 20 percent, and, at the same time, the corporation's request to store radioactive waste in dry casks. Permission for each request required approval of both the NRC and PSB. If the advocates could win with either one of the institutions on any one of the issues (sale, uprate, or dry cask storage), they would achieve their policy goal of closing the reactor.

Moreover, the Vermont legislature had the power to approve or reject any new storage of radioactive waste in the state, and thus the advocates had a third target and means for blocking that decision.

The advocates' initial research and analysis was largely dictated by the jurisdictions and powers of the different policy institutions. Federal law gives the NRC sole jurisdiction over issues of nuclear safety as well as the power to evaluate environmental impacts of nuclear reactors and related issues. The PSB's powers were, in general, limited to determining if the decisions were in the economic interests of the rate payers.

Thus, when involved with NRC policy making, the advocates needed to present data and analysis that addressed safety and the environment. Moreover, their research needed to include understanding and attempts to counter the data, analyses, and recommendations, often very technical, generated by researchers working for their target (the NRC) and their opponent (Entergy) and its allies (the Nuclear Energy Institute and other groups supporting the industry). While several people in the advocacy network had developed significant expertise on these matters through self-education, it was also necessary to engage a number of nuclear experts and lawyers in various volunteer or paid capacities to carry out the research and make the arguments.

When involved with PSB policy making, the research and analysis needed to shift to issues related to PSB's jurisdiction and to respond to a different set of data and recommendations from Entergy and its allies. To do so, additional expertise (for example, from economists) was also necessary.

On the other hand, neither policy institution was likely to accept the advocates' arguments and recommendation. The NRC had never denied a power plant's application related to power uprates, dry cask storage, or license extension; most advocates viewed the NRC as a pawn of the nuclear industry. Likewise, it was relatively easy for Entergy to gain PSB approval by selling Vermonters a portion of the total output at below-market rates (while making significant profits selling the majority of its output on the open market).

Thus the combination of policy and political analyses informed the strategic decision to refocus on influencing the legislature with regard to the next and most defining policy decision: whether the reactor can continue operation after 2012 when its NRC license and PSB certificate expire. That process is discussed later in this chapter.

Intersections of Policy/Politics and Strategy

At each point when the complex, iterative process between policy and politics results in a specific policy change goal and a clear targeting of a policy institution, the arena of strategy may seem straightforward: identify a combination and sequence of methods (organizing, coalition building, use of media, lobbying, and so forth) that will influence the policy makers and achieve the policy change goal. Yet once again, the intersections are multiple and complex (see figure 4.2).

Strategy at the Outset of Policy/Political Analyses
The policy change goal is the product of an analytic process that begins with the identification of a problem or set of problems. If advocates are to be accountable to the communities affected by a problem that is to be

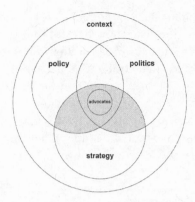

Figure 4.2 Intersections of
policy/politics with strategy

solved through policy change, they cannot complete even this first step
of the policy analysis process without a strategy to engage community
members in defining and prioritizing their own problems.

Moreover, if the advocacy is to be *by,* and not only *on behalf of,* a
marginalized community, members of that community must be able to
be actively engaged in both the policy and political analysis processes.
Where this capacity is undeveloped, as is frequently the case, an even
more developed strategy is needed, one that builds capacity through
some combination of community outreach, education, organizing, and
leadership development.

Strategy Informing Decisions About
Policy Goals and Political Targets

As the policy and political analysis processes begin to focus on a desired
goal and specific target, strategic analysis asks the question, can we win?
Or, more accurately, do we have a reasonable chance of achieving the
policy change goal in light of the larger context and our own capacities
and resources? Can we address gaps in our capacity and resources?

The strategic analysis may result in modifications of the goal or target. More often, the result may be the formulation of a multiphase plan
that requires parts of the policy or political analysis to be deepened, expanded, or refined.

Likewise, advocates may return once again to policy analysis, or at
least the way the analysis is presented, when developing their communications strategy.

Other Strategic Goals

In some cases a policy change goal cannot be achieved without a change
in policy-making processes or, more generally, in governance. Frequently

a policy goal cannot be achieved without shifts in power; advocacy organizations, marginalized groups, and the general public need to build their people power, capacities, and resources to challenge elite groups.

Strategic analysis should ensure that in addition to policy change goals, these other goals are clear.

The process of advocating for a policy change can simultaneously shift power and change governance where appropriate. However, with limited resources and time constraints, advocates are often faced with choices: win a specific policy change or build people power.

CLOSE VERMONT YANKEE CASE: INTERSECTIONS OF POLICY/POLITICS AND STRATEGY

Strategy. During the initial phase of this case, the advocates used a variety of methods to stop the sale, block the uprate, and slow down if not block dry cask storage as a means to achieve the policy goal: close the reactor. Some of the strategies involved formal engagement in the NRC and PSB processes (gaining party status to intervene in the official hearings, providing testimony, and so forth). Other strategies focused on public outreach, education, and engagement. Materials were published, including letters written to local newspapers. Hundreds of citizens attended NRC open meetings. Town meeting day resolutions were passed. A group of activists committed to civil disobedience were arrested for trespassing at the reactor and the corporation's local headquarters.

Given the grassroots history and structure of the advocacy organizations, coupled with public outreach, the campaign was largely by and for those most affected. On the other hand, the technical nature of the policy research and analysis limited the importance of the communities' involvement beyond the most general statement of the problem.

The strategic arena was central to the shift in the campaign's focus in 2006. Having lost the sale and uprate policy decisions, attention turned to the next and most important decision: whether the reactor would be allowed to operate after its license and certification ended in 2012. Unfortunately by then the advocates had an increasingly clear answer to the main strategic question of can we win? It was: if it requires influencing the NRC or PSB, not likely.

When the legislature also approved dry cask storage, the advocates might have also added them to the "not likely" category.

However, the advocates' strategy related to public education and engagement created the capacity to view the decision as a strategic opportunity. The political leader most identified with the poor handling (sellout) of the dry cask decision was also the top candidate in the next election for Vermont's seat in the US Congress. It would be difficult to win if the anti-Vermont Yankee forces opposed him. And thus the advocates were able to secure his critically important support for a bill that would give the legislature the power to decide on the future of the reactor.

To prevent a repeat of the dry cask vote, the advocates now needed to expand and refine their policy analysis as well as the strategic framing of that analysis. Given the NRC's sole jurisdiction regarding safety, research and policy arguments focused on other concerns that legislators might have, such as the overall state economy, the feasibility of alternatives to nuclear power, and public health. To pass the legislation that would give the Vermont legislature the power to decide the fate of Yankee Vermont after 2012, these arguments needed only to raise reasonable questions, because the message became the following: good governance and due diligence require that elected representatives ensure the decision is based on facts that can be debated by the public and in the state house.

The advocates also needed to refine and expand their political analysis to understand the power relations and processes involved in passing legislation. To expand that analysis, new strategic alliances need to be built and solidified with organizations like VPIRG that work closely with the legislature on multiple issues. Some of the same groups were also critical in building support among their members and supporters in other parts of the state.

Passing the bill, Vermont General Assembly Act 160, would not have been possible if the advocates had not effectively interconnected the arena of strategy with the arenas of policy and politics.

Note

1. It would have been equally appropriate to have viewed the case from the perspective of any one of those organizations, or of one on the multi-issue, staffed organizations that are here viewed as allies of the local network, or even of the yet larger and more informal network of all those organizations.

PART TWO

CASE C

BRAC Advocacy Unit, Bangladesh: What Next?

Sheepa Hafiza, coauthor

The Bangladesh Rehabilitation Assistance Committee (BRAC) was formed by F. H. Abed and a group of fellow Bangladeshis in 1972 in the aftermath of a devastating cyclone and the new nation's brutal struggle for liberation from Pakistan. It has since evolved from a small relief effort in one part of the country to what it is today, one of the world's largest and most respected nongovernmental organizations (NGOs) in the field of development.[1]

In 2002 the BRAC Advocacy Unit (BAU) was formed as part of a major initiative to address the conditions of ultra-poor women (see page 73 for the definition of *ultra poor*) who are unable to take advantage of even the microcredit programs that BRAC and other Bangladeshi organizations, such as the Grameen Bank, have made available to the poor in nearly every village across the nation.

Over the course of the next eight years, the BAU developed innovative approaches to social communication, media mobilization, and advocacy that resulted in over a thousand village-level associations and projects to support the ultra poor in their communities, millions of students learning about ultrapoverty through school quizzes and debates; several thousand news reports in print and electronic media, including television talk shows; and hundreds of government officials participating with academics, religious leaders, and other influential members of civil society in workshops, forums, on television talk shows, and in field visits focused on how to address ultrapoverty.

During that time, the BAU expanded its focus and applied similar approaches to address a number of different health issues (tuberculosis and malaria control, water and sanitation, and infant and child nutrition) and the human rights abuses experienced by Bangladeshis who seek work abroad.

But BAU's leadership and staff were not satisfied with their many accomplishments. In 2010 they invited an external resource person to review their work and make suggestions about how they might improve and increase their impact.[2] The exercise for this case asks you to assume the role of that external resource person. Your focus will be limited to BAU's work related to ultrapoverty. In addition to your knowledge of advocacy from Part One of this book, your responses should reflect the following information about Bangladesh, BRAC, and its BAU.

Context

Bangladesh is one of the poorest and most densely populated countries in the world, with about 160 million people living in an area that is slightly smaller than the US state of Iowa (in fact, five countries the size of Bangladesh could fit into the area inside Pakistan's borders) and is prone to floods, cyclones, and other natural disasters.

About 98 percent of the population is of the same ethnic heritage (Bengali) and speaks a common first language (Bangla). About 90 percent of Bangladeshis are Muslim, and about 9 percent are Hindu. There are also a number of ethnic and religious minorities.

With regard to the focus of this case, about 40 percent of Bangladeshis are "poor according to the national poverty line. About 25 percent live in extreme income poverty, and about 10 percent subsist on two meals or less for several months every year. Almost one-third of the rural population has suffered the indignity of chronic poverty for over a decade—low consumption, hunger, illiteracy, and lack of access to basic health and other services."[3]

But in the field of development, Bangladesh is also a source of inspiration. The Chronic Poverty Research Centre, an international partnership of universities, research institutes, and NGOs, begins its overview of Bangladesh as follows:

> Following independence in 1971, Bangladesh—ravaged by war, natural disaster and destitution—was viewed in the international community as a "basket case" that would remain dependent on foreign aid for the foreseeable future. Yet the country went on to achieve extraordinary improvements in social and economic development indicators, based on consistently high growth rates, some government success, particularly in large-scale infrastructural development, and concerted action by NGOs.
>
> In the 1970s Bangladesh was also populated by a significant cadre of young activists full of hope, energy and commitment to reconstruction and nation-building, and as the substantial challenges overwhelmed the new government, even with overseas assistance, small NGOs emerged to organize relief, rehabilitation, and eventually development. Today Bangladesh is host to many of the most well-respected and successful local NGOs and microfinancial institutions and models of alternative service delivery in the world.[4]

Advocates

Of the many well-respected and successful local NGOs in Bangladesh, BRAC is one of the oldest and without question the largest in terms of the scope and scale of its work. Its scope and orientation are reflected in its vision-mission-values statement:

> Our Vision: A world free from all forms of exploitation and discrimi-
> nation where everyone has the opportunity to realise their potential.
> Our Mission: Our mission is to empower people and communities in
> situations of poverty, illiteracy, disease and social injustice. Our interven-
> tions aim to achieve large scale, positive changes through economic and
> social programmes that enable men and women to realise their potential.
> Our Values: Innovation, Integrity, Inclusiveness, Effectiveness.[5]

Soon after the organization was founded, BRAC's leadership chose to move away from a general community development model (through which local elites often gained the most) to one that works directly with the poor, especially rural women, and provides a comprehensive set of supports. Today those supports include village-level, group-based microcredit loans, income generation skills training, health education and services, human rights education and legal services, and nonformal preprimary and primary education. The quality of the programs and the identification of lessons for further innovation are enhanced through studies conducted by the large and well-trained Research and Evaluation Division in BRAC.

However, BRAC's leadership concluded that a comprehensive scope was not enough by itself. In the often quoted words of F. H. Abed, who has continued as the organization's primary leader for nearly forty years, "Small is beautiful, but big is necessary." In the context of Bangladesh, that means very big. In the late 1970s, BRAC developed an innovative approach for providing home-based training in oral rehydration therapy (a simple combination of water, salt, and sugar to treat diarrhea, one of the primary causes of infant mortality) that successfully reached at least one woman in almost every household in every village in the country. That effort and the lessons learned gave BRAC the capacity to scale up most of its programs. BRAC describes this capacity as one of its core strengths: "Unprecedented Scale and Reach—Working in countries where the poor number in the tens of millions, we cannot afford to be satisfied with small-scale projects. We are specialists in taking an idea, testing it, perfecting it and then expanding it rapidly to national scale cost-effectively and without compromising quality."[6]

Data from BRAC's 2009 annual report provide an indication of what that means: over US$1 billion in microcredit loans were made to six million households (with historical repayment rates exceeding 99 percent), volunteer health workers provided education or services to over one hundred million people (nearly two-thirds of the entire population), and BRAC operated twenty-six thousand preprimary schools and thirty-eight thousand primary schools for children from poor households. To provide these and other services, BRAC employs over 120,000 staff members, about 48,000 full-time (nearly 20 percent women) and 72,000 part-time village teachers and health workers (over 99 percent women).[7]

BRAC also created an extensive network of business enterprises, many of which are at the end of supply chains that begin with village-level income generation activities initiated through microcredit and training (for example, a dairy plant that makes yogurt and other products for urban consumption gets its milk from women who have used loans to purchase one or two cows). A very significant portion of BRAC's revenue is derived from their profits.

BRAC has recently become an international NGO, helping to build poverty-related institutions in other countries. The first major initiative was in Afghanistan after the Taliban lost power. Today BRAC is also providing microfinance, education, and other development support in Pakistan, Sri Lanka, Liberia, Sierra Leone, Southern Sudan, Tanzania, Uganda, and Haiti.

Compared to its innovative and enormous programs, BRAC is not well known for its policy advocacy. However, it does in fact have a long and impressive track record of influencing the policy agenda of and policy formulation, enactment, and implementation by the Bangladeshi government. Some of those experiences are described in the section on strategy (page 75).

Politics

Bangladesh's political system went through considerable turmoil for nearly twenty years following independence, with a series of assassinations, coups, and military governments. However, since 1991 democracy has been relatively stable and secular. Although Bangladesh has a multiparty system, two main political parties have traded power about every five years when national elections are held. Prior to each election, a caretaker government acceptable to all parties is formed, and one of its purposes is to ensure neutrality in the election process.

The legislative body is a unicameral parliament with 345 members, 45 of whom must be women. The executive body consists of a prime minister and cabinet as well as multiple ministries headed by appointed ministers, most of whom are members of parliament. Each ministry is managed by a secretary and other civil service officials. There is also an independent judicial system. The press, which is mostly private, has been relatively free.

Administratively, below the level of central government, Bangladesh has seven divisions consisting of sixty-four districts. These are divided into about five hundred subdistricts (the Bangla word *upazila* is most often used even in English) and nearly 4,500 unions, each of which is divided into a number of wards and many villages. Most ministries have offices and staff at all levels down to wards. Each union has an elected governance structure, the Union *Parishad* (or council), composed of a chairman and twelve members, three of whom must be women.

However, while the formal systems of governance appear stable, a deeper examination reveals significant problems. According to a study from the Institute of Governance Studies at BRAC University,

> over almost two decades, Bangladesh moved from what may be considered "minimalist democracy"—regular free and contested elections, peaceful transfer of power, fundamental freedoms, civilian control over policy and institutions—to what has been called illiberal democracy—misuse of state power for partisan and personal gain . . . [which has] severely undermined the accountability mechanisms of the political system and rendered it largely dysfunctional. . . . Bangladesh is further characterized by high levels of competition between major parties, absence of intra-party democracy, highly centralized decision-making, and personalization of internal party structures.[8]

The study discusses how the interparty competition is based on a winner takes all approach to control over public resources and the patron-client relationships in their allocation, leading to high levels of corruption.

Policy—Ultrapoverty

As previously noted, Bangladesh is one of the poorest countries in the world. As with all policy issues, there are multiple and competing analyses of the causes of poverty and what must be done to resolve the problem. In fact, in the field of development there is no consensus over how to define *poverty* and its various levels, including ultrapoverty.

When BRAC designed its new initiative targeting the ultra poor, it defined the target group as households that suffer from two or more of the following conditions:

- Own less than 10 decimals of land (i.e., one-tenth of an acre)
- Have no productive assets
- Adult women in the household are selling their labor or begging
- There are no active adult male members
- School-going aged children are selling their labor[9]

In a baseline survey of the households identified by these characteristics, women were the head of 40 percent of the households, 98 percent of the households owned no cultivatable land, less than 6 percent had access to a sanitary latrine, and the literacy rate of the heads of households was barely 4 percent.[10] According to BRAC, there are multiple causes of such ultrapoverty.

> Apart from deprivation in access to economic assets, resources and opportunities, poverty is also caused by [the] ultra-poor's weak socio-political assets, lack of power to influence policy decisions, ineffectiveness of state institutions and the interactive intricate social equations that severely limit or even deny [the] ultra-poor's access to most social services like health and education. All these accentuate their powerlessness, thus reducing their ability to assert their rights and claim their entitlements.[11]

A specific example of the effects of powerlessness is the allocation of vulnerable group development (VGD) cards, which provide access to food subsidies and are essential for the very survival of many ultra-poor households. The VGD cards are distributed by local administrators and government officials. According to BRAC staff, it is common that these do not reach those members of the community with the greatest need; in some cases it is because an official is not aware of who the people in need are, and in other cases the cards are sold or given to relatives and political supporters. Similar inefficiencies or corruption is present in the local implementation of many other national policies, such as the rights of the poor to unused government (or *khas*) land.

As made evident in the strategy section (page 75), BRAC's leadership believes that an important part of the solution to ultrapoverty involves changing the power relations between the poor and the local government officials and other power holders. Specifically, the strategy seeks to change the implementation of existing policies so they are more transparent, fair, efficient, and accountable.

However, BRAC documents on ultrapoverty do not include an equivalent analysis of national policy. While they include references to Bangladesh's need to meet its Millennium Development Goals (the first of which is to reduce the poverty rate by 50 percent from 2000 to 2015) and other references to the national Poverty Reduction Strategy Paper (required of aid-recipient countries by the World Bank and many bilateral agencies), the documents do not identify which if any specific policy changes are necessary to achieve the poverty reduction goals in the Millennium Development Goals or the poverty reduction strategy.[12] Likewise, with regard to parliament and the major ministries, the documents do not identify current policies that need to be protected or strengthened, revised, or abolished, or new policies that need to be enacted and implemented. While other advocacy groups in Bangladesh, as have coalitions in many other countries, integrated such efforts around creating a pro-poor budget, the BRAC documents do not include recommended changes in national expenditure or sources of income.

Strategy

Challenging the Frontiers of Poverty Reduction—Targeting the Ultra Poor (CFPR-TUP) is the long but descriptive title of the BRAC strategy launched in 2002. It recognizes the need to address the multiple challenges faced by the ultra poor (landlessness, poor health, social marginalization, etc.) and to intervene at multiple levels: direct services to poor women and their households, building a supportive environment in their communities, and influencing policies that affect them.

The CFPR-TUP program documents describe the strategy as both "pushing down" and "pushing out." The first consists of "a proven targeting strategy to provide the ultra poor with a mix of economic instruments—asset transfers, stipend, loans and saving facilities. For each member, these inputs will be complemented over a two-year period by enterprise training, social development support and subsidized essential health care."[13] As of 2010, over 326,000 women had received this package of services.

The pushing out strategy includes efforts to create a "pro-poor environment" through interventions that increase understanding and support for the "plight of the ultra poor" throughout the country. A highly related element is to "strengthen support for pro-poor policies and effective implementation of existing policies within communities and at all levels of government, focusing on the lowest tiers of government."[14]

When planning the part of its strategy focused on pro-poor policy advocacy, CFPR-TUP planners could draw on the experiences and lessons from several decades of advocacy work by BRAC and the organizational infrastructure, human capital, and other resources that developed through those efforts. Several of those efforts are described in the following section.

BRAC Policy Advocacy Strategies

When asked to identify BRAC's most important overall accomplishments related to policy advocacy, Abed described its contribution to ensuring that poverty and other forms of marginalization occupy a central place in the national policy discourse and the policy-making agenda (personal communication). That success can be attributed, among other factors, to the effectiveness of its programs, the depth and quality of its research, the integrity of its leadership and staff, and its international profile, which have allowed BRAC to influence policy makers through demonstration of new program models, collaboration, dialogue, and other relatively low-profile advocacy methods.

During the 1990s different divisions and programs in BRAC became more visibly engaged in advocacy. At the national level, its education program was instrumental in forming the Campaign for Popular Education (CAMPE), a coalition of more than four hundred NGOs concerned with basic education in Bangladesh. The BRAC Research and Evaluation Division (RED) took on a central role in one of CAMPE's highest-profile advocacy initiatives, Education Watch. Each year RED conducts a large-scale research project on some national educational issue chosen by the coalition. CAMPE then launches the research report at a national workshop with high-level government officials and extensive media coverage, and subsequently uses the evidence to lobby education policy makers.[15] BRAC and CAMPE have successfully influenced a number of specific policies (e.g., expanding the government's policy on providing textbooks to schools to include nongovernmental schools, including but not limited to the thousands of nonformal primary schools that BRAC has initiated) and also target more comprehensive policies (e.g., the government's multiyear Primary Education Development Plans).

At the national and international levels, BRAC staff members in the Gender Justice and Diversity Section and other departments became active in advocacy related to women's rights, in some cases acting as individuals. For example, as members of national coalitions, they made a significant contribution to enacting the National Women's Development Policy and then protecting it from attacks by religious fundamentalists. The policy legalizes equal rights for women, including property rights, and requires a 40 percent quota of women in the government's high executive, judiciary, and legislative branches, parliament, and local government bodies. At the international level, BRAC advocates have helped prepare shadow reports and lobbied at United Nations meetings on the Convention on the Elimination of all Forms of Discrimination Against Women.

At the local level, or the lowest tier of government, the BRAC Social Development Programme took on a leadership role. Its strategy was to organize poor women who were already members of BRAC's village-level microfinance groups. Members of groups from several villages in an administrative ward were trained and organized into an association, or *Polli Shomaj.* One of its main functions was to monitor the implementation of local government policies and advocate for access to the resources and services that poor women and their families were entitled to. There are now over twelve thousand such associations. Representatives from four Polli Shomaj in one administrative union form higher-level associations, or Union Shomaj, to have yet greater impact. The associations also encourage their members to seek election to the twelve-member Union Parishads (councils), the most decentralized policy-making bodies in Bangladeshi government. Nearly six thousand Union Shomaj members have been elected. The Social Development Programme provided leadership training for those and all other women who had been elected to a Union Parishad. The program has also helped the women from the same subdistricts to create an Upazila Forum to support each other and further enhance their effectiveness.

CFPR-TUP Advocacy Strategy and the BRAC Advocacy Unit

Part of CFPR-TUP's push down strategy of providing direct support to ultra-poor women was to help them develop the level of financial stability, skills, and confidence that would allow them to join their local Polli Shomaj and become involved in the advocacy work described earlier, and thus become part of the push out strategy. At the same time, the CFPR-TUP strategy involved creating of another type of local-level association. In every village where the program was providing services, its staff members worked with local elites—teachers, religious leaders, businesspeople, and others—to establish a village poverty reduction committee (Gram Daridro Bimochon committee or GDBC). The committees mobilize voluntary labor and donations to assist some of the ultra-poor households, and they help monitor local government departments to ensure that the ultra poor receive the resources and services they are entitled to.

The BAU was established to build on and extend all the other elements of the CFPR-TUP strategy. It was responsible for targeting the vast majority of Bangladeshi villages where BRAC would not be able to provide the full package of direct support or organize GDBCs because of the program's resource limitations. It was also responsible for targeting every relevant ministry at every level of government across the country. In so doing, it was assigned the following broad objectives:

- To inform and make people aware of, and sensitive to, the plight of the poor and ultra poor, and create a pro-poor environment, which will bear positive influence on programmatic interventions undertaken by the CFPR-TUP Programme.
- To mobilize and motivate people to act in favour of the poor and ultra poor.
- To motivate officials of service-providing government departments and mobilize NGOs and members of civil society to ensure that the poor and ultra poor gain access to services that they are entitled to but are unable to access due to social, structural and official constraints.
- To influence and trigger changes in policy making and implementation by advertising the condition of the ultra poor as well as achievements of the programme at the grassroots and national levels.[16]

To achieve these objectives, the unit designed an innovative strategy that they call participation, interaction, and mobilization (PIM). It incorporates social communication, media mobilization, and advocacy methods.

At the village level, one of the main PIM methods is built around popular theater. In a very intentional process, BAU communication workers first collaborate with members of a village to research and document specific experiences of the ultra poor who live there. They then work with a team of local actors to choose and dramatize one or more of those experiences, culminating in a play performed in that village. At the end of the event, the audience is invited to attend a meeting scheduled for the following day to discuss the play with the actors and talk about what they might do to help alleviate ultrapoverty. Most often the meetings result in the formation of a *jogajog* forum (direct translation is "communication forum") which, like a GDBC, is primarily composed of local elites who are willing to volunteer time and resources to alleviate the problems in their village.

In addition to popular theater and jogajog forums, BAU uses many other awareness-raising methods. These include posters, pamphlets, and other print media; audio and video programs played in village markets, tea stalls and other venues; quizzes and debate competitions about ultrapoverty in primary and secondary schools; and various special events and fairs. In addition, BAU organizes national, district, and union-level workshops on ultrapoverty, which involve elected policy makers (MPs, Upazila chairmen and Union Parishad members) and high government officials, who are often designated as special guests and invited to open, close, or give the keynote address at the event. Other participants include staff of different NGOs, academics, religious leaders, businesspeople, and other elites. Immediately after workshops, BAU organizes field visits for all workshop participants, including MPs and other high-level government officials, to learn about ultrapoverty and interact with participants in BRAC's village-level interventions.

Media mobilization methods complement the preceding activities and include securing media coverage of the workshops and field visits, as well as initiating television and radio talk shows on the topic of ultrapoverty. Other methods focus directly on journalists, including training in development journalism, field trips, fellowships, and awards for the best reporting on the topic.

Level of Effort

The scale as well as the breadth and creativity of BAU's work is impressive. For example, BAU reports indicate that community members have established 1,256 jogajog forums, each involving twenty to thirty people; at present, 465 of the forums are running without any external support from BAU. Forums have mobilized about US$71,000 in local donations, provided seed funds for over 33,000 income generation efforts of ultra-poor members of their communities, and established 350 preprimary schools serving nearly 10,000 children. Debates and quiz competitions have exposed two million school and college students to the challenges of the ultra poor. Media mobilization has resulted in 1,711 reports on the ultra poor in local print media, 556 reports in national daily newspapers, and twelve TV talk shows and twenty other programs broadcast by national television stations.

Outcomes

The outcomes of the BAU strategy are difficult to measure but likely quite significant. Admittedly, while the fund-raising and initiatives of jogajog forum members are inspiring, the level of effort pales in light of the level of financial resources needed to adequately address the problem; but, on the other hand, those efforts may be helping reignite a spirit of community self-reliance that has waned as a result of growing dependence on government and NGO services. More importantly, from an advocacy point of view, the forums (and GDBCs) are creating a new and accessible group of local constituents to advocate for policy change. The Polli Shomaj and Union Shomaj identify and organize poor women. The forums identify and organize local allies who can join them when advocating for pro-poor policy decisions and implementation in local government, which also reduces opportunities for corruption. While some forums have already been active in this way, as of yet no systematic training and support for their role as advocates have been provided.

While even more difficult to measure, another significant outcome of BAU efforts is on setting policy agendas. Efforts from popular theater productions in villages, national workshops, talk shows, and the high level of media attention are likely having a significant impact on the awareness of the general public and policy makers with regard to the existence of and need to address ultrapoverty. Moreover, to date at least some policy changes can be traced to BAU advocacy, such as the decision by the Bangladesh Bureau of Statistics to conduct a separate census on ultrapoverty.

LEARNING EXERCISE

As best you can, given the limitations of the information presented in this case, create a list of ideas on how BAU might improve and expand the effectiveness of its policy advocacy. (Even if you have the background of the external reviewer and access to all the information that was collected during the actual review, your ideas should at most be offered as sources to stimulate dialogue and decision making by BRAC leadership and staff.)[17]

As you formulate your ideas, give special consideration to the fact that BAU leaders would like to have an impact on all levels of policy (local to national and even international) related to ultrapoverty and all four stages of the policy-making cycle (i.e., agenda setting, formulation and enactment, implementation, and evaluation). They are interested in ideas for improvement in any of those areas.

However, as may be evident from the content in the Policy and Strategy sections they have yet to directly influence national policy formulation and enactment on ultrapoverty. Thus they are especially interested in your ideas related to building that capacity.

Notes

1. As such, BRAC has been the subject of numerous studies, articles, chapters, and at least three books, the latest of which is Ian Smillie's *Freedom from Want: The Remarkable Success Story of BRAC, the Global Grassroots Organization That's Winning the Fight Against Poverty* (Sterling, VA: Kumarian Press, 2011).

2. Jeff Unsicker, Rapid External Review of BRAC Advocacy Unit (Internal report, October 2010).

3. "Introduction to Chronic Poverty in Bangladesh," Chronic Poverty Research Centre, http://www.cprc.abrc.co.uk/2/partners-pages.php.

4. "Introduction to Chronic Poverty."

5. "Who We Are: Mission and Vision," BRAC, http://www.brac.net/content/who-we-are-mission-vision.

6. "Who We Are," BRAC, http://www.brac.net/content/who-we-are.

7. See http://www.brac.net/sites/default/files/Annual-Report-2009/brac-ar-2009-programme-update.pdf

8. Institute of Governance Studies, *The State of Governance in Bangladesh 2008: Confrontation, Competition and Accountability* (Dhaka, Bangladesh: IGS, BRAC University, 2011), xv.

9. BRAC, *Challenging the Frontiers of Poverty Reduction: Targeting the Ultra Poor, Targeting Social Constraints, 2007–2011* (Dhaka, Bangladesh: BRAC, 2006), 12.

10. BRAC, *Challenging the Frontiers,* 12.

11. BRAC, *Challenging the Frontiers,* 22.

12. BRAC, *Challenging the Frontiers,* 18–20.

13. BRAC, *Challenging the Frontiers,* 7.

14. BRAC, *Challenging the Frontiers,* 7.

15. BRAC University was created in 2005 and has provided additional policy research and advocacy capacity. In particular, the university's Institute of Governance Studies has produced a series of reports, "The State of Governance in Bangladesh," that are used in ways similar to those of Education Watch.

16. BRAC, *Challenging the Frontiers,* 87.

17. The resource person had developed joint programs with BRAC and taught advocacy courses for NGO managers in Bangladesh over a seven-year period. The review involved two weeks of meetings and workshops with leadership and staff of BAU, other BRAC programs, BRAC University, and other Bangladeshi NGOs; observation at several jogajog forum meetings and some of their community support projects; and access to a large number of English-language program documents and materials.

5

Advocates
Building Capacity

AT THE CENTER OF THE ADVOCACY PROCESS ARE THE PEOPLE, GROUPS, ORGANIZATIONS, networks, and coalitions that seek to solve problems by changing policies of governments, corporations, and other powerful institutions. There is incredible diversity among advocates in terms of issue focus, size, structure, culture, and many other characteristics. However, to be effective every advocate needs to either have, develop, or access some common capacities. The introduction to the advocates circle in chapter 2 includes a basic list of what advocates must be able to do:

- analyze and act in accordance with the larger context;
- carry out policy research and analysis;
- identify, analyze, and navigate a political system composed of numerous different actors;
- develop and carry out various strategies and tactics for influencing policy makers;
- monitor, evaluate, and learn from all of the above; and
- manage the integration of those capacities to support a long-range vision and specific initiatives that build on organizational strengths.

The list is organized around the rest of the Advocacy Circles framework and can provide a useful starting point for any organization that is ready to assess and then build its advocacy capacities. You may have referred to it when doing the learning exercise for Case C.

There are of course other frameworks for conceptualizing the capacity assessment and building process. A growing number of external support organizations and consultants have focused on these capacities, and new conceptual frameworks, concepts, tools, and resources are emerging. One of the best is the International NGO Training and Research Centre (INTRAC), which works with nongovernmental organizations (NGOs) in the global North and South.[1] It produced a relatively comprehensive overview of practitioner experiences and current literature in this area. To broaden and refine our understanding of capacity building, the next section of this chapter presents the list of what INTRAC identified as core advocacy competencies and then compares and contrasts it with the preceding list.

The subsequent section discusses some challenges to building capacity related to management, which is the sixth and final item on the preceding list. The other items are addressed in chapters 6–10.

INTRAC's Framework

In INTRAC's *Capacity Building for Advocacy,* the authors write that capacity building, while often viewed as simply an issue of staff training, should focus on multiple levels: "Before planning an intervention it is necessary to have an idea of what capacity exists already. A helpful way of doing this is through identifying the different qualities that 'capacity' as a whole can possess. There is sufficient evidence to support the idea that advocacy capacity can best be understood to operate at six interlinked levels. Capacity building interventions are normally targeted at one or many of these levels."[2] See table 5.1.

The authors discuss more specific capacities in each of the six areas. With regard to the sixth level, they note that capacity-building interventions should

seek to achieve a range of outcomes, involving a combination of the following:

- key individuals have enhanced capacity to engage and represent
- the strength of organisation's advocacy is enhanced
- organisations better facilitate and strategically situate advocacy within wider organisational contexts and approaches
- local communities and marginalised groups are empowered to engage and advocate;
- more effective collaboration takes place between organisations
- state bodies are better able and/or more willing to engage meaningfully with community organisations and their representatives.[3]

Table 5.1 Six levels of advocacy capacity building

Level of intervention	In an advocacy context, focus would be on:
1. Individual	• individuals' relevant skills and abilities
2. Projects and programmes	• single-issue campaigns • broader advocacy programmes
3. Organisational	• organisational structures, processes and resources • management and governance issues
4. External linkages	• extent and quality of coordination between organisations • extent and quality of links between organisations and the groups and communities they are supporting and representing
5. Enabling environment	• the political and policy context within which advocacy processes take place
6. Multiple	• the connections between each of the levels and how they work together to enhance advocacy capacity

Source: Chris Stalker with Dale Sandberg, *Capacity Building for Advocacy* (praxis paper 25, Oxford, UK: INTRAC, 2011), 5–6, www.intrac.org/data/files/resources/698/Praxis-Paper-25-Capacity-Building-for-Advocacy.pdf. Reprinted by permission.

The levels and outcomes for capacity building identified by INTRAC have much in common with the capacities listed at the beginning of this chapter, and many of the differences are simply in terminology. However, there are also some useful differences. One is their focus on individual capacity development in the larger process of organizational development.

Another is their significant emphasis on external linkages with people and communities affected by a policy and with other organizations. The list of capacities based on the Advocacy Circles includes these critical elements as part of the capacity that corresponds with the strategy circle: develop and carry out various strategies and tactics for influencing policy makers. The INTRAC framework will ensure that an assessment of capacity includes the amount and quality of external linkages.

On the other hand, organizations also need to assess and build their capacities to carry out still other important strategies and tactics for influencing policy makers, such as the ability to frame messages, work with media, lobby policy makers, and so forth. These are not highlighted or even included in the INTRAC framework.

Another key difference is the fact that INTRAC's *Capacity Building for Advocacy* includes an "enabling environment" and "state bodies" (and presumably other policy-making institutions) as a focus for capacity building. That makes some sense from the perspective of civil society support organizations (CSSOs) and others that provide external support to advocacy organizations, since "[the] capacity to influence and seek change cannot be delinked from issues about the opportunity to influence. CSSOs must bear this in mind when supporting advocacy work. Even if an organisation has the internal capacity to influence, many of the external, 'opportunity' challenges being faced may limit its advocacy success."[4]

However, from the perspective of most advocacy organizations, making the state and other policy-making bodies more enabling is not a matter of capacity building.[5] From their perspective (and that of this book), improving governance through increased transparency, citizen participation, accountability, and so forth is a matter of advocacy, of using information and people power to influence policies and practices related to policy making and policy implementation.

Ultimately, the frameworks and ideas in *Capacity Building for Advocacy,* and indeed those in other literature generated by the growing field of advocacy capacity building, are useful additions to an advocate's conceptual toolbox, to be used, adapted, or combined with others depending on the needs of a specific advocacy organization and situation.

Management Capacity

While subsequent chapters address issues related to most of the items on the list of advocacy capacities (policy research and analysis, political systems analysis, framing, strategy development and monitoring, evaluation and learning), there is no equivalent attention paid to the challenges related to management and staffing. These are addressed in the following section.

These challenges will vary. For example, small organizations, often with limited human and financial resources, must often pay significant attention to using others' resources. Recall in Case A how the Tambogrande Defense Front in Peru led the advocacy to stop the open pit mine in its town, but to be successful it needed to fill gaps in its technical resources. Thus it approached the church and national and international NGOs for support ranging from media access to an external review of the mining corporation's claims about environmental impact. On the other hand, larger organizations with more resources often face challenges related to communication and collaboration across departments. Case C, on the advocacy for the ultra poor in Bangladesh by BRAC, a *very* large organization, highlights some of these.

Organizations, large or small, for which advocacy is just one part of their mission, often face challenges related to developing a synergy between advocacy and the organization's programs, services, and other activities. This is especially so when advocacy has been initiated after those activities were established. In some cases these challenges are made more difficult by apolitical worldviews of many service providers and by associated concerns that advocacy will politicize and therefore jeopardize the integrity of their work. Often programs and advocacy must compete for finite organizational resources.

Nearly all organizations face one or more challenges in securing adequate resources for advocacy. Grassroots associations of people most affected by social injustice face the challenge that their communities by definition have limited resources to contribute. Many of the organizations that raise direct contributions from social classes with more resources do so by highlighting crisis relief, humanitarian aid, and other activities that appeal to individual donors who most often do not understand what advocacy is. Frequently, those same organizations confront a related tension: advocates who wish to tap the donor base not only for funds but also to become engaged in organizing and lobbying on public policy issues, and fund-raisers who fear that such efforts may jeopardize continued support from some segment of the donors they have so carefully cultivated.

Further complicating the challenges of fund-raising is the fact that most external funding sources that support organizations' services—foundations, government agencies, corporations, and others—do not understand the complementary role of advocacy or simply do not wish to support such activities. Fortunately there are some very notable exceptions, and the trend appears to be greater understanding and support among many donors. But in any case, there are yet more challenges for organizations that receive funds from governments or corporations and that also advocate for changes to the policies of those powerful institutions.

In terms of staff development, relatively few professional education programs prepare advocates. As noted in chapter 1, the opportunities that are available tend to be short-term training sessions organized around a single definition and framework of advocacy. Less available is education that gives leaders, managers, and other professionals a comprehensive and critical understanding of advocacy that contextualizes more specific, skills-based training. Graduate schools and programs focused on policy studies, oriented to issues (development, natural resources, public health, education, and so forth) or oriented to general public policy, purport to educate such professionals. However, their focus is nearly exclusively on policy research and analysis; rarely do they even have a single course on how to link that work with the realities of policy change. We return to this issue in chapter 6 on policy.

Notes

1. INTRAC, based in the United Kingdom, is an important center for research, publications, short courses, and consultancies contracted by international development agencies and NGOs (http://www.intrac.org). Capacity building and advocacy are two of its primary foci.

2. Chris Stalker with Dale Sandberg, *Capacity Building for Advocacy* (praxis paper 25, Oxford, UK: INTRAC, 2011), http://www.intrac.org/data/files/resources/698/Praxis-Paper-25-Capacity-Building-for-Advocacy.pdf.

3. Stalker, *Capacity Building*, 14.

4. Stalker, *Capacity Building*, 11.

5. Even from the perspective of external support organizations, it is rarely possible to do capacity building interventions with the advocates and the institutions that constitute the advocates' political and policy context. Some exceptions occur within the politics of international aid, where a northern donor can recommend or require changes in the recipient state's governance processes as part of an aid agreement, in which case the donor often identifies which support organization(s) should be engaged in building state capacity, including its capacity to engage citizens and civil society organizations in governance.

CASE C

Conclusion
BRAC Advocacy Unit

The learning exercise that culminated the first part of Case C asked you to make a list of ideas about how the BRAC Advocacy Unit might improve and expand its work related to ultrapoverty. If you wish, you can now amend or add to that list based on the discussion of capacity building in chapter 5. This conclusion to Case C will allow you to compare your ideas with those contained in the report of the rapid external review.[1] However, it is important to reiterate that the goal of the review was to stimulate longer-term and internal dialogue among BRAC leaders and advocates; obviously their process would incorporate information and various factors that could not be known or understood after a rapid external review.

The Assessment

The introductory paragraphs of the external review report provide a context for the various recommendations:

> The findings of this review of the BRAC Advocacy Unit (BAU), within the larger context of BRAC, suggest that the unit and organization are well positioned to assume a leadership role in advocacy regarding policies—local, national and international—that impact the poor, ultra-poor and otherwise marginalized groups within Bangladesh and partner nations.
>
> If BRAC makes the strategic decision to take on that role, and mobilizes the necessary resources, it can build on a long (if not widely recognized) history of influencing public policies at the national and local levels in Bangladesh, as well as on the more recent social communication and media mobilization work of the BAU.

To successfully implement such a decision, BRAC would need to make an ongoing, high-level commitment and create internal systems for yet greater communication and collaboration across program divisions. The BRAC Advocacy Unit could provide, facilitate and support those systems, especially if it is able to hire and/or develop human resources to fill several gaps in current capacity.[2]

According to the report, BRAC is well positioned to take on a leadership role in advocacy because of numerous experiences, learning, and development over many years resulting in a set of capacities that can be organized in terms of the first four items in the list on page 81 of chapter 5. For example, BRAC's capacity

- to analyze and act in accordance with the larger (historical, political, economic, cultural, etc.) context is demonstrated by its ability to function and grow under conditions ranging from military dictatorships to the more recent shifts in power between political parties every five years;
- to carry out policy research and analysis is institutionalized through its professional Research and Evaluation Department (demonstrated through its annual Education Watch research projects) and several units of BRAC University;
- to identify, analyze, and navigate the Bangladesh political system and its many actors is demonstrated in its ultra-poor strategies, which engage with all levels of government structures and with key government officials, social elites, members of the media, and other actors in local and national contexts; and
- to develop and carry out various strategies and tactics for influencing policymakers is demonstrated through the range of advocacy approaches used to promote the rights of the poor, ultra poor, women, migrant workers, and others that have established ongoing committees at local levels and national networks with other organizations.

The report provided a number of ideas for how the capacities in these areas could be improved and are noted at the end of this section.

With regard to the fifth item, BRAC has also demonstrated a very significant capacity to monitor, evaluate, and learn with regard to its programs and overall approach to poverty alleviation through rigorous formal research and through reflection and planning activities. One of the report's recommendations is to add expertise in the still emerging practice of evaluating the more complex processes and outcomes of advocacy work.

However, the report suggests that if it is to reach its full advocacy potential, BRAC must first focus on the sixth item on the list: manage and support the integration of those [other] capacities into both a long-range vision and specific initiatives that build on organizational strengths. It needs to make a "strategic decision," an "ongoing, high-level commitment." It also needs to mobilize more resources and to create "internal systems for yet greater communication and collaboration across program divisions."

This dimension of capacity building may be less obvious when reading the case study; however, the need for greater organizational commitment is suggested by the lack of any reference to policy or advocacy in two of BRAC's organizational materials: BRAC's mission statement and the description of its unprecedented scale and reach.[3] While the former states a commitment to empowering people and communities affected by social injustice, it indicates that the means to do so are "economic and social programmes." The latter also suggests that programs—tested, perfected, and rapidly expanded— are how BRAC can respond to tens of millions of poor people. A simple addition of "and policy change" after "programmes" in the mission statement would help signal such a strategic commitment. Even more so would be the addition of policy change as a second and complementary approach to scaling up programs whenever leaders and organizational documents discuss "small is beautiful, but big is necessary."[4]

The review identified some of the challenges BRAC would need to address as part of a strategic decision to institutionalize advocacy as a core component of its mission and methods. Some were the common challenges noted in the preceding chapter: resistance to change when an organization is initiated to provide programs, services, and community-level interventions; related issues of competition for available funds; and large organizations often face challenges related to communication and collaboration across departments or other organizational units. It appeared that the lack of an organization-wide definition and thus understanding of policy advocacy was an obstacle for resolving some of those challenges.

Responding to this assessment, three of the nine recommendations in the report focused on building organizational or managerial capacity and systems:

- Develop internal structures and processes within BRAC that allow for (a) regular, inclusive and cross-program/division regular consultations to agree on major policy change goals, macro strategy and resources for every area of BRAC's advocacy; (b) for policy advocacy to be considered as a possible element of every new BRAC program plan and/or funding proposal, at the point of it first being developed, and (c) for policy advocacy to receive a portion of core or block grant funds, overhead funds, and funds from other discretionary sources.
- Form Policy Advocacy Teams (most likely cross-departmental) to plan, coordinate and implement the specific elements of advocacy

strategies; teams would ideally include a point person for each of the
following: Policy Analysis, Government Relations, Network Relations, Media Relations, and Social Mobilization.
- Develop advocacy plans for each policy issue area of significant importance to BRAC that include sections on context, policy analysis,
political map, strategy (including message framing), monitoring and
evaluation, learning and resources.[5]

In the process of refining and expanding such organizational and management systems, the report encouraged BRAC to "build future advocacy on
the foundation of its historical strengths, but to be prepared to develop new
strategies that are consistent with new external realities, the specific policy
goals and relevant political dynamics."

With regard to BRAC's advocacy for the ultra poor, the case study highlighted a key gap: policy research and analysis that identifies specific policy
change goals at the level of national government. Effective goals should be
keyed to specific policy change opportunities, such as reviews of the Millennium Development Goals, the annual cycle for formulating and approv-
ing national budgets, and so forth. The latter would be enhanced if adequate
staffing was dedicated to government relations.[6]

Other recommendations in the report focused on strategy and tactics relevant for BRAC advocacy in general. Some suggested possible ways to build
on the range of local groups, committees, forums, and so forth created by different departments and programs.[7] For example, the report suggested examining how these are "*duplicating* and/or *reinforcing* (synergy) each other in
terms of influencing policy making and policy implementation. If possible,
simplify, but also recognize the benefits of redundancy given the inevitability
of changes in leadership, funding, etc." An examination should ensure that
the committees or forums that directly represent the poor are not dominated
by those composed of social elites who seek to support the ultra poor.

The report also suggested that BRAC assess the potential for local groups
to be involved in influencing the formulation of national policy decisions in
addition to influencing the implementation of those policies by local government structures. This would require more training. It might involve paying
special attention to building the capacity of local advocates in the home or
constituent districts of key policy makers. And it might involve taking advantage of social networking tools, especially for people who use mobile phones,
which are now pervasive in nearly every rural village across the country.

Whether social networking technology is used to mobilize village and
other local-level advocates, BRAC could use it to build and expand its middle-class support base, especially among tech-savvy youths.

The report also suggested ways to be more systematic in its networking and coalition building. It encouraged BRAC to recognize the potential

of dominating (or being perceived to dominate) such structures because of its relative size and resources. But it also suggested that BRAC consider using those resources to fund other organizations to carry out complementary advocacy.[8]

Finally, the report suggested that the BRAC Advocacy Unit and BRAC University collaborate together and with other institutions to provide in-depth professional education for advocates in Bangladesh and other countries.

Notes

1. Jeff Unsicker, "Rapid External Review of BRAC Advocacy Unit" (Internal report, October 2010).

2. Unsicker, "Rapid External Review."

3. "Who We Are: Mission and Vision," BRAC, http://www.brac.net/content/who-we-are-mission-vision; "Who We Are," BRAC, http://www.brac.net/content/who-we-are.

4. The external review report uses nonformal primary education (NFPE) to make this point: "no matter how many thousands of NFPE schools BRAC develops [38,000 by 2009], they are not likely to ever meet the total national need; on the other hand, successfully influencing policy (including budgetary) decisions of government could lead to educational opportunity for every girl and boy child in every village. In addition, many social problems of concern to BRAC are directly or indirectly caused by public policy decisions. In those cases, services alone, no matter how many, cannot produce a sustainable solution."

5. The report included specific suggestions for the third and fourth items, that is, composition and management of teams and the content to be included in each section of the advocacy plans.

6. Even as the review was in progress, the BRAC Advocacy Unit was securing funds to support specific policy research and seeking funds for a staff member with the background and time needed for government relations and lobbying.

7. In addition to the Polli Shomaj, Gram Daridro Bimochon committees, and jogajog forums described in the case, other local groups have been created as part of initiatives that address a number of other issues (for example, safe migration and water and sanitation).

8. Oxfam America adopted this approach to funded allies in several recent campaigns. We return to the idea in Case E (p. 119).

CASE D

Research and Advocacy
for a Ghana AIDS Commission

Nikoi Kote-Nikoi, coauthor

During the 1990s the HIV/AIDS pandemic was devastating many countries in east, central, and southern Africa—the so-called "AIDS Belt." Nikoi Kote-Nikoi, a politically progressive economist, relocated home to Ghana in 1999 to serve as research director of the Institute of Economic Affairs (IEA) and was concerned the disease could have an equally negative impact on his and other nations in West Africa. The region still had relatively low rates of infection; for example, from 1990 to 1995, the HIV seroprevalence in urban areas of Ghana was estimated to be 2.2 percent, while the equivalent rates in Malawi, Uganda, Zambia, and Rwanda ranged from 23.3 percent to 30.3 percent. However, the nonlinear, potentially exponential manner by which the disease is spread could quickly change that reality. Yet those low infection rates are precisely the reason there had been no policy response by the Ghanaian government to prevent such an outcome.

This case study examines the policy advocacy process Kote-Nikoi, the IEA, and a network of allies used to convince the national government to establish a national AIDS commission and through it to take a series of steps to carefully monitor and prevent the spread of the disease in Ghana. One of the first and most important elements in the process was policy research and analysis completed in 2001 and reported by Kote-Nikoi in an IEA paper, "The Potential Macroeconomic Impact of HIV-Seropositivity in Ghana."[1]

Following a brief overview of the context and the IEA, the case poses a challenge to the reader: what types of economic evidence would be most effective for arguing that Ghana should establish a national AIDS commission?

Context

Led by Kwame Nkrumah, one of the great leaders of the African independence movement, Ghana in 1957 became the first nation in West Africa and the first British colony in all of Africa to win its freedom. Nkrumah was overthrown by a coup in 1966, and Ghana began a long period of mostly military rule. However, since 1992, following a referendum that approved a new constitution, the country has had a relatively stable multiparty democracy.

Ghana has a population of about 24 million. It has considerable gold and other mineral resources and significant agricultural capacity.[2] In terms of export crops, it is the world's second largest producer of cocoa. The fluctuation in world prices for its primary products (gold and cocoa in particular) has created boom and bust periods in Ghana's economic growth. Subsistence agriculture remains a major sector of the economy. Overall, agriculture produces about one-third of Ghana's gross domestic product and involves over half of its work force. Other sectors, including manufacturing and especially services, are growing.

International organizations consider Ghana a lower-middle-income country, which is considerably better than most African nations. While the poverty rate had decreased in the 1990s, it was still about 30 percent in 2000. In the period leading up to 2000, progress had been made in relation to many of the other development indicators (life expectancy, infant mortality, literacy, primary school enrollment, etc.).

Advocates

In the preface to each of the IEA's policy papers, it describes itself as having been

> founded in 1989 as an independent, non-governmental institution dedicated to the establishing and strengthening of a market economy and democratic, free and open society. [The IEA] considers improvements in the legal, social and political institutions as necessary conditions for sustained economic growth and human development. The IEA supports research and promotes and publishes studies on important economic, socio-political and legal issues in order to enhance understanding of public policy.[3]

The director, staff, and other researchers are Ghanaians with advanced academic credentials. Many have studied or worked in Europe and in the United States. While IEA officials clearly hope to influence policies, they do not view IEA as an advocacy organization. During IEA's first ten years the primary method of influencing policy makers was to provide them with high-quality policy research findings through publications and by inviting them to attend presentations and discussions on their content.

The methods for influencing the national government's HIV/AIDS policy went beyond IEA's standard practice, beginning with the formation of a close network with other civil society and professional organizations, some of which had a more explicit advocacy focus. Some of those organizations are described briefly in the conclusion of the case that follows chapter 6.

Politics

Ghana has a tripartite democratic government. National elections are held every four years. A president and vice president are directly elected as a single ticket. The 230 members of Ghana's unicameral parliament each represent a single constituency. The court system is independent.

The locus of health policy is in the Ministry of Health, headed by officials appointed by the party in power. The Ghana Health Service, composed largely of career civil servants, is responsible for implementing policy and managing government hospitals, clinics, and other services.

The two major political parties are the National Democratic Congress (NDC) and the New Patriotic Party (NPP). The NDC was elected in 1992 and 1996 and thus was in power in 1999 when Kote-Nikoi relocated back to Ghana. The NDC, which had its origins in Ghana's nationalist independence movement, has a populist or progressive orientation in some ways similar to that of the British Labour Party and the Social Democrats in Scandinavia. Kote-Nikoi identified with the NDC's policies and politics and was well connected to a number of its leaders. However, he found the party reluctant to consider his concerns about HIV/AIDS prevention. Not only was the low incidence rate a factor, but at the time malaria was a much greater public health concern to the NDC. Moreover, from the perspective of social equity, the party's leaders were aware that most of the people suffering from malaria were from poor rural areas, while those affected by AIDS were primarily in urban centers and often economically better off. Thus the NDC argued that its finite health budget should prioritize malaria and similar diseases.

The political context changed dramatically in 2000 when the NPP won the national election. The NPP, which identifies with the US Republican Party—and at the time, the new administration of George W. Bush—has a conservative pro-business and free-market policy orientation. Kote-Nikoi realized that to be successful, he would now need to shift from social justice to economic growth arguments. While he has often described traditional or neoclassical economic methodology as nonsense, he was well trained in the field and willing to use economic growth as an argument if it would result in the broader policy change he was seeking.

LEARNING EXERCISE

Imagine it is the year 2000, and Kote-Nikoi has asked you to help him think about what types of economic evidence and arguments might be most persuasive for the NPP government. (Keep in mind that the government sees business as the primary engine of economic growth and development, and market allocation as the most efficient means of using the country's productive resources.)

Jot down your ideas. If you are familiar with economic research methods, include your ideas about how the evidence might be gathered and analyzed. When finished, compare your ideas to the approach taken by Kote-Nikoi as summarized in the conclusion of this case, following chapter 6.

The summary is followed by a brief description of IEA's strategy, the outcome, and lessons based on the connections between Ghana's experience and the content of chapter 6.

Notes

1. Nikoi Kote-Nikoi, "The Potential Macroeconomic Impact of HIV-Seropositivity in Ghana" (Accra, Ghana: Institute of Economic Affairs, 2001). Unfortunately, this paper is no longer accessible.

2. Significant reserves of crude oil have since been discovered, and exploitation is expected to have a major impact on Ghana's economy and politics.

3. Kote-Nikoi, "The Potential Macroeconomic Impact," preface.

6

Policy
Problems, Causes, and Solutions

IN ITS MOST BASIC SENSE, POLICY IS ABOUT THE *WHY* OF ADVOCACY. TO BE EFFECTIVE, advocates must clearly define the problem they wish to address, analyze its causes, and identify one or more policy changes that will solve or help solve the problem. As indicated in table 3.1 in chapter 3, there are different types of policy change goals. The advocates' goal might be to block a proposed policy that would be harmful, to repeal or amend such a policy that already exists, or to block its implementation. Or the goal might be to help pass a new policy that would be helpful (possibly also helping to formulate the policy proposal itself), to protect such a policy that already exists, and finally to ensure its implementation. In some cases, the desired policy change is about the rules and procedures used to enact, amend, or implement policy.

To do this, the advocates must have, develop, or access the ability to carry out policy research and analysis.[1] Depending on the specific problem and its scale, the research and analysis process can be relatively straightforward or quite complex.

The primary reasons for undertaking this process are to determine which policy changes are most likely to achieve the desired outcomes; a worst-case scenario is for advocates to succeed in achieving a policy change goal and then find it is ineffective or even counterproductive. The second reason is to identify or generate evidence about the problem, its causes, and the efficacy of the proposed solution, which the advocates can use when communicating with various audiences and lobbying policy makers. In some cases, a third reason is to educate and mobilize people and communities that are affected by a problem through directly involving them in the research and analysis.

96

It is also important for advocates to understand the formal and informal ways research is used (or not used) by policy makers. Effective advocates monitor the work of others who are doing policy research and analysis related to the same problem, its causes, and possible policy solutions. They follow the work of researchers based in the relevant policy-making institutions, in universities and research centers, and in organizations or institutions that either support or oppose the advocates' values and goals. As appropriate, the advocates either incorporate or counter others' evidence and policy recommendations as they conduct their own research, analysis, and advocacy.

Policy research and analysis is not a linear process. It is almost always intertwined with the context, politics, and strategy arenas. An effective policy change goal must be formulated and often reformulated in relation to one or more specific policy-making bodies and to events and changes that are beyond the control of either the advocates or policy makers. Depending on political and strategic variables, the advocates' policy change goals may need to be divided into a set of related objectives that are ordered in terms of timing and feasibility.

The first section of this chapter discusses the relationship between policy research and actual policy change in theory and in reality. It summarizes work by a program of the Overseas Development Institute (ODI), which suggests why research has had a limited impact on policy and what researchers in universities and think tanks need to do if they wish to increase the impact. The section concludes with how advocates can use that knowledge.

The second section discusses the process of doing policy research and analysis. It summarizes a very useful primer on the topic from *The Democracy Owners' Manual* and adds some additional ideas from *A New Weave of Power, People and Politics.*[2]

The final section discusses the role of policy research and analysis in the book's first three case studies. The conclusion to Case D on research and advocacy for the National AIDS Commission in Ghana provides a yet more in-depth grounding of these concepts in the context of practice.

Theory and Reality of Research and Policy Change

Theoretically, policy researchers and analysts are neutral professionals who use their scientific or technical expertise to study a problem and its causes, then generate a menu of alternative solutions, and finally use a cost-benefit calculation to determine which alternative maximizes the best interests of the majority of citizens. Policy makers follow their recommendation. That policy is then implemented, monitored, and evaluated by the same or other experts and then adjusted based on the findings. This theory is based on a number of assumptions, including that it is possible for policy researchers, policy makers, and others responsible for implementing and evaluating policies to be unbiased, that all policy issues and choices can be monetized and then assessed in terms of their costs and benefits, and that a single public has common interests.

Today, few would fully subscribe to that theory. On the other hand, too often graduate schools and programs in policy studies (either issue oriented, such as international development, public health, natural resources, and so forth, or oriented to general public policy) have continued to focus almost exclusively on policy research and evaluation as the means to solve economic, social, and environmental problems. Many of the graduates work as policy analysts in governments and other policy institutions where they conduct the type of research and evaluation work they were trained for. Many of their professors, as well as other researchers based in universities, think tanks, and other settings, continue to produce policy papers and other reports they hope will influence policy decisions.

Of course, the research produced by some of those professionals and experts sometimes becomes the basis of decisions by policy makers. But not often. An ODI publication cites a study of seventy thousand research projects on education that found that just seventy of them had "a significant influence on education policy and practice."[3] One in a thousand may be on the extreme end of the spectrum of ineffectiveness. But it is safe to say that (despite a recent wave of calls by policy makers for evidence-based policy that rigorously uses research findings) the vast majority of the reports end up on bookshelves, gathering dust or in some equally marginalized space in today's digital world.

Through its Research and Policy in International Development (RAPID) program, ODI has sought to increase our understanding about when and why some research does in fact significantly influence policy when most does not. The program asks, "Why are some of the ideas that circulate in the research/policy networks picked up and acted upon, while others are ignored and disappear?" The program staff and consultants have completed extensive reviews of relevant literature and conducted field studies in multiple countries.[4] They have also translated those findings into a number of practical tools and offered workshops and other training for policy researchers, policy makers, and civil society organizations.

Most of that work is focused on researchers based in universities and think tanks (including ODI, which itself has generated hundreds of policy papers and other research reports on a range of international development policy issues) and what they can do to increase the likelihood that their evidence and recommendations will be acted on.

Those involved in the RAPID program concluded that if researchers are serious about policy change, they need to understand not just their own but also the contrasting realities of those who will (or will not) use the outcomes of their research. Table 6.1 is often used in RAPID training sessions and presentations to highlight some of the salient differences. While they should not sacrifice their integrity, they need to let go of some of their scientific biases and find ways to bridge the gap.

RAPID's analytical and practical framework provides a comprehensive and very useful map for researchers who want to bridge that gap.[5] The framework states that they need to understand "a wide range of inter-related factors" that can be "broadly divided into three overlapping areas: the political context; the evidence; and the links between policy and research communities. These three areas occur within a fourth set of factors: external environment."[6] Figure 6.1 illustrates the interplay of these areas.

A corresponding table in the same document, titled "How to Influence Policy and Practice," includes a column of suggestions on what researchers need to do in each of the areas.[7] With regard to the political context, they need to

- get to know the policy makers, their agendas, and their constraints;
- identify potential supporters and opponents;

Table 6.1 Different notions of evidence

Researchers' Evidence	Policy Makers' Evidence
• Scientific (context free)	• Colloquial (contextual)
• Proven empirically	• Anything that seems reasonable
• Theoretically driven	• Policy relevant
• As long as it takes	• Timely
• Caveats and qualifications	• Clear message

Source: Phil Davies, "Different Notions of Evidence." Presentation at Impact to Insight: The Policy, Research and Practice Interface, Government Social Research Unit, Cabinet Office/Overseas Development Institute, October, 17, 2005. Used with permission.

Figure 6.1 The RAPID framework

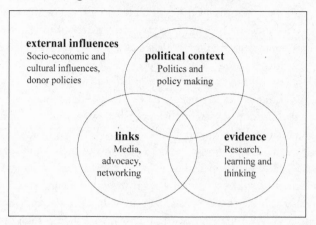

Source: Julius Court, Ingie Hovland and John Young, *Bridging Research and Policy in Development: Evidence and Change Processes* (London: Practical Action Publishing, 2005), http://pra.stylus pub.com/Books/BookDetail.aspx?productID=100830. Reprinted by permission.

- keep an eye on the horizon and prepare for opportunities in regular policy processes; and
- look out for—and react to—unexpected policy windows.[8]

With regard to evidence, researchers need to

- establish credibility over the long term,
- provide practical solutions to problems,
- establish legitimacy,
- build a convincing case and present clear options,
- package new ideas in familiar theory or narratives, and
- communicate effectively.[9]

With regard to links, researchers need to

- get to know other stakeholders,
- establish presence in existing networks,
- build coalitions with like-minded stakeholders, and
- build new policy networks.[10]

While most of RAPID's work is focused on researchers, it can also be very useful for advocates. If nothing else, the program's findings should effectively dissuade any advocates who still believe that research and evidence alone are effective strategies to achieve their policy change goals.

More proactively, the RAPID framework provides useful insights into many of the issues advocates must address. The conceptual as well as visual similarities between the framework and the Advocacy Circles map presented in this book (evidence generally correlates with the policy circle, political context with politics, links with strategy, and external influences with context) can make the connections all the more evident.

Advocates can also use RAPID's work to improve the effectiveness of policy research and analysis in their larger advocacy process. For example, advocates also benefit from understanding policy makers' notions of evidence (see table 6.1) when they are doing and communicating their own research. And the list of things researchers need to do regarding the evidence area of the RAPID framework is an equally insightful list of what advocates need to do when conducting their own policy research and communicating with policy makers.

Especially since advocates often do not have the internal capacity to do a significant amount of their own research, particularly on more complex problems, there is a second way they can draw on RAPID's work: to better understand and communicate with university and think-tank-based researchers who do have the expertise, time, and resources to conduct policy research relevant to their concerns. In this context, the advocates can benefit from understanding the researchers' (and not just the policy makers') notions of evidence.

When they have identified researchers who share their values, advocates can use the RAPID framework as a tool to orient or educate them about ways to improve the likelihood that their research will be acted on. In particular, advocates can point out the suggestions on what researchers need to do with regard to the links area of the framework. A win-win strategy is for the advocates to help researchers establish a presence for themselves and their networks and coalitions as key like-minded stakeholders and to directly engage those researchers in relevant activities (from public education forums to lobbying) that are part of the advocates' overall strategy.

Conducting Policy Research and Analysis

It is important for advocates to understand the basic elements of policy research. This is true even if the main source of the research they will use is a report written by someone else. But it is especially important if the advocates (or some members of the advocacy team) are going to conduct new research.

As noted at the beginning of this chapter, depending on the nature and scale of the problem, there can be great variation in the amount and complexity of the research required to accomplish one or more of the purposes listed: choose policy goal(s), collect evidence to use when conducting advocacy, and engage constituents. Thus there is no single formula or approach for conducting policy research.

On the other hand, numerous books and manuals provide generic models for comprehensive policy analysis, many written by faculty who teach public policy or related fields. Of these, I recommend the clear, practical discussion of an eight-step framework (what the author calls the eightfold path) by Eugene Bardach.[11]

However, the resource I have found to be the most cogent and insightful, an assessment shared by nearly all of my students, is chapter 6 in the *Democracy Owner's Manual*.[12] The majority of the chapter is what Shultz calls a primer on the subject. He breaks down the process into five steps and offers many useful tips for completing each one. The steps and some of the tips are discussed in the following section. Lisa VeneKlasen and Valerie Miller include two chapters in *A New Weave of Power, People and Politics* that are relevant to policy research and analysis, and some of their content is incorporated when relevant to a specific step.[13]

Step 1: Define the Problem

Shultz, as well as VeneKlasen and Miller and nearly all others writing about policy research, emphasizes the critical importance of beginning the process with a clear understanding of the problem the advocates wish to solve. His approach is to first define the problem in "a very basic way." Next, add three types of facts about the problem: *how much*, which provides perspective on the scope of the problem; *why*, which explains the causes of the problem; and *so what*, which explains why it is important to solve the problem. This leads to a short but more specific definition of the problem that guides the rest of the process. One of the examples he provides is:

> Pollutants are seriously damaging our rivers. A more specific definition after the facts have been added is: As more and more factories locate along the Ohio River, pollution levels have increased and are beginning to contaminate local drinking water supplies.[14]

In their chapter "Identifying and Defining Problems," VeneKlasen and Miller suggest slightly more detailed definitions, such as the following example about advocacy planning in Zimbabwe:

> Basic health care is too expensive for low-income and poor people, and inaccessible to most rural residents. Drugs are unavailable and costly. Hospitals and clinics are understaffed or staffed by poorly qualified personnel. People are not educated about their health and are unable to demand better treatment or clarify what ails them and their families. The problem has greater impact on women and children, who have specific health care needs, and who must look after other family members when they are ill.[15]

They argue that the key to a good problem definition is that it "helps avoid confusion and conflicting interpretations of the problem later on in planning."[16]

Among the tips offered by Shultz, perhaps the most essential is to be sure the problem has not been defined "in a way that presumes a solution,"[17] in particular, as the absence of a predefined solution. An example of this I have often used in classes is making the mistake of defining the problem of drug abuse in a community as a lack of or inadequate drug education and treatment programs. The actual cause of the abuse might well be economic, in which case more or improved programs, at least by themselves, would be inadequate to resolve the situation; policies that generate well-paying jobs might be needed.

While these guidelines are all well and good, it is important to remember that most problems are highly complex and interconnected with others. Thus, before focusing on a short problem definition, it will often be helpful to do a more detailed analysis and perhaps create a diagram or problem web of as many issues as seem relevant to the advocates' initial concern.

Step 2: Get the Information You Need

While information was needed to produce the facts during problem definition, this stage expands and deepens that process. Shultz suggests advocates begin by gathering information about the bigger picture, the history and context of the issue. Next "start assembling your inventory of specific facts" that "will help you to both understand the problem and talk about it effectively."[18] These facts (or evidence) should further clarify the nature and scale of the problem, including who or what is suffering as a result of the problem.

Shultz suggests that advocates next gather information about specific strategies (or policy solutions) that have been used elsewhere or are being proposed by other actors concerned with the same immediate problem. "Collect information about the widest variety of approaches possible, including data about their costs and their effectiveness in solving the problem." Finally, "take a careful look at the politics of the issue."[19] This information will help in steps 3, 4 and 5.

Shultz provides a number of tips about how to actually gather the information. An approach he calls "Paper, People, Produce Your Own" (describing the sources and order for the research) is very useful. The first source, paper, refers to already published or available reports and documents, including those on the Internet. He suggests beginning with paper (or digital) sources for several reasons, because of its efficiency (no need to duplicate what is already available) and the fact that it allows the advocates to gain a better sense of who else is thinking about their issue. People refers to "direct contact with experts, officials, advocates, journalists or other people who have important information to share." Sometimes identified through the paper research, these people can help fill in gaps in that information or refer you to others who can. In some cases, they can become formal or informal allies throughout the advocacy process. Produce your own refers to any number of different forms of primary data collection (for example, surveys, focus groups, or interviews with people affected by the problem) that the advocates plan and carry out themselves. Shultz suggests doing this last because it often consumes significant amounts of time and other limited resources. Thus, if paper and people have already generated the needed information, it may not be necessary to produce your own at all. If more information is needed, the advocates will be able to be very focused and efficient in this process.[20]

No matter what the source (paper, people, or your own), advocates might be especially alert to any particularly powerful statistics—*killer facts* is a phrase use by some—that will be particularly useful in communicating with the public, policy makers, or any other audience that has minimal patience with research evidence.

VeneKlasen and Miller add another perspective about this step of the process, that of grassroots, people-centered advocacy groups, especially those concerned with the full range of problems facing a population group or community. In such cases, advocates often directly engage primary constituents (members of the affected community) in the production of their own research. When most fully implemented, the engagement involves an active or lead role in the design as well as in the implementation of the research. Most often this research is carried out at the beginning or early in the information-gathering process, and almost always before any paper and people research is completed. In many cases, this research is used to identify a number of problems and then to prioritize the ones that will be the focus of the advocacy; in those cases, it actually precedes even step 1 in Shultz's primer.

Through approaches such as participatory assessments and other forms of action research, the advocates are not only able to gather useful information, but they can also help the constituents become more critically aware of and informed about their problems. Engagement in the research process can also help organize those constituents and prepare them to mobilize and take action when appropriate.[21]

Step 3: Interpreting the Information You Get

This step involves finding meaning within the numbers and other information the advocates have gathered. Shultz provides several tips in doing so. He suggests making comparisons: "this versus that; now versus before; here versus there; with or without; this group versus that one." He also cautions about the use of secondary sources of data (prioritize those that have the latest data and are closest to the original data source) and about the limitations of cost-benefit analyses (as noted earlier, a cost cannot be calculated for many important factors or variables).[22]

Step 4: Developing and Judging the Policy Options

This step involves reviewing and possibly expanding the list of policy strategies or policy solutions developed in step 2, as well as generating new options. Shultz suggests grouping options according to a basic menu. When the goal is to reduce some situation or behavior (his examples are pollution and smoking), policies can involve (a) prohibition, (b) taxes or other financial disincentives, and (c) public relations or education. When the goal is to increase some situation or behavior (his examples are health care and public transit), policies can involve (a) financing and providing the service, directly or through contracts; (b) tax breaks or other financial incentives; and (c) public relations or education. In both cases, Shultz suggests that doing nothing be included as a policy option, if only because it "provides a useful point of comparison."[23]

Step 5: Making a Choice

Finally, advocates must decide what policy change they will pursue, at least initially, since in long and complicated advocacy initiatives, new information may lead to changes in the problem definition, new inter-pretations, or new policy choices. Shultz provides a basic list of criteria to use when choosing between policy alternatives, formulated as questions:

- What is most likely to solve the problem?
- How much will it cost, who will pay for it, and is it worth it?
- What other problems will it solve or create?
- Can it be implemented?
- Who will support and oppose each alternative?
- Which ones could attract enough political support to be adopted?[24]

VeneKlasen and Miller offer an overlapping but different list of cri-teria that can be used to expand or refine Shultz's list. Some of the dif-ferences reflect concepts and terms that are part of an analytic process they discuss in their chapter, "Analyzing Problems and Selecting Priority Issues," which cuts across the five steps.[25] The process appears to begin at step 1 with the identification of a problem. But unlike the approach in their chapter "Identifying and Defining Problems" (and in the exam-ple about Zimbabwe under step 1), in this chapter the problem is de-fined very generally; among their examples are corruption and domestic abuse. Having identified one or more general problems, advocates next analyze the multiple causes of each problem, their consequences (specific impacts on people and the environment), and possible solutions. Using that analysis, they identify parts of the problem or the issues they might focus on. Each issue is associated with one or more solutions or in terms of Shultz's steps, policy alternatives. Advocates "should choose the issues whose solutions will best further their values, credibility, opportunities and impact." More specifically, they should choose issues whose solution will do the following:

- Result in a real improvement in people's lives.
- Give people a sense of their own power.
- Be widely felt.
- Be deeply felt.
- Build lasting organization and alliances.
- Create opportunities for women and marginalized people to get involved in politics.
- Develop new leaders.
- Promote awareness and respect for rights.
- Have a clear political and policy solution.

- Have a clear target and timeline.
- Link local concerns to global issues.
- Provide opportunities to raise funds.
- Enable you to further your vision and mission.
- Be winnable.[26]

Case Studies

While the case studies of advocacy by the Tambogrande Defense Front, the Close Vermont Yankee network, and BRAC did not focus on the role of policy research and analysis, each illustrates some of the connections between the ideas discussed here and the actual practice of advocates. The chapter's final section discusses some of those. Additional insights and lessons from the advocacy for a national AIDS commission in Ghana are included in the concluding section of Case D, which follows this chapter.

The Tambogrande and Close Vermont Yankee cases are similar in that in fact very little research was involved in the choice of the policy solution, even though this is often the primary reason for doing such research and is the major focus of the five-step policy analysis process in the preceding section. However, Tambogrande Defense Front members did not need extensive or complex data to decide social and environmental problems would result if an open pit mine was constructed in the middle of their town or to arrive at a policy solution: block its construction. Likewise, most of the individuals and organizations in the Close Vermont Yankee network used commonly known facts about nuclear power to choose their policy solution: close the nuclear reactor and replace it with safe and clean alternatives.

On the other hand, both cases demonstrate the important role research can play in generating evidence useful in the advocacy process, which is the second reason for doing policy research and analysis. While it was conducted well after the Tambograndinos had formulated their policy change goal, research on the mine's potential environmental impact by a Canadian expert provided data and credibility that was very useful for achieving that goal. The antinuclear advocates in Vermont and surrounding states were constantly doing research to generate the evidence needed at different points in the campaign, for example, about alternative sources of energy and their costs.

The research to generate evidence about the potential impact of the mine in Tambogrande was an example of what Shultz calls produce your own. Moreover, while it required someone with technical expertise members of the Defense Front did not possess, it was accessible either because the researcher had done one of the things recommended by ODI's RAPID program (that is, build relationships with advocates) or because Oxfam America had done what is recommended at the end of that section (that is, build relationships with researchers). Most of the evidence to support closing Vermont Yankee has been limited to what Shultz calls "paper and people," with the latter including nuclear power experts who had grown critical of the industry.

BRAC is a case in which a development organization has built up considerable internal expertise in research. Historically, that expertise was focused on program-level evaluations and used to improve the quality or reach of the organization's support for the poor. However, BRAC has disseminated reports (from some of its program research and other more general studies on development issues in Bangladesh) to external audiences. The expert quality of the information is only one reason BRAC has been able to influence policy debates in the larger development community, thereby contributing to decisions by national and international policy makers to support microfinancing, basic education, community health, and other areas. A second reason is the additional legitimacy of information from BRAC, an organization directly and successfully engaged in development work. The case study mentions how this expertise in BRAC was then used to carry out complex, large-scale Education Watch research projects on an annual basis, each of which provided evidence central to a new round of policy advocacy with the government of Bangladesh and other policy makers. Most of the research by BRAC, including the Education Watch studies, includes a substantial produce your own component. Moreover, it is likely the national Education Watch coalition chooses the specific issues in education using criteria similar to the list from VeneKlasen and Miller.

Notes

1. The advocates must also conduct other research (broadly defined as systematic collection and analysis of information and knowledge through experience and reflection, observations, review of literature, interviews, surveys and other methods), for example, researching the political system to identify the policy makers and possible opponents and allies, researching strategies developed by others to borrow ideas, and monitoring and evaluation research related to the progress of an advocacy initiative. These are addressed in chapters 7–10.

2. Jim Shultz, *The Democracy Owner's Manual: A Practical Guide to Changing the World* (New Brunswick, NJ: Rutgers University Press, 2002); Lisa Vene-Klasen with Valerie Miller, *A New Weave of Power, Politics and People: The Action Guide for Advocacy and Citizen Participation* (Warwickshire, UK: Practical Action Publishers, 2007).

3. The study was by J. Molas, P. Tang, and S. Morrow, "Assessing the Non-Academic Impact of Grant-Funded Socio-Economic Research: Results from a Pilot Study." *Research Evaluation* 9, no. 3 (2000); quoted in E. Crewe, I. Hovland, and J. Young, "Chapter Two. Context, Evidence, Links: A Conceptual Framework for Understanding Research-Policy Processes," in Court, J., I. Hovland and J. Young, editors, *Bridging Research and Policy in Development: Evidence and the Change Process* (London: ITDG Publishing, 2004).

4. A good synthesis of the early findings is Emma Crewe, Inge Hovland, and John Young, "Context, Evidence, Links: A Conceptual Framework for Understanding Research-Policy Processes," in *Bridging Research and Policy in Development: Evidence and the Change Process,* ed. J. Court, I. Hovland, and J. Young (London: ITDG Publishing, 2004). However many other and more current papers and related materials produced by RAPID are available from the ODI website, http://www.odi.org.uk/work/programmes/rapid/.

5. While the framework is included in many of RAPID's publications, one of the most accessible sources is ODI's "Bridging Research and Policy in International Development: An Analytical and Practical Framework" (Research and Policy in Development Briefing Paper No. 1, London, UK: Overseas Development Institute, 2004), http://www.odi.org.uk/resources/docs/198.pdf.

6. ODI, "Bridging Research and Policy," 2.

7. ODI, "Bridging Research and Policy," 4.

8. ODI, "Bridging Research and Policy," 4.

9. ODI, "Bridging Research and Policy," 4.

10. ODI, "Bridging Research and Policy," 4.

11. Eugene Bardach, *A Practical Guide for Policy Analysis: The Eightfold Path to Effective Problem Solving* (Washington, DC: CQ Press, 2009). Bardach is a professor at the University of California, Berkeley.

12. Jim Shultz, "Research and Analysis: Advocacy by Fact, Not Fiction," in *The Democracy Owners' Manual: A Practical Guide to Changing the World* (New Brunswick, NJ: Rutgers University Press, 2002), 83–95.

13. Lisa VeneKlasen with Valerie Miller, "Identifying and Defining Problems" and "Causes, Consequences and Solutions," in *A New Weave of Power, People and Politics: The Action Guide for Advocacy and Citizen Participation* (Warwickshire, UK: Practical Action Publishers, 2007), 125–146, 147–162.

14. Shultz, *Democracy Owner's Manual,* 84–85.

15. VeneKlasen and Miller, *New Weave,* 127.

16. VeneKlasen and Miller, *New Weave,* 127.

17. Shultz, *Democracy Owner's Manual,* 85.

18. Shultz, *Democracy Owner's Manual,* 85–86.

19. Shultz, *Democracy Owner's Manual,* 85–86.

20. Shultz, *Democracy Owner's Manual,* 87–88.

21. While not explicitly stated in *New Weave,* it is also possible to involve some secondary constituents (who are not members of the affected community but care about the same problems), perhaps especially students, in the research process, and in the process increase their understanding and commitment to the advocacy work and organize them for future action.

22. Shultz, *Democracy Owner's Manual,* 89–90.

23. Shultz, *Democracy Owner's Manual,* 90–91.

24. Shultz, *Democracy Owner's Manual,* 92.

25. VeneKlasen and Miller, "Analyzing Problems and Selecting Priority Issues," in *A New Weave, People and Politics: The Action Guide for Advocacy and Citizen Participation* (Warwickshire, UK: Practical Action Publishers, 2007), 147–162. They describe the process and include several exercises.

26. VeneKlasen and Miller, *New Weave,* 159–161.

CASE D

Conclusion

Research and Advocacy
for a Ghana AIDS Commission

The learning exercise that culminated the first part of Case D asked you to jot down ideas about what types of economic evidence and arguments might be most persuasive in influencing the new government of Ghana to establish a national AIDS commission. If you wish, you can now modify your ideas based on the discussion of policy research and analysis in chapter 6.

Now compare your ideas with the evidence and arguments in the actual policy paper produced by Kote-Nikoi, which are summarized in the following policy section.[1] The strategy section then describes how the paper was used in the larger advocacy process and the outcome. The case ends with a section on lessons.

Policy

Among the primary and most obvious economic aspects of an HIV/AIDS policy are the budgetary costs of addressing a potential AIDS pandemic. These costs are for prevention education and what are often referred to as the three Ts—tracking, testing, and treatment.[2]

Such services were of course very important. However, Kote-Nikoi felt that at the end of the day, their costs were short term, static, and not adequately persuasive. Moreover, the international donor community had demonstrated a willingness to significantly subsidize such costs, which reduced the policy makers' motivation to develop Ghana's own national policy regarding HIV/AIDS.

He felt that a stronger case for a national policy, especially with the New Patriotic Party, would be made by providing evidence of the longer-term, more dynamic impact that a threshold level of HIV/AIDS infections could have on the entire Ghanaian economy, not just on health, national budgets, or the labor market.

To make the case, Kote-Nikoi analyzed HIV/AIDS from the perspective of "the exogenous supply-side shock to the typical African economy through its impact on the labour market." Based on what was happening elsewhere in Africa, he argued that "the disease is likely to decimate the most productive sectors of the labour force (men and women between the ages of 15 and 45)."[3] High rates of illness (morbidity) and death (mortality) would lead to increases in the costs of labor. He offers an economist's description of the impact:

> This rise in the cost of this crucial production input will initiate three systemic responses and/or induced effects: firstly, producers and employers will attempt to minimize the amount of this increasing-cost input they hire. Unemployment in the formal sector is thus likely to rise as a result, which will be further exacerbated by the consequent fall in aggregate demand. Secondly, as most production processes in Ghana are labour-intensive, the added labour costs will be passed on to consumers as higher output prices. Generalized inflation and lower household purchasing potential, hence even a lower standard-of-living than currently exists in the country, are very real possibilities. . . . Thirdly, there will, in the long-run, be a desertion by producers of labour-intensive production for capital-intensive industries, if the relative prices of labour and capital change significantly enough. In short, both output and factor markets will be adversely affected, as will the composition of investment as resources get shifted inter-sectorally in response to relative price changes in (factor) markets.[4]

For policy makers and other readers who are not economists, Kote-Nikoi provides a simplified schema of the impacts on the per capita GDP in figure D.1.

But none of this suggests the scale of the impacts on the overall economy. Kote-Nikoi argued that this can be best approximated by using a "multi-sectoral Computerized General Equilibrium (GCE) model"[5] to simulate the impact of the disease across the country and over a period of time. He goes on to provide a number of technical arguments on why this is the best approach, with multiple references to and examples from the relevant literature, as well as an appendix with details on the specific GCE approach he would use. Kote-Nikoi realizes that few readers who are not economists, including most policy makers, would understand these technical points; on the other hand, one of its purposes was in fact to convince policy makers that the analytic process was sound and thus they should view the findings as credible.

The subsequent description of how the GCE was implemented was more accessible to noneconomists. It uses data on the

- relative size of the eleven most important sectors of the economy, and factors such as the import/export ratio for each;[6]

Figure D.1 Impact of morbidity and mortality on per capita GDP

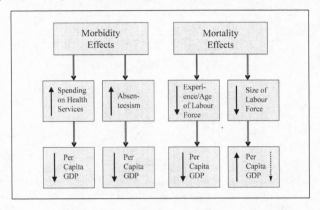

Source: Nikoi Kote-Nikoi, "The Potential Macroeconomic Impact of HIV-Seropositivity in Ghana" (Accra, Ghana: Institute of Economic Affairs Publications, 2001), 3.

- composition of labor in each sector, divided between rural, urban un-skilled, and skilled; and
- HIV/AIDS infection rates for each category of labor.

As indicated in table D.1, the simulation showed a massive impact.

The first two cells in the GDP row were more than enough to get the attention of policy makers. A decrease of 44 percent in the rate of GDP growth would have devastating effects on the population's standard of living. Moreover, the simulation suggested there would be a negative effect in terms of every other important economic variable and a very dramatic one with regard to government saving, the main source of public investments.

Kote-Nikoi concluded, "There are three principal (and interrelated) arguments issuing from these simulations and analyses of the macroeconomic effects of AIDS-induced labour shortages in Ghana's (and, perhaps, much of the African) economy. . . .

(1) There would be a negative impact on the capacity of the economy to produce and expand, with the degree of that impact dependent on factors such as labor intensity in a given sector's production processes;

(2) Labor shortages would cause an increase in wages and thus the general price level, with multiple implications for the balance of trade and foreign exchange rate; and,

(3) There would be declines in government revenue and private spending, which subsequently translate into lower investment demand and a further contraction of the (long-term potential of the) economy."[7]

Based on these findings, Kote-Nikoi closed with the following statement: "We at the IEA [Institute of Economic Affairs] wish to sound the alarm

Table D.1 Ghana's performance with and without the HIV/AIDS shock, 1996–2001

Variables	No AIDS	AIDS	RR[a]	UU[b]	US[c]
GDP	4.3	2.4	4.3	4.3	2.6
Consumption	4.6	4.3	4.5	4.6	4.4
Fixed investment	5.1	1.4	5.1	5.0	1.7
Exports	5.9	3.9	5.9	5.9	4.1
Imports	4.4	2.8	4.4	4.4	3.0
Private saving	3.6	3.2	3.6	3.6	3.3
Government saving	10.2	−25.2	10.1	9.3	−20.6

Source: Nikoi Kote-Nikoi, "The Potential Macroeconomic Impact of HIV-Seropositivity in Ghana" (Accra, Ghana: Institute of Economic Affairs Publications, 2001), 17–18.
a. Rural labor
b. UU (Urban) Unskilled labor
c. US (Urban) Skilled labor

that HIV-AIDS might well become the single most important economic, political, public health and *development* issue for Ghana (and the rest of the sub-continent) for at least the next generation. More is the pity that recent governments have not seen fit to offer the country a comprehensive programme of intervention to tackle the issue head on."[8]

Note that the paper did not include any specific policy recommendation on what would constitute a comprehensive intervention. According to Kote-Nikoi, that should be defined by public health experts and not by an economist. Thus he believed the best policy solution would be for government to establish a national AIDS commission with a comprehensive mandate, adequate funding to pursue it, and the involvement of relevant professionals in and outside government. But he wanted that goal to emerge from consultations with allied advocacy organizations, policy makers, and other relevant stakeholders.

Strategy

It is common for many policy research centers and think tanks, such as the IEA, to complete policy-relevant studies, pass them on to policy makers, and hope they will make a difference in policy decisions. To date, the IEA had been no different. However, it was to break new ground in advocating for the national AIDS commission.

The process to create an informal advocacy network of the following people, organizations, and groups most directly concerned with HIV/AIDS was very intentional:

- internal allies in government, especially civil servants responsible for responding to health and related problems on the ground on a daily basis, the most important of whom were members of the Ghana Health Service, but others included the women and juvenile departments in the police force;
- the Christian Health Association of Ghana, for similar reasons;
- social-justice-oriented NGOs with advocacy experience, such as the Center for Democracy and Development and the Ghana Chapter of the International Federation of Women Lawyers; and,
- the Ghana Radio Broadcasters Association.

The allies were fully briefed on the findings and implications of the IEA research. They discussed possible policy goals and agreed to advocate for a national commission.

The public was informed through very popular radio talk shows that involve guests and opportunities for listeners to call in their questions and comments. Kote-Nikoi and people from the allied organizations participated in numerous programs that reached different parts of the country, which included areas where at that time HIV/AIDS was not yet well understood. In those areas, many Ghanaians called it "the thinning disease" because they only knew that persons become ill and slowly wither away.

Roundtables organized for policy makers were typically held over a weekend at a hotel near enough to Ghana's capital city to make them feasible but far away enough that organizers had a relatively captive audience for the sessions.[9] The IEA was able to engage some of the most influential people—the heavy lifters—including the health minister (one of Kote-Nikoi's schoolmates) and adviser to the vice president of Ghana. Members of parliament who attended were on the health subcommittee. Also present were members of the Ghana Health Service, including the internal allies noted in the preceding list, as well as representatives from other organizations in the advocacy network.

During the roundtables, the evidence in Kote-Nikoi's paper was discussed and its arguments for action were made. That led to processes of collective brainstorming and deliberations about appropriate policy responses. The importance of responding was made more personal when, during one session, a representative from IEA reported that a recent study had found a "shocking" fact (which really did not shock anyone present): African parliamentarians had a particularly high incidence of HIV/AIDS. This opened the door for the advocates to pose the question: "Have *you* been tested?"

The roundtables provided a forum for representatives of the IEA and the other advocates to introduce or support the idea of a national AIDS commission and for the policy makers to feel ownership of the idea. They provided an opportunity for the advocates to help shape the specifics of the policy, such as the commission's specific mandate, its structure, membership of different committees (e.g., it called for the Ghana Health Service and the Christian Health Association of Ghana to be fully represented), and so forth.

The processes ensured that HIV/AIDS was an issue on the national policy agenda, and it soon led to the official formulation and introduction of the advocate's policy solution. At that point, the advocates focused on supporting internal allies and lobbying fence sitters as the policy made its way through parliamentary committees and the relevant ministries.

Within six months the policy recommendation was passed as an act of parliament and signed by the president. The Ghana AIDS Commission was officially launched in 2002. The advocates had succeeded and were well positioned to guide or influence the implementation of the policy.

Lessons

One important aspect of the case is the relationship between research and the formulation of the advocates' policy change goals. Kote-Nikoi, as director of research at IEA, and others in the network recognized that relatively extensive and complex public health policy research would be necessary to adequately understand the relevant problems, their causes, and possible solutions or policy options. They were in no position to identify, much less to choose, which policies would have the best chance of preventing the eruption of an AIDS pandemic in Ghana. That would require new expertise and resources that had not been prioritized by the national government.

Thus the advocates formulated an initial policy change goal that did not require such expertise and resources: the government should create and fund (along with the international community) a national AIDS commission to carry out the public health policy research and formulate well-informed policy change recommendations.

And therefore the major policy research challenge became, what evidence will be most effective in influencing the government to establish a commission?

At the time, the IEA was a think tank with most of the limitations identified by the Research and Policy in International Development (RAPID) program, which were discussed in chapter 6. In terms of RAPID's "Different Notions of Evidence" (table 6.1), the left column generally described the IEA's biases and perspective evidence; the right column did the same for the government policy makers.

However, Kote-Nikoi took a new approach. He understood and took many of the actions included under the political context, evidence, and links in RAPID's "How to Influence Policy and Practice" table.[10] For example, in terms of political context, he knew "the policy makers, their agendas and constraints" and reacted to "unexpected policy windows" in light of the dramatic change in government and thus the national political agenda following the elections of 2000. With regard to evidence, his research on the economic impact of AIDS was designed to "build a convincing case," one that could be packaged for the new government in a "theory and narrative" that they would find "familiar." And in terms of links, he knew many of the "other stakeholders" and joined or helped build networks or loose coalitions with those who shared his values, concerns, and policy goals.

On the other hand, Kote-Nikoi's "Potential Macroeconomic Impact of HIV-Seropositivity in Ghana" policy paper did not include specific "practical solutions" or "present clear options" as recommended by ODI. In fact, it never even mentioned a national AIDS commission. Nor did the research process follow Shultz's five steps or any other guidelines for moving from problem to solution (though the author knows these well and in fact offers students his own guidelines when teaching policy analysis).[11] Yet he and his colleagues succeeded in achieving their policy goal in a rather short time frame.

The lesson is that no single approach is appropriate for every situation. Successful research and its dissemination will vary with the issue, the political and cultural context, the historical moment, and other related factors. In this case, the research generated evidence that could then be discussed among stakeholders, in public forums (newspapers, radio talk shows, etc.), and with policy makers. It also allowed for the policy solution to emerge from that process and to be owned by all the involved actors.

Notes

1. Nikoi Kote-Nikoi, "The Potential Macroeconomic Impact of HIV-Seropositivity in Ghana" (Accra, Ghana: Institute of Economic Affairs, 2001). Unfortunately, this paper is no longer accessible.

2. It is likely that when doing the case study's exercise, most if not all the economic evidence and arguments you identified were budgetary or similar costs, such as for orphanages or other services for children whose parents have died of AIDS and for whom the traditional family and community support systems have been overwhelmed or broken down.

3. Kote-Nikoi, "Potential Macroeconomic Impact," 2.

4. Kote-Nikoi, "Potential Macroeconomic Impact," 2.

5. Kote-Nikoi, "Potential Macroeconomic Impact," 16.

6. The eleven most important sectors of the economy are food crops, cash crops, forestry, food processing, consumer goods, intermediate goods, cement and base metals, capital goods, construction, private services, and public services.

7. Kote-Nikoi, "Potential Macroeconomic Impact," 19–20.

8. Kote-Nikoi, "Potential Macroeconomic Impact," 20.

9. The IEA secured funding to cover not only the direct costs but also a per diem that provided an additional incentive for policy makers to allocate a weekend to such an activity.

10. Overseas Development Institute, "Bridging Research and Policy in International Development: An Analytical and Practical Framework" (briefing paper, Research and Policy in Development (London, UK: Overseas Development Institute, 2004), 4, http://www.odi.org.uk/resources/docs/198.pdf.

11. For the five steps, see Jim Shultz, *The Democracy Owner's Manual: A Practical Guide to Changing the World* (New Brunswick, NJ: Rutgers University Press, 2002).

CASE E

Oxfam America Climate Change Campaign: Political Mapping

Gabrielle Watson, coauthor

The United Nations Climate Change Summit in Copenhagen, December 2009, was to be the culmination of a decade of efforts to reach an international agreement adequate to address the growing crisis of climate change. Thousands of advocacy organizations and special interest groups had worked hard to influence the outcome. Oxfam America and other affiliates of the Oxfam International confederation were among the advocates. They launched a campaign focused on achieving an agreement that would be a "fair and safe deal" for the countries and communities that, due to poverty and other forms of marginalization, are the most vulnerable to floods, droughts, and other effects of "unprecedented climate stress."[1]

Oxfam America's Climate Change Campaign (CCC) is the subject of two case studies. This one focuses on the process of identifying the political systems and the actors who need to be influenced and the other actors who support or oppose the advocates' efforts to do so. Following an introduction to the context, the advocates, and their policy analysis and goals, you are invited to imagine you are a member of Oxfam America's campaign team and have been asked to draft an initial list of the policy institutions and policy makers the campaign will need to influence, the types of allies the campaign might work with, and the types of opponents they must overcome.

The second case, Case H, which precedes chapter 10, describes the strategy of the campaign and its outcomes (including but not limited to the well-known fact that no substantive agreement, much less a fair one, was reached in Copenhagen). The learning exercise for this case asks you to think about how to evaluate and learn from the campaign.

Context

In response to growing concerns about global warming, the United Nations Framework Convention on Climate Change (UNFCCC) was created in 1994. The 190 plus countries ratifying the UNFCCC treaty, the parties to the convention, agreed to work together to monitor climate changes and develop goals and plans for reducing emissions of carbon dioxide and other greenhouse gases and for responding to the impacts of changes that were already set in motion. The treaty recognized that industrialized countries were the major source of harmful emissions and that they should have primary responsibility for achieving the treaty's goals.

With support from a UNFCCC secretariat and three different expert groups, and based on the work of various preparatory committee meetings, international agreements and other major policy decisions are made during an annual Conference of the Parties (COP). All member countries send delegations, and their decisions are supposed to be made by consensus.

In practice, the size and capacity of the delegations from the rich countries, which are active before and during all preparatory meetings as well as during the COPs, far exceed those that developing countries are able to send. To some extent, the disadvantaged countries attempt to compensate through forming their own regional or special interest caucuses and coordinating their efforts. But the rich countries also have their own networks, with even more resources and often coordinate their efforts as well. And since decisions are made by consensus, and any meaningful responses to climate change require the rich countries to make the major reductions in emissions, any one or group of those countries can ultimately determine the nature and scope of all UNFCCC responses.

On the other hand, the COPs provide a forum for developing countries to present evidence and proposals for action that emphasize the mutual self-interest of all countries and people. Moreover, over six hundred observer organizations (multilaterals, environmental nongovernmental organizations, and others) can attend COPs and provide information and otherwise attempt to influence those decisions.

The most important agreement to date was made during the third COP in Kyoto, Japan, in 1997. While the UNFCCC treaty encouraged industrialized countries to take responsibility, the Kyoto Protocol committed them to achieve by 2012 national emissions levels below what they were in 1990. It provided various mechanisms the countries could use (for example, emissions trading and clean energy investments in developing countries) to achieve their targets, and it established a global fund for helping developing countries cope with the growing consequences of climate change. In subsequent years, the COPs focused on the protocol's details and resolving differences with regard to its implementation.

Most of the industrialized and developing countries ratified the Kyoto Protocol, and it went into force in 2005. However, several key countries, most notably the United States, backed out. US President Bill Clinton had signed the agreement but was unable to convince the Senate to ratify it before the end of his second term. President George W. Bush took office in 2000 and opposed its ratification; in 2001 a Senate vote rejected the protocol.

Even with members of the European Union and other industrialized countries taking some steps toward emissions reductions, the overall level of greenhouse gases continued to rise, and the pace of climate change increased. To resolve the deteriorating situation, many countries and thousands of advocacy organizations pointed to the fifteenth COP slated for Copenhagen in 2009 as a critical moment for creating a new, more effective, and fully inclusive treaty that would replace the Kyoto Protocol upon its expiration in 2012.

The possibility that the United States would become more engaged and even provide leadership in the post-Kyoto negotiations improved in 2006. Popular support for the Bush administration had waned, and in the midterm elections Democrats regained control of the House for the first time since 1994, winning back the slim majority in the Senate they had lost in 2002. The Democrats fared even better in 2008 with the election of President Barack Obama and attaining a large majority in the Senate. Obama and many Democrats and some Republicans in Congress pledged to actively pursue a solution to climate change.

Advocates

Oxfam America, based in Boston, describes itself as "an international relief and development organization that creates lasting solutions to poverty, hunger and injustice. Together with individuals and local groups in more than 90 countries, Oxfam saves lives, helps people overcome poverty, and fights for social justice. We are one of 15 affiliates in the international confederation, Oxfam."[2]

The original Oxfam, the Oxford Committee for Famine Relief, today called Oxfam Great Britain, was founded in 1942 to respond to the plight of refugees in Greece. Nearly thirty years later, the humanitarian crisis resulting from Bangladesh's war of liberation was the impetus for the founding of Oxfam America. While most of the other Oxfam affiliates are also based in the Global North (Ireland, France, Spain, the Netherlands, Germany, Australia, New Zealand, Canada, and a separate Oxfam in Quebec), the confederation now also includes affiliates in India, Hong Kong, and Mexico.

Soon after it was founded, Oxfam America's leadership decided to not accept funding from the US government and instead decided to "build broad-based, grassroots support that would remain independent of government foreign policy."[3] And they decided Oxfam's development support would be through partnerships, most often long term, with locally created and run nongovernmental and community organizations. Two of those partnerships are subjects of other case studies in this book: Case A on the Tambogrande Defense Front in Peru (recall Oxfam's role in funding the external review of the environmental impact report) and Case B on BRAC in Bangladesh (which Oxfam has helped support, and has learned from, for nearly forty years).

In the 1980s Oxfam America expanded its focus to include advocacy on issues such as debt relief and fair trade, targeting the policies of the US government, and in collaboration with others including other Oxfam affiliates, the policies of the World Bank and other multilateral organizations. In 1994 it opened an office in Washington, DC, to support those advocacy initiatives. During the past decade, Oxfam has successfully influenced the Starbucks Corporation to change the way it buys coffee from producers in Ethiopia. It sought significant changes in the 2005 reauthorization of the US Farm Bill; while not able to achieve its primary goals related to food aid reform, Oxfam did contribute to other changes in the interest of small farmers. It has played a lead role in a coalition that has successfully advocated for US legislation and other actions that force multinational corporations involved in mining and other extractive industries to act in more transparent and responsible ways.

Today one of Oxfam America's two vice presidents is in charge of the Policy and Campaigns Division, which includes fifty staff members involved in policy research and analysis, outreach and organizing, alliance building, government affairs (lobbying), private sector engagement, and monitoring, evaluation, and learning. The Oxfam Communications and Constituency Engagement Division works closely with Policy and Campaigns on advocacy-related communications (media relations, publications, website development, and social networking) and outreach (training and mobilization of Oxfam constituents, including Action Corps volunteers and student groups). A comprehensive campaign strategic framework provides guidelines for planning and evaluating campaigns.

At any given time several campaign teams, each headed by a campaign manager, draw members from many if not all the different practice areas in each of the two divisions. The CCC team was initiated in 2007. While it was working, another campaign team was focused on aid effectiveness (or aid reform), and a relatively smaller team was focused on extractive industries (the Right to Know, Right to Decide campaign).

The CCC, part of a coordinated advocacy campaign by the entire Oxfam federation, was planned by policy and advocacy staff from many of the affiliates, and its strategy involved some common actions (in the different countries or together, such as in New York City during preparatory meetings at the UN offices). However, each affiliate was expected to also focus on its own unique resources, opportunities, and capacity in ways that would be most effective for achieving the fair and safe deal in Copenhagen.

Policy

A series of policy papers defined the policy goals for the campaign, provided evidence, and expanded or refined the key arguments for supporting the goals. The first, "Adapting to Climate Change: What's Needed in Poor Countries, and Who Should Pay," is a forty-seven-page paper published in May 2007 by Oxfam International, which begins with a strong, concise summary of the confederation's position:

> Climate change is forcing vulnerable communities in poor countries to adapt to unprecedented climate stress. Rich countries, primarily responsible for the problem, must stop *harming*, by fast cutting their greenhouse-gas emissions, and start *helping*, by providing finance for adaptation. In developing countries Oxfam estimates the adaptation will cost at least $50 billion each year, and far more if global emissions are not cut rapidly. Urgent work is necessary to gain a more accurate picture of the costs to the poor. According to Oxfam's new Adaptation Financing Index, the USA, European Union, Japan, Canada and Australia should contribute over 95 per cent of the finance needed. The finance must not be counted toward meeting the UN-agreed target of 0.7 per cent [of gross domestic product] for aid. Rich countries are planning multi-billion dollar adaptation measures at home, but to date they have delivered just $48 million to international funds for least-developed country adaptation, and have counted it as aid: an unacceptable inequity in global responses to climate change.[4]

The need to cut carbon emissions was consistent with the policy goals of most environmental and other advocacy organizations working on climate change. However, as an international development organization focused on ending poverty and defending human rights, Oxfam's special contribution to the policy debates on climate change was its focus on international aid policy. Oxfam staff drew from their on-the-ground knowledge of the problems that vulnerable populations were already experiencing and the costs of addressing them. They had a deep understanding of past international aid agreements (for example, the UN targets) and the gaps between those agreements and actual performance, including the way donor countries often manipulate the way they report aid. Oxfam's solution included a clear rationale and equitable formula for how much each donor country should contribute to meeting the overall international aid costs for adaptation, that is, a percentage equal to the percentage of global carbon emissions released by that country.

The following year, 2008, Oxfam America published a shorter policy paper that focused specifically on US international aid for adaptation: "Adaptation 101: How Climate Change Hurts Poor Communities—and How We Can Help."[5] Produced for a wider audience, including policy makers (or their aides), the paper's author devotes a substantial section to clarifying what adaptation looks like.

> No one solution or approach will work for everyone. In all countries facing the impacts of climate change, the key is to build resilience at the community level; communities must be able to respond and adapt to the shifting and frequently unexpected conditions that climate change brings. Climate change will be essential in a few key areas:
>
> • Addressing water scarcity that jeopardizes safe drinking water and agriculture;
> • Coping with excessive water, including from floods and sea level rise;
> • Reducing disaster risks from severe weather events;
> • Improving agricultural practices and diversifying agricultural livelihoods;
> • Improving health systems to address climate-related diseases and other health impacts;
> • And addressing social impacts that stem from climate change, including migration and conflicts over natural resources.[6]

Based on an understanding of US culture and politics, Oxfam America provided "compelling reasons" why the US government should contribute its equitable share of the costs.

> The US should provide funding for adaptation because . . . it would demonstrate global leadership . . .
>
> • it would help safeguard global security . . .
> • responding now would save money down the road . . .
> • climate change brings with it the spread of hunger and disease . . . [and]
> • promoting economic development in developing countries should be a national priority.[7]

The paper identifies several possible ways to fund adaptation. If the legislative proposals that use the cap and trade approach to reduce emissions are adopted, then the permits to industries and utilities should not be given away but rather sold, and the revenue used for a number of public needs, including international aid for adaptation. Alternatively, "the costs of adaptation can also be funded through other revenue-generating policies, such as carbon fees and taxes on major industries and utilities, or by shifting subsidies and tax breaks away from fossil fuel energy to adaptation funding."[8]

In addition to arguing for dramatic increases in international aid for adaptation, Oxfam America advocates argue that the ways the greenhouse gas emissions are cut should also be sensitive to the needs of vulnerable populations. Financing and deploying clean energy technologies should be done "in an equitable manner that benefits poor people around the world and neutralizes any negative consequences for poor Americans" and provides "new 'green job' opportunities in the US and abroad."[9]

A year later, 2009, three other publications refined Oxfam America's positions and arguments to appeal to US policy makers. The most detailed provided more data and analysis in support of many of the same points in the previous paper, but framed some of them as a "Green New Deal" that would benefit US businesses and developing countries.[10] A short piece focused entirely on the "green economic growth" potential for the United States in responding to "climate change preparedness" and "adjustment" needs in the United States and the developing world.[11] A third paper focused on "social vulnerability and climate change" in the United States, specifically the thirteen-state region of the Southeast, which is highly prone to one or more of four "climate hazards": drought, hurricane force winds, sea-level rise, and flooding.[12]

LEARNING EXERCISE

You have joined the Oxfam America's CCC team and understand that the campaign's ultimate goal is a fair and safe deal emerging from the fifteenth COP in Copenhagen, which you now know must include an increased commitment to adaptation funding.

A meeting has been scheduled to specify the policy-making institutions and, if possible, the policy makers the campaign will need to influence. Moreover, given the hundreds of other advocacy organizations Oxfam might collaborate with, the meeting will identify the most important types of potential allies (by sector or interest) and, in general, their opponents.

As with all other team members, you have been asked to draft a set of notes. You can augment your notes after reading chapter 7. The conclusion of Case E, which follows that chapter, will allow you to compare your notes with Oxfam's actual analysis of their targets, allies, and opponents.

Notes

1. Kate Raworth, "Adapting to Climate Change: What's Needed in Poor Countries, and Who Should Pay" (Oxfam Briefing Paper 104, Oxford, UK: Oxfam International, 2007).

2. "Who We Are," 2012, http://www.oxfamamerica.org/whoweare.

3. Click on the "Our History" link at http://www.oxfamamerica.org/whoweare.

4. Raworth, "Adapting to Climate Change," 1.

5. Oxfam America, *Adaptation 101: How Climate Change Hurts Poor Communities—and How We Can Help* (Boston: Oxfam America, 2008).

6. Oxfam America, *Adaptation 101,* 11.

7. Oxfam America, *Adaptation 101,* 5.

8. Oxfam America, *Adaptation 101,* 9.

9. Oxfam America, *Adaptation 101,* 19.

10. Oxfam America, *Adapting to Climate Change: How Building Stronger Communities Can Save Lives, Create Jobs and Build Global Security* (Boston: Oxfam America, 2009).

11. Oxfam America, *The New Adaptation Marketplace: Climate Change and the Opportunities for Green Economic Growth* (Boston: Oxfam America, 2009).

12. Oxfam America, *Exposed: Social Vulnerability and Climate Change in the US Southeast* (Boston: Oxfam America, 2009), 5.

7

Politics

Formal and Nonformal Power

IN ITS MOST BASIC SENSE, POLITICS IS ABOUT THE *WHO* OF ADVOCACY. IF ADVOCATES are going to solve problems by changing policies, they must know who makes policies and how they are made. This includes knowing the relevant policy-making institutions and the specific person or body (for example, a legislature or council) in an institution that has the formal power to make the policy decision they seek. It also includes knowing the formal or official processes by which policies are considered, enacted, implemented, and evaluated.

The advocates must know not only who makes policy decisions but also who and what influences them—the wielding of nonformal power. In some cases another person or group has so much influence on the official policy makers that they are in fact the real decision makers. In almost all cases, in addition to the advocates other people, groups, organizations, and coalitions seek to persuade or pressure the decision makers. Often there are many. Nearly always, many others are excluded. One of the major factors that determines a policy decision is the relative power in terms of the connections, resources, knowledge, and people (consciousness and mobilization) of the advocates, their allies, and those who oppose them.

The advocates must effectively integrate their understanding of politics and power with the policy analysis processes discussed in chapter 6. For example, if advocates are able to generate convincing evidence and analysis, that knowledge can increase their power and influence. Likewise,

127

at the point in a policy analysis process when the advocates must choose the policy changes (solutions) they will pursue, the best decisions are based on an understanding of the political and power realities. Thus, of the six criteria that Shultz provides for making those choices, two are specifically political: "Who will support and oppose each alternative? Which ones could attract enough political support to be adopted?" The same is true for the last criterion in VeneKlasen and Miller's list, which is simply: "Is it winnable?"[1]

In this chapter, the first section focuses on understanding policy institutions, their formal processes, and the official decision makers. It stresses the importance of being precise about who or what body has the formal power or authority to make the decision the advocates are seeking. It also introduces the policy cycle (agenda setting, formulation and enactment, implementation, and evaluation), which can help advocates understand the multiple points where decisions are made.

The chapter's third focus is on the nature and dynamics of nonformal power that shape the official and especially the unofficial processes of policy making. In some cases, the distribution and use of power are easy to see and understand. In most cases, they are not. Even when power dynamics are visible and simple, but especially when they are opaque and complex, advocates need concepts and tools for analyzing institutions, systems, and actors.

However, some of the language and concepts the advocates, policy makers, and other actors commonly use in thinking about policy making can obscure rather than clarify the deeper relations of power. Thus the chapter's second section highlights two of these: stakeholder participation and the three sector (state, market, and civil society) model.

The chapter's third section focuses on a conceptual framework that illuminates relations of power and their role in policy making. Developed by John Gaventa and colleagues, it distinguishes three forms or dimensions of power (visible, hidden, and invisible), the political spaces (closed, invited, claimed/created), and the levels (local, national, global) where decision making takes place and represents their relationships in the form of a power cube.

The fourth section of the chapter discusses tools advocates can use to apply their understanding of politics and power when planning a campaign or initiative. While there are many, it summarizes one I find useful. This final section draws connections between the preceding material and the exercise in Case E about the Oxfam America Climate Change Campaign.

Policy Makers and Policy Making

To influence policies, advocates need to know what institution or institutions have the formal power to make the decisions they seek. While most often the institution will be one or more parts of government, there are many other possibilities (multilateral institutions, corporations, universities, hospitals, and so forth). The following concepts can be applied to all, but since government is the most common and usually the most complex of the policy-making institutions, it is our focus.

It is never enough to simply identify the relevant institution as "the government." Advocates must know at which level and which branches agencies or other units of government can make the policy decisions the advocates are seeking. They need to be able to answer the following:

- Will the decision be made by one or more parts of the national government? Subnational units of government (state, province, district, municipality, and so forth)? Multigovernmental global institutions? Or does a decision require action at multiple levels? If so, is there a hierarchy or sequence for such decision making?
- Within each of those levels of government, what are the different units (for example, executive, legislative, and judicial branches) and in which one(s) will the decision be made?
- If there is a legislative branch (national congress or parliament, state assembly, city council, etc.), are there specific committees or other bodies that must make the initial decision before it goes to the full membership?
- If there is an executive branch, will the decision be made by the chief executive or by one of its agencies (department, ministry, etc.)? If by an agency, will the decision be made by the top official, another official, or some committee?

Advocates must also know the official rules and processes for making policies in every part of government relevant to their issue. For example, what steps must a legislature go through to pass a law? Are there stated guidelines for what needs to be considered before an agency issues a certain type of regulation? Is there a formal requirement and are there procedures for securing public input, and if so, what does that involve?

Legislatures enacting laws and agencies issuing regulations to implement a law are examples of two phases of what is commonly conceptualized as a four-phase policy cycle. Advocates should be familiar with all four. They are depicted in figure 7.1, which also shows what type of advocacy intervention is appropriate in each phase. The large arrows indicate the logical sequence of the phases. In reality the process is nearly always more dynamic and multidirectional, as indicated by the smaller arrows.

Knowledge of the different institutions, levels, branches, and agencies of government, and especially the identification of the official rules or processes for decision making, often focuses on the formulation and enactment of policies and their implementation.

However, the other two phases are also important. If the advocates' policy issue is not a priority for the policy makers, it is necessary to focus on the agenda setting phase. This phase is also important because, as discussed in chapter 9, it is often when an issue is framed by the advocates, their opponents, or others, and the dominant frame can significantly shape what occurs in all the other phases.

In practice, the evaluation phase is sometimes neglected in the policy-making process; in those situations the advocates may need to focus on ensuring that a thorough assessment of whether a policy is having its intended impact is conducted. They may do this by pressuring the responsible body of government to do the assessment and then monitoring how well it is carried out. Or depending on resources, policy evaluation might be undertaken by the advocates or an allied organization. In any case, the findings of an evaluation can often be very useful for getting a policy issue back on the agenda for further action; when a policy is being

Figure 7.1 Four phases of the policy cycle: An advocate's perspective

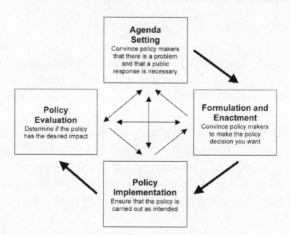

reviewed, the findings can be used to defend or strengthen a policy the advocates support or to reform or eliminate a policy they oppose.

Power: Concepts That Can Obscure Understanding

Since the relative power of the advocates and others seeking to influence the formal policy-making process is a major factor in determining the outcome, advocates need to clearly understand the nature and dynamics of power. In so doing, they need to be attuned to implicit or subtle assumptions about power that are embedded in language and concepts they often hear and use. In many cases these have been initiated or popularized by those with power or by those who support them. Unless approached with a clear and critical understanding, some concepts and language can impede effective power analysis.

Stakeholder participation is one example. In itself, the concept of a stakeholder is basically neutral; the term simply refers to anyone or any group that has a stake or interest in a policy decision or its outcome. And, as discussed later, effective power mapping begins by identifying stakeholders, followed by using various methods for analyzing each person's or group's interest, their strengths and weaknesses, whether they will support or oppose the advocates, and so forth.

However, a more dominant approach to stakeholder participation, often employed by liberal governments and institutions (or those that wish to appear liberal) ignores or at least plays down differences in power. It assumes that everyone with a significant stake in a policy outcome has an equal right to have input in policy making and that the best policies are those that maximize benefits to all. The approach assumes conflicting interests can be mediated in a fair way. In some cases, there may indeed be little or no difference in the relative power of the different stakeholders and it may be possible to reach a fair decision. But more often the process actually facilitates the ability of the most powerful stakeholders to have unequal influence.

That is not to say that a critical understanding of stakeholder participation should lead advocates to reject any effort by policy makers to involve them as stakeholders; in fact, they may be the ones who advocate for the participation of all stakeholders. Since the most powerful actors will almost always have access through informal channels, they may as well be invited to participate in the open. But decisions to participate or to advocate for greater participation should be done with full awareness of the potential for the process to be manipulated. Thus advocates need to push for participation rules and methods that enhance their influence and limit that of their more powerful opponents.

The *three sector (state, market, and civil society) model* is a second example of a concept that can obscure power. Since the 1990s that framework has been used widely in the field of international development and in other contexts. The concept or at least the term *civil society* is even more widely used, including by progressive advocacy organizations.[2] Figure 7.2 provides a simple overview of the three sectors.

One of the most basic assumptions of the framework is that in healthy societies each of these sectors is strong and there is a balance between all three. Thus, it is common to represent the sectors as circles to visually depict the relative strength of each sector (size of each circle) and to show relationships of the sectors (the distance or in some cases overlap between the circles).

Of course, much more specific and nuanced analyses build on the overall framework. However, the conceptual trap for power analysts is not questioning this most general level of analysis and its most basic assumptions. If one thinks in terms of *a* market, then important power differences between a multinational corporation and local enterprise are lost. Likewise, important power and ideological differences between a professional association of corporate executives and a trade union of marginalized workers, or between a fundamentalist and a progressive faith

Figure 7.2 Three sector model

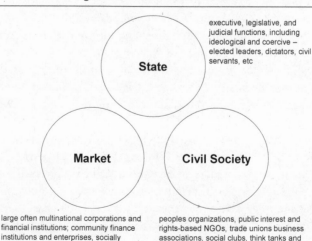

institution (including a fundamentalist and a progressive institution of the same faith) are lost if one thinks in terms of *a* civil society.

As a tool for rethinking the three sector model, I have found it helpful to reorganize the diagram based on wealth, power, and social class interests. As depicted in figure 7.3, civil society organizations and institutions now appear in all three circles, based not on their form or function, but on their class interests; the same is true for market organizations and institutions.

The relationship between the different classes and the state cease to be understood as one in which a harmonious relationship is a given or even possible. Instead, the state is a contested terrain in which each class seeks to gain advantage through influencing policy decisions.

As with the concepts and language of stakeholder participation, the rethinking exercise is not to suggest that advocates should never use the three sector model; even if they tried, it would be nearly impossible to do so in light of how ubiquitous the concepts have become. The point is to not allow that usage to obscure their understanding of power and conflict.

Power: Concepts That Illuminate Understanding

In contrast, many conceptual frameworks insightfully illuminate power differences. Several of these are presented in *A New Weave of Power* and

Figure 7.3 State as contested terrain model

State: executive, legislative, and judicial structures

Market: parastatal enterprises

Civil society: government-run NGOs

State
"contested terrain"

battle for control

Owning class
its institutions
and allies

battle for power
over middle classes

Marginalized classes
their institutions
and allies

Market: large, often multinational large corporations and financial institutions

Civil society: business associations, elite social clubs, right-wing think tanks and organizations, "astro-turf" organizations

Market: community finance institutions, micro-enterprises, socially responsible businesses

Civil society: peoples organizations, public interest and rights-based NGOs, trade unions other publications by Lisa VeneKlasen, Valerie Miller, and their colleagues at Just Associates.[3]

One framework distinguishes between *power over,* the mechanisms for dominating others; *power within,* the mechanisms for building self-worth and confidence of the dominated groups; *power to,* harnessing their potential; and *power with,* the mechanisms for creating alliances among the dominated.

Another and more comprehensive framework was developed by John Gaventa in collaboration with others, including VeneKlasen and Miller.[4] It began by distinguishing three forms or dimensions of power: visible power, hidden power, and invisible power. In a number of his works, Gaventa draws on VeneKlasen and Miller to describe these:

Visible power: observable decision making
    This level includes the visible and definable aspects of political power—the formal rules, structures, authorities, institutions and procedures of decision making.

Hidden power: setting the political agenda
    Certain powerful people and institutions maintain their influence by controlling who gets to the decision-making table and what gets on the agenda. These dynamics operate on many levels to exclude and devalue the concerns and representation of other less powerful groups,

Invisible power: shaping meaning and what is acceptable
    Probably the most insidious of the three dimensions of power, invisible power shapes the psychological and ideological boundaries of participation. Significant problems and issues are not only kept from the decision-making table, but also from the minds and consciousness of the different players involved, even those directly affected by the problem. By influencing how individuals think about their place in the world, this level of power shapes people's beliefs, sense of self and acceptance of the status quo—even their own superiority or inferiority. Processes of socialisation, culture and ideology perpetuate exclusion and inequality by defining what is normal, acceptable and safe.[5]

Just Associates developed a power matrix that integrates both of the preceding frameworks.[6] It "presents how different dimensions of power interact to shape the problem and the possibility of citizen participation and action," while adding the caution that "the distinctions among the different dimensions are not neat or clean." For each of the three dimensions—visible, hidden, and invisible—the matrix describes the "mechanisms through which dimensions of *power over* operate to exclude and privilege," and provides examples of how the dominant groups do this. For each of the dimensions, the matrix also describes possible responses and strategies by advocates to challenge dominant power with transforming forms of power or power with, to, and within.

The following is adapted from the matrix:

Visible Power: Making and Enforcing the Rules

Mechanisms: policy makers in government and other institutions of power, and "instruments: policies, laws, constitutions, budgets, regulations, conventions, agreements, implementing agreements, etc."

Examples of power over: "biased laws/policies (for example, health care policies that do not address the poor or women's reproductive health needs); decision-making structures . . . [that] favor the elite or powerful and are closed to certain people's voices and unrepresentative."

Advocates' responses and strategies: "confronting, engaging, negotiation" including policy research and recommendations, monitoring, lobbying, negotiation, collaboration, litigation, voting, running for office, etc.

Hidden Power: Setting the Agenda
Through Exclusion and Delegitimization

Mechanisms: unwritten rules and political control of dominant and vested interests; intimidation, co-optation, and misinformation

Examples of power over: leaders of marginalized groups labeled trouble makers or unrepresentative; issues related to the environment are deemed elitist/impractical; feminism blamed for male violence/breaking families; domestic violence, childcare seen as private, individual issues not worthy of public action; peasant land rights/labor rights are "special interests" and not economically viable

Advocates' responses and strategies: "building collective power"—including organizing communities, strengthening organizations, coalitions, movements, and accountable leaders; participatory research and dissemination of information/ideas/images that validate and legitimize the issues of excluded groups

Invisible Power: Shaping Meaning, Values, and What's
"Normal" Through Socialization and Control of Information

Mechanisms: schooling, media, advertising, and other forms of popular culture shape people's understanding of their needs, rights, and status in ways that prevent the marginalized classes from believing they can or should be involved in change, that reinforce privilege-inferiority, blame the victim, and "manufacture consent"

Examples of power over: women blame themselves for domestic abuse; poor farmers blame themselves for their poverty, despite unequal access to markets, decent prices, or wages; crucial information is misrepresented, concealed, or inaccessible

Advocates' responses and strategies: "building individual and collective power," including popular education, consciousness-raising, sharing stories, speaking out and connecting with others, affirming resistance, analyzing power and values, linking concrete problems to rights.[7]

Gaventa's framework distinguishes not only these three forms or dimensions of power, but also different types of spaces where power is acted out, and the different levels where that occurs, each of which "should also be seen as a flexible adaptable continuum, not as a fixed set of categories."[8] He represents their interrelationships in the form of a cube, which is shown in figure 7.4.

At each level of power, at any one moment, an institution's formal policy-making processes will be somewhere on a continuum of closed to open in terms of the space the institution allows for meaningful engagement with those most affected by its policies. Closed spaces exclude direct engagement by citizens.

Figure 7.4 The "power cube": The levels, spaces, and forms of power

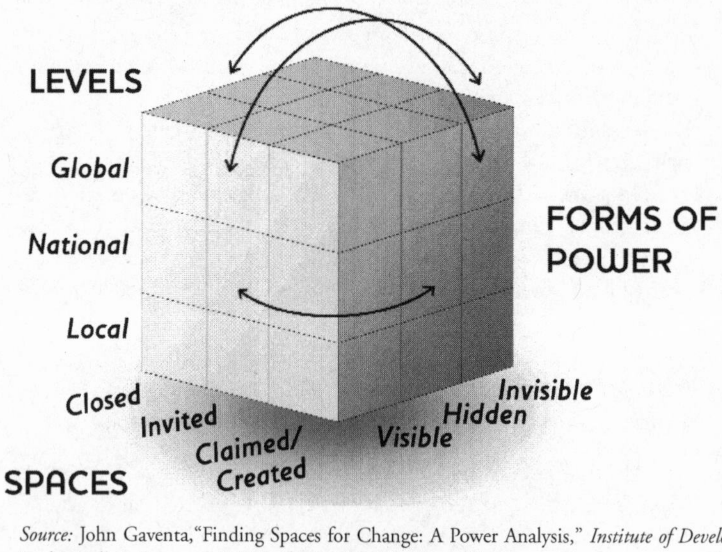

Source: John Gaventa, "Finding Spaces for Change: A Power Analysis," *Institute of Development Studies Bulletin* 37, no. 6 (2006): 25. Reprinted with permission.

Gaventa distinguishes between two types of open spaces: invited and claimed or created. Invited spaces are provided by those with visible power and allow citizens (including advocates) some level of opportunity to engage in the policy-making or governance process. As suggested in the discussion of stakeholder participation on pages 131–133, it is possible for an invited space to be truly open, transparent, and democratic. However, as also noted in that discussion, invited spaces most often favor the more powerful. The Just Associates' power matrix provides examples of how power over is exercised in the arena of visible power and also draws attention to the fact that the hidden power and invisible power mechanisms of power over are most likely occurring at the same time.

Claimed or created spaces are established through advocacy. This form of open space is achieved when advocates focus not only on changing policies but also on changing policy-making processes and then protecting and expanding those changes in the face of opposition from the powerful groups that benefit from closed space. The way this is done will vary with the form through which power over is being exercised; the responses and strategies in the power matrix are relevant for advocating for changes in policies and policy making.

Gaventa also uses the term *created space* to refer to public spaces outside the policy-making process, where advocates and allies have the opportunity for dialogue, learning, collaboration, and building their capacity and power to intervene in policy making.

The different elements of the power cube and their multiple interrelationships are useful for advocates seeking to integrate their work into a more comprehensive, long-term process of social change. Gaventa writes: "Transformative, fundamental change happens, I suggest, in those rare moments when social movements or social actors are able to work effectively across each of the dimensions simultaneously, that is when they are able to link the demands for opening previously closed spaces with people's action in their own spaces; to span across local and global action, and to challenge visible, hidden and invisible power simultaneously."[9]

Tools for Doing Power Analysis

The three dimensions of power and the overall power cube have been adapted for training and practice.[10] However, a number of resources for doing power analysis are more structured as tools (charts, checklists, and so forth) that advocates can immediately use or adapt when planning or reassessing a specific campaign. The process is often called *power mapping*. A quick Internet search with the key words *advocacy* and *power map* will lead to many different tools.

Any good tool will ensure that advocates precisely identify the policy makers they need to influence, often referred to as *targets*. It will also ensure that they identify all important stakeholders and other actors who might support, oppose, or possibly play another role in terms of influencing the targets. In some cases, this basic analysis is adequate given the context of a specific advocacy effort and its policy change goals. However, when the context is complex or there is significant conflict, a good tool will provide more nuanced categorizations or require more information about the different actors.

For example, several power analysis tools in *A New Weave* differentiate between a primary target (the person or body with the power to make the decision) and secondary targets (the people who are trusted by and advise the primary targets), especially but not only in situations where the advocates are not able to directly communicate with the primary target.[11] However, a different tool might also cue the advocates to identify the media as a secondary target if the nature of news coverage has a strong influence on the primary target.

In terms of other stakeholders, the tools in *A New Weave* differentiate between different types of allies and opponents. Allies are divided between individual and organizational allies, and primary (those who will collaborate with the advocates, possibly through forming a coalition) and secondary (those who are sympathetic and may endorse, but will not become directly involved). The authors provide a chart for advocates to fill in three columns for each ally: level of support, motivation/agenda, and degree of influence. There is a similar chart for opponents, who are classified as either primary, secondary, or fence sitters (potential opponents the advocates might be able to influence if only to prevent them from being active opponents).[12] On the other hand, a different tool might define fence sitters as stakeholders who are potential opponents or allies. Yet another tool might also have a category for internal allies (those in the target institution who support their position).

Advocates should select and adapt tools based on their context. The main criterion is whether the map allows the advocates to effectively plan and carry out a strategy that will result in the policy makers/targets' making the decision they seek. Thus, no one tool is the best.

One example of a tool that can be very useful in certain contexts is the power mapping grid originally developed by Strategic Concepts in Organizing and Policy Education, better known by the acronym SCOPE (www.scopela.org). Based in Los Angeles, it is directly engaged in social justice campaigns and movements and provides research, training, and publications to support organizers from around the United States. The power mapping grid is included in its Power Tools Manual (see http://scopela.org/section.php?id=66). A good example of the grid in use can be accessed on the website of the US National Community Tax Coalition (NCTC). The coalition is "a voice for low-income workers and the organizations that meet their tax and financial services needs. We advance and support policies that, ultimately, will secure greater financial stability and economic opportunity for the families we serve."[13] The power mapping grid is the focus of a slide presentation for a workshop on "Mapping Your State Coalition's Power."[14] One of the final slides (see figure 7.5) provides an example of a grid completed for a campaign to create a federal cap on interest rates, countering the opponents' support for an unregulated predatory lending market.

The grid has two axes that are used to plot key decision makers, organized opponents, organized supporters, and unorganized groups.

Figure 7.5 Power mapping grid example

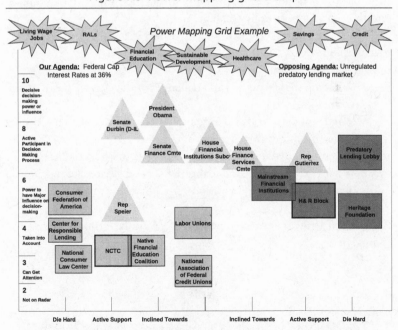

Source: National Community Tax Coalition, "Mapping Your State Coalition's Power," accessed March 15, 2010, http://tax-coalition.org/take-action/advocacy-toolkit/build-your-coalition/Power_Mapping_Toolkit.pdf, 14 . Reprinted with permission.

The NCTC presentation recommends completing the grid through an interactive meeting with groups and individuals who share the advocates' agenda, and suggest writing the names of the different actors on shapes that correspond to their status (triangles for decision makers, rectangles for organized groups, circles for unorganized groups).

Advocates write "our agenda" at the top left of the grid, remembering that "the agenda should be a clear and concise policy position. It should not be a broad mission or vision nor should it be a list of all your policy priorities." At the top right, advocates write "opposing agenda."[15]

Recorded previously these are "*other issue debates or active policy battles* that are currently happening [and] relate to the agenda just defined. . . . These will serve as a reminder of the power that can be pulled from current active campaigns that affect a shared constituency."[16] (For NCTC, the constituents are low-wage workers.)

The presentation suggests first plotting decision makers with their location defined by their level of power and their position with regard to the advocates' agenda. Then plot organized opposition (they will be on the right) and organized supporters (they will be on the left). Finally, unorganized groups, "the kinds and categories of people in the community that the coalition believes are the most important to be organized and to involve in this policy change," are plotted.[17]

Once the grid is complete, the advocates step back and ask the following questions:

- What are the strengths and challenges of the current position and your allies?
- What opportunities for organizing (recruiting and developing leadership) does this picture show us?
- Where are there opportunities and needs to build alliances?
- What strategies can your coalition take and what relationships can be developed to build your power and affect change?[18]

Answers to those questions become the foundation of an advocacy campaign.

Notes

1. Jim Shultz, *The Democracy Owner's Manual: A Practical Guide to Changing the World* (New Brunswick, NJ: Rutgers University Press, 2002); Lisa Vene-Klasen with Valerie Miller, *A New Weave of Power, Politics and People: The Action*

Guide for Advocacy and Citizen Participation (Warwickshire, UK: Practical Action Publishers, 2007).

2. Uncharacteristically, VeneKlasen and Miller include a section in *New Weave* that uses the three sectors as the basis for analyzing politics.

3. A current list of publications is available at http://www.justassociates. org/publications.htm.

4. A concise overview of that work through 2006, including an overview of Gaventa's background as a scholar activist, can be found in John Gaventa, "Finding Spaces for Change: A Power Analysis," *Institute of Development Studies Bulletin* 37, no. 6 (2006): 23–33. Lately, Gaventa and many colleagues from around the globe have collaborated through the Development Research Centre on Citizenship, Participation and Accountability, producing volumes of studies and publications that draw on his and related power frameworks. See http:// www.drc-citizenship.org.

5. Gaventa, "Finding Spaces," 29.

6. Just Associates, *Making Change Happen: Power* (Washington, DC: Just Associates, 2006), 11.

7. Just Associates, *Making Change,* 11.

8. Gaventa, "Finding Spaces," 28.

9. Ibid., 30.

10. The website http://www.powercube.net includes several training workshop designs and handouts for this purpose, as well as a rich collection of papers and articles that have been collected and organized by some of Gaventa's former colleagues at the Institute of Development Studies at the University of Sussex.

11. VeneKlasen and Miller, *New Weave,* 221–227.

12. VeneKlasen and Miller, *New Weave,* 221–227.

13. NCTC, "Impact," 2011, http://tax-coalition.org/about-us/impact.

14. NCTC, "Mapping Your State Coalition's Power," http://tax-coalition. org/take-action/advocacy-toolkit/build-your-coalition/Power_Mapping_Toolkit.pdf.

15. NCTC, "Mapping," 6.

16. NCTC, "Mapping," 7.

17. NCTC, "Mapping," 15.

18. NCTC, "Mapping," 17.

CASE E

Conclusion
Oxfam America: Political Mapping

The learning exercise that culminated the first part of Case E asked you to make notes about who you think might be the targets (policy-making institutions and policy makers), allies, and opponents for Oxfam America's Climate Change Campaign (CCC). If you wish, you can now augment those notes based on the discussion of these different types of political actors in chapter 7.

Unless you were really a member of campaign team, your notes will be much more general than the following description of the advocates' actual analysis of targets, allies, and opponents. However, comparing your notes with their analysis will still produce significant learning. (Remember that the strategy Oxfam used to build alliances, mobilize pressure, lobby, and so forth is described in the second part of Case H that precedes chapter 10.)

Politics

Policy Makers

United Nations Framework Convention on Climate Change

Oxfam's ultimate goal of a "fair and safe deal" would ultimately require action by the 194 members of the United Nations Framework Convention on Climate Change (UNFCCC) Conference of the Parties, ideally at the fifteenth conference in Copenhagen in 2009.

Based on its long-term development work in Africa, Asia, and Latin America, Oxfam America chose to provide funding to and collaborate with local partners in three of those countries: Ethiopia, Cambodia, and Peru. Ethiopia was particularly important, since it was the lead for the African caucus during UNFCCC meetings. One goal was to strengthen the national policies and plans regarding adaptation efforts in each country in ways that are responsive to the realities of their poorest and most marginalized communities. Its second goal was to enhance the effectiveness of those countries' delegations during UNFCCC proceedings, partially through presenting their own domestic policies as potential elements of a larger international agreement.

On the other hand, given the imbalance of power among UNFCCC member countries, Oxfam International's primary targets were the United States, Australia (one of the few other countries that refused to ratify the Kyoto Protocol), and Great Britain. It would be up to the national affiliate in each country to influence its own government.

US Government

Because the United States is the richest, most powerful country and the biggest greenhouse gas emitter in the world, and because its refusal to ratify the Kyoto Protocol was a major factor in the growing climate change crisis, Oxfam America had the most important and most difficult advocacy challenge of any Oxfam affiliate. As they mapped the formal systems of power, the CCC advocates knew they must influence the president and his administration and Congress.

Congress

For several reasons, the campaign team's political analysis led it to focus initially on Congress. Perhaps the most important reason was that when the campaign was launched in 2007, Republican George W. Bush was still president. Given his close relationships with the oil industry and other corporate special interests that worked against the ratification of the Kyoto agreement, it made little sense to focus on his administration; it was better to wait and see who would be elected in 2008. Another reason for focusing on Congress was the lessons from the Kyoto experience. Passage of a bill that supported a fair and safe deal would have two effects: it would strengthen the ability of the president and administration to negotiate a new international agreement that includes Oxfam's priorities, and it would increase the likelihood of ratification when it was subsequently submitted to the Senate. The decision to focus on Congress was made all the easier by the 2006 elections and the Democrats' regaining control of both chambers.

To influence Congress, the CCC advocates knew they would need to influence the new Democratic leadership groups in the two chambers and, most importantly, the Senate Majority Leader, Henry Reid of Nevada, and Speaker of the House, Nancy Pelosi of California. The people in these positions have primary control over which bills reach the full chamber, and they have primary responsibility for getting enough votes to pass (or defeat) them. Likewise, the advocates knew they must influence the members and especially the new Democratic chairs of committees and subcommittees, which would need to formulate or approve climate change legislation before it could go for a vote in the full chamber. To reach those policy makers, it would sometimes be necessary to target their staff, especially those assigned to the relevant committees. When the political leadership decided to move climate change legislation through the House and hold off in the Senate, Oxfam focused on House committees and their members; particularly important were the House Energy and Commerce Committee, chaired by representative Henry Waxman of California, and the Energy and the Environment Subcommittee, chaired by representative Edward Markey of Massachusetts.

The next step in the mapping involved determining which of those key legislators was already on record as supporting or opposing Oxfam's position, who else might support or oppose it, and who was a fence sitter who might end up casting a swing vote. In the process, the advocates sought to identify internal allies or champions—legislators who would not only support adaptation and other key elements Oxfam sought in a bill, but who also had the commitment and ability to convince their peers to support those elements and to secure their votes. Pelosi, Waxman, and Markey were identified as being "very favorable." In fact, an internal campaign document stated that "Congressmen Waxman and Markey who will lead the way on a climate bill are two of the Congress's most progressive members and this is the best imaginable piece of legislation we can see for at least 5 years."

It was beyond the capacity of Oxfam (and most advocacy organizations in the United States) to do a similar analysis for the hundreds of other representatives who were not in leadership positions or on the most important committees. But by working through coalitions, it was possible to pool information about many more representatives than would otherwise be possible. Based on its contacts and advocacy resources, OA could then target some of those considered important for passing legislation, and it could rely on other advocacy groups to target others.

The CCC advocates knew they would need to repeat the preceding actions in order to identify the senators it would target. However, according to an internal campaign document:

> In contrast to the House, the climate in the Senate is difficult and uncertain. Passing a climate bill will need 60 votes and would currently be 16 votes shy of 60. These 60 votes will need to include some Republicans as well as Democrats from coal and oil producing states, and therefore calls for us to focus and try to create champions and allies from within the "Gang of 16," mostly through faith-based groups and large constituency organizations that represent women, African Americans and Latinos.[1]

President and Executive Branch

Once Obama was in office, the CCC advocates began mapping the new Democratic administration. They quickly determined that the Department of State would be given primary authority for the US position and negotiations on climate change. Thus their primary focus became Secretary of State Hillary Clinton and her top officials, including the president's special envoy for climate change. However, it soon became evident that the administration would allow Congress to take the lead on climate change policy, especially since the president was focused on addressing the economic recession inherited from the Bush administration and pushing for a new national health policy.

Allies

Oxfam made a list of key influencers, types or groups of organizations that might support its climate change policy goals, and if so, whose voices could play an important role in influencing the US government. (Some of these are identified in the assessment of the Senate in the preceding section.)

- *Environmental organizations.* These were at the forefront of climate change advocacy; some had been engaged for decades. Several national coalitions had been formed to consolidate their efforts. However, nearly all were primarily focused on the mitigation of climate change. Relatively few had a strong focus on the most vulnerable populations.
- *Other international development organizations.* Many of Oxfam's traditional allies on international aid policy had also recognized if not yet made major investments of their advocacy resources related to climate change and adaptation funding.
- *Women's organizations.* Most victims of poverty and thus those most vulnerable to the impacts of climate change are women and children, and women are among the strongest supporters of humanitarian work. Some women in Congress were potential champions for adaptation funding.
- *Latino and African American organizations.* The most vulnerable to the adverse effects of climate change, including in the United States, are people of color. The Congressional Hispanic Caucus and Black Caucus were potential sources of swing votes and possibly internal champions.
- *Faith organizations.* These organizations are increasingly active and effective in influencing certain members of Congress, and many mainstream and evangelical Christian organizations are concerned about poverty and the environment.
- *National security organizations.* These organizations are well positioned to communicate how the human impacts of climate change can lead to conflict and destabilize international relations.
- *Domestic organizations.* Those focused on domestic adaptation and green jobs, especially those in the hurricane-prone Gulf Coast, might

be effective in making the global-local linkage and in influencing their representatives in Congress.

- *Businesses.* Business leaders have always had significant influence on US policies. While some were highly active in blocking or weakening climate change policy (see the following section on opponents), a number of other businesses and their networks recognized that strong policies were in their own, as well as the world's, long-term interest (or, more accurately, that those were one and the same interest).

Opponents

The CCC advocates were of course aware that large corporations, especially in the energy sector (oil, gas, and coal), consistently opposed any legislation that would restrict their short-term profitability, and that they viewed climate change policies as having that effect. The corporations had made massive investments in lobbying and election campaign support. Among their tactics was funding biased research that questioned the nearly unanimous scientific consensus about the human causes of climate change. The US chamber of Commerce, dominated by large corporations but representing a wider number of businesses, was also an active opponent of climate change policies.

With regard to financing adaptation aid, the corporations and chamber of commerce were especially opposed to many of Oxfam America's policy positions, for example, selling rather than giving away permits with a cap and trade policy, carbon fees, and taxes on polluting industries. In this regard they were joined by yet other organizations that oppose any kind of tax increase and actively lobby for tax reductions.

Note

1. The "gang" referred to in the assessment was an informal group of sixteen moderate Democrats formed in 2008 whose primary interest was ensuring that a climate change bill would not harm the special interests (including polluting industries) in their own states.

CASE F

Safe Power Vermont Coalition:
Phase Two of Advocacy to Close
the Nuclear Reactor

This is the second case study of the multidecade effort to close the Vermont Yankee nuclear power reactor and replace it with safe and green alternatives. Case B, which preceded chapter 4, described the loose network of antinuclear, environmental, and public interest organizations that helped pass landmark legislation giving the Vermont legislature the power to block the continued operation of the reactor after its forty-year license expired in March 2012. The case ended with that victory—the enactment of Act 160 in May 2006.[1]

It is assumed you have read and reviewed Case B, which provides background information about the context, advocates, policy, and politics arenas, and the advocacy strategies used to help pass the legislation. This case addresses the advocates' next and much greater challenge: convincing the legislature to vote against allowing the reactor to continue operation. This case begins with an overview of the new advocacy context and the initial stages of forming a coalition to coordinate the advocacy. The learning exercise invites you to join one of the early meetings of the coalition and help plan its strategy.

The New Challenge

To continue operation of the reactor after March 2012, the Entergy Corporation needed to receive a new license from the federal Nuclear Regulatory Commission (NRC) and a certificate of public good from the quasi-judicial Vermont Public Service Board (PSB). The PSB is required to base its decision almost solely on what is in the best interest of the state's electricity customers.

Act 160 would prevent the PSB from issuing its certificate of public good unless the elected members of the Vermont legislature voted in favor of extended operation. The democratic process would determine what was in the best interest of the state's citizens. Moreover, since the house and senate would both need to approve the extension, a "no" vote in either chamber would allow the advocates to achieve their goal.

The act also required the state's Department of Public Service to carry out a series of fact-finding studies and a public engagement process prior to any vote in the legislature. The studies were to address the following:

- long-term accountability and financial responsibility issues, including guardianship of nuclear waste after licensure but before removal of nuclear waste from the site; closure obligations, dates of completion, and assurance of funds to secure fulfillment of those closure obligations; emergency management requirements and evacuation plans before and after plant closure; any other financial responsibility related to any periods in which the facility is out of service; and
- long-term environmental, economic, and public health issues, including issues relating to dry cask storage of nuclear waste and decommissioning options.[2]

None of these topics, or any deliberations in the Vermont legislature, could include an assessment of safety, which is the sole authority of the NRC.

The earliest the studies and public engagement could be completed was early 2008, possibly in time for consideration during the January–May 2008 legislative session. A final vote could take place in that or in any subsequent session. The senators and representatives in office during the 2008 session would have been elected in November 2006. If the vote were to occur during the 2009 or 2010 session, the legislators would be those elected in November 2008.

The advocates knew Entergy would use its vast wealth in an effort to persuade the public and legislators to support continued operation. Based on past experience, they anticipated that the corporation would spend millions of dollars to underwrite a front organization (of some business and labor groups), fund its own studies, pay public relations firms, and hire more lobbyists than any other interest group in the state. It might seek to influence the elections through campaign donations or other means.

The advocates also knew their best chance was a highly coordinated, broad-based campaign on their part. And thus three of the organizations that had played key roles in passing Act 160—the Citizens Awareness Network, Nuclear Free Vermont, and the Vermont Public Interest Research Group— convened a conference of antinuclear, environmental, and public interest groups to plan and carry out a joint strategy through a new coalition. They named the coalition Safe Power Vermont.

LEARNING EXERCISE

You are affiliated with one of the member organizations of Safe Power Vermont and have been asked to participate in a meeting to plan the strategy for the next round of advocacy to close and replace the nuclear reactor. To prepare, you are to make a set of notes related to the following questions:

- What set of actions on our part are most likely to convince at least one chamber of the Vermont legislature to vote against allowing the nuclear reactor to continue operation after 2012?
- Should we focus on the house, the senate, or both? Why?
- Do we need to change or expand our policy argument and message to convince the legislators? If so, what should they be?
- Do we need to find or produce new evidence to support our argument?
- What type of coalition organization and leadership will be most effective in helping us achieve our goal? Do we need to expand our coalition membership? If so, whom should we target?

Notes

1. An Act Relating to a Certificate of Public Good for Extending the Operating License of a Nuclear Power Plant, 2006 Vt. Acts & Resolves No. 160, http://www.leg.state.vt.us/jfo/envy/ACT160.pdf.

2. An Act Relating to a Certificate of Public Good, Section 4(b).

8

Strategy
People Power and Other Methods

IN ITS MOST BASIC SENSE, STRATEGY IS THE *HOW* OF ADVOCACY. IN CHAPTER 3, I DE-scribed it as "the planning and actions the advocates use to seek to (partially) solve problems by influencing policy institutions to accept their policy change goals." Marshall Ganz, whose work is discussed here, describes strategy as "how we turn what we have into what we need to get what we want."[1]

What constitutes an effective strategy depends on the context; the advocates' organizational capacity; the problem, its cause, and possible policy solution; the political systems; and the specific actors who must be influenced.[2] Depending on those factors, the strategy might involve any combination of a very large number of possible actions. The actions can range from collaborative to confrontational. They can involve direct or indirect contact with the policy makers. Some require significant resources; others do not. Some can be implemented quite quickly; others take years if not decades to fully carry out.

A representative but necessarily incomplete list of such actions is provided on page 151. A discussion of all possible actions, or even just those on the list, is beyond the scope of this chapter. Fortunately, most of the specific actions (for example, media work and lobbying) are addressed at length in other books and manuals.

In this chapter I discuss several general concepts on how to think about and approach strategy development in general and about two types of actions on the list: constituency development and building networks and coalitions. Those foci were chosen from the larger list because they are primary ways to build the people power to counter and overcome the economic power of opponents.

The Building Blocks of a Strategy

This section contains some of the actions that can be incorporated into a strategy but do not include actions or work related to the other arenas in the circles map. Some other frameworks for thinking about advocacy include one or more of them as elements of strategy. Here the assumption is that as advocates plan and launch a strategy, they have already analyzed their context, developed their capacity, done the research and analysis to have formulated one solution or a set of policy solutions, and identified and analyzed who can make the decisions they want, who might support them, and who might oppose them.

However, it is important to keep in mind the reason the circles are depicted as nonsequential and overlapping. Effective advocacy is an iterative process. As they carry out a strategy or set of actions, effective advocates monitor and respond to changes in the larger context, learn more about and may make adjustments in terms of political targets, carry out additional research as policy goals are refined or changed, develop or enhance their capacity, and so forth. The new knowledge or capacities will in turn lead to improvements and sometimes significant shifts in strategy.

All the actions in the list involve communication with some audience. Effective strategies give significant attention to a core message that will be consistent in all those communications, especially how the message will be framed or how the story will be told. Given the importance of this element of strategy, as well as relatively recent developments related to (re)framing and storytelling, Case G and chapter 9 address the topic of advocacy communications.

Nearly every advocacy strategy involves at least one and often many of the actions listed here, roughly from the most collaborative to the most confrontational. The process of choosing one of the following actions is discussed in the next section.

- *Pilot or model programs.* These demonstrate the need for or viability of what a new policy can create.
- *Joint initiative with the target institution.* This is most possible when the advocates have resources or expertise a government or other target lacks. A joint initiative can demonstrate need and viability for a policy and influence decisions about what will be prioritized.
- *Public education via various media.* Public mass media, online blogs and social media, and folk or popular media (e.g., songs and plays)

can all be used to raise public awareness of an issue, influence public opinion, and recruit potential constituents.

- *Constituency development.* This is the use of media, meetings, workshops, and other methods to increase the number of citizens who identify with the advocacy organization and enhance their readiness to take part in its strategy.

- *Empowerment.* This should focus on citizens who are most directly affected by a problem and thus have the greatest stake in policy changes that address the problem. It involves consciousness-raising, building skills, and leadership development to increase effective engagement in the change process.

- *Building networks, alliances, and coalitions.* This is developing and deepening relationships among advocates, their organizations, allies, and other key actors to share information, pool resources, and coordinate collective action.

- *Indirect persuasion of policy makers.* This can involve public events, media coverage, and influencing how issues are framed in public discourse and among thought leaders.

- *Direct persuasion.* This involves communications addressed to policy makers in the form of petitions, letters, phone calls, formal visits, informal meetings, and other methods.

- *Litigation.* This means legal challenges to decisions by policy makers.

- *Protests in the forms of demonstrations, marches, and other public actions.* In many ways these are similar to indirect persuasion, the difference being that the actions are more confrontational and are often taken after other efforts have failed.

Strategy Development

Effective advocates carefully choose some combination and sequence of actions (not limited to those just mentioned) that are most likely to achieve their policy change goals. They also review and adjust those choices as the campaign evolves.

A rigorous approach to choosing actions is important because advocates rarely have enough resources to do everything that might work. The visual image should be that of a laser beam, not a shotgun. A rigorous approach takes discipline in collective thinking and planning. It prevents the all-too-common case in which a group of advocates simply choose the action or set of actions they know best or are most comfortable doing. For example, regardless of the situation, some researchers tend toward evidence and recommendations, while some activists tend toward demonstrations, regardless of what is most appropriate for a specific advocacy initiative.

Shultz suggests that in light of limited resources, most often the best choice is the action or set of actions that requires the least amount of investment (time, political capital, funds, and so forth) to achieve a given objective.[3] A related suggestion is that most often the best choice is the one that involves the least amount of confrontation or conflict to achieve the objective. The benefits of the second suggestion go beyond resource management; even if unsuccessful, a nonconfrontational first attempt may win allies and increase support for subsequent efforts that scale up the level of confrontation.

VeneKlasen and Miller offer a set of criteria for choosing strategies and specific actions, presented in table 8.1.

The process of making such choices is often described as formulating a theory of change. But whatever the terminology, advocates should begin strategy planning by clearly identifying the policy goal and specific policy maker or policy-making body with the power to make the decision the advocates are seeking. If the advocates have other goals (for example, strengthening the capacity of advocates and coalitions for long-term change and creating new political space for meaningful citizen engagement in future policy-making processes), it is important to also identify them. In some cases, a series or interrelated set of decisions needs to be made by different policy makers. In the Oxfam case, the advocates recognized they would need to get the US Congress and the White House to make significant policy decisions before they could even hope to influence the United Nations Framework Convention on Climate Change to adopt their policy goal of a fair and safe global deal.

The next step is to determine what actions or other factors will most likely result in the policy maker's agreeing to accept their recommended policy. In some cases, this may involve influencing others who are more likely than the advocates to have access to or credibility with the policy maker. In nearly all cases, it involves a series of actions that lead to an interim outcome, which may be necessary before some other action can be taken.

However, if a theory of change, or strategy development process more generally, is approached as a purely rational or technical exercise, even if the choices are consistent with the five criteria for good strategies

Table 8.1 What good strategies should be

Appropriate	Will the strategy further your [organization's] vision and mission? Will it make good use of your organization's strengths? Will it fit the community conditions where your [organization] operates? Will your constituency be able to participate? Will it exacerbate or reduce social tensions within the community?
Adequate	Will the strategy be sufficient to address the problem given its magnitude? Does [it] justify the effort and resources you will expend?
Effective	Will the strategy achieve the stated objective? Will [it] further your mission *and* address the problem in a reasonable timeframe?
Efficient	Will the strategy make optimum use of the organization's material and human resources? What are [its] costs in terms of people's time, energy and materials in relation to the benefits?
Sensitive to side effects	Will the strategy increase demand for basic services or resources? Will [it] generate resistance due to traditions, religion, etc. [Can] this resistance be minimized? How will those in power respond to shifts in social relationships, demands for change, etc.? What will happen if violence breaks out? Will the negative consequences be counterbalanced by positive benefits?

Source: Lisa VeneKlasen with Valerie Miller, *A New Weave of Power, People and Politics* (Warwickshire, UK: Practical Action Publishing, 2007), 175. Reprinted by permission.

and even if the process is then repeated at different points throughout a campaign, it will likely fall short. Effective advocates approach strategy as an exercise in creative thinking. In the words of Marshall Ganz, such thinking is "reflexive and imaginative, based on ways leaders learn to reflect on the past, attend to the present and anticipate the future."[4] Such thinking is a distinguishing quality of advocates who are able to respond quickly and effectively to major shifts in opportunity or resistance.

In a series of books and papers, Ganz offers a general conceptual framework and numerous insights about strategy that draw on decades of work in the civil rights movement and with Cesar Chavez and the United Farm Workers.[5] He is now a lecturer at Harvard and an active adviser to advocacy organizations and campaigns (including the constituent organizing strategy in Barak Obama's 2008 campaign for president).

Ganz often uses the biblical story of David and Goliath to illustrate his key concepts about strategy development.

When Goliath, veteran warrior, victor of many battles, arrayed in full battle gear, challenges the Israelites, their military leaders cower in fear. It is David, the young shepherd boy, to whom God gives the courage to face the giant. David's success begins with his courage, his commitment and his motivation. But it takes more than courage to bring David success. Reminded by five stones he finds in a brook, he reflects on previous encounters in which he protected his flock from bears and lions. Based on these recollections, he reframes this new battle in a way that gives him an advantage. Pointedly rejecting the king's offer of shield, sword and armor as weapons he cannot use effectively against a master of these weapons, David conceives a battle based on his five smooth stones, his skill with a sling, and the giant's underestimation of him.[6]

In the story, David's strategy to defeat Goliath used three elements Ganz considers essential to effective strategy development. One element is task motivation. "David knew why he had to do it before he knew how he could do it."[7] A second element is salient knowledge, which includes what Ganz calls *domain-relevant skills.* "David did not know how to use King Saul's weapons, but he did know how to use stones as weapons."[8] The most effective strategists have a mastery of key tactics relevant to their domain (context, policy, and politics). They also have deep local knowledge and understanding of their domain.

The third element is heuristic processes. "David found his skill with stones useful because he could imaginatively recontextualize the battlefield, transforming it into a place where, as a shepherd, he knew how to protect his flock. . . . he saw resources others did not see and opportunities that they did not grasp."[9] This capacity for imagination, for seeing new ways of combining the familiar to make novel interpretations and new pathways conceivable, is essential if advocates are to overcome more powerful opposition. It requires a better understanding of the local domain than their elite opponents have.

An imaginative approach to strategy development is enhanced by diverse points of view and experiences, which in turn stimulate and inform the generation of multiple ideas and possible solutions. If well managed, teams provide such diversity. Ganz notes,

> To take advantage of heterogeneity, however, a team must learn both to foster minority expression that encourages divergent thinking associated with creativity—learning by discovery—and to switch to convergent thinking required to make decisions—learning by testing. Managing these differences is especially challenging when planning

and action occur simultaneously. . . . They are managed more successfully by leaders tolerant of ambiguity who employ distinct organizational mechanisms for creative deliberation and decision making, rely
on multiple sources of resources and authority, and resolve conflict by
negotiation rather than by fiat or consensus.[10]

Task motivation, salient knowledge, heuristic processes, and heteroge-
neous teams are important elements and approaches when planning,
implementing, and adapting an overall strategy and each of its building blocks. The remainder of this chapter deals with concepts related
to two of those: constituency development and advocacy networks and
coalitions.

Constituency Development

Social justice advocates have a number of different resources to creatively
employ as part of their strategy, including evidence and moral argument.
However, their primary resource, which most often gives them an advantage in relation to their opponents, is people power—the power of
citizens acting together and speaking with a common voice. Citizens can
influence policy makers directly through methods such as voting, signing
a petition, writing letters, or meeting with policy makers and intermedi-
ary targets; less direct methods range from boycotting products to participating in vigils, rallies, and marches to civil disobedience. As noted in
the following section, one of the advantages of networks and coalitions
is that a strategy can involve the grassroots person power of multiple organizations in coordinated actions.

Effective advocacy organizations reach out to and connect with citizens who identify with the organization and are willing play a role in its
overall strategy. Many (but not all) advocacy organizations refer to those
citizens as their constituents.

The term *constituent* is more commonly used in formal politics to
refer to a citizen who lives in a political district represented by an elected
leader. A citizen is typically a constituent in multiple districts (a group
of neighborhoods that are represented by a member of the city council,
which are part of a group of cities that are represented by a member of
the state legislature, which are part of a whole state that is represented
by a governor and US senator, and so forth). It is helpful if some or all
of an advocacy organization's constituents are also political constituents

of an elected policy maker they seek to influence, because the representative may need their support for reelection or is truly dedicated to serving the needs and interests of the representative's constituency. For these reasons, when building its constituency, an advocacy organization might focus its citizen outreach and organizing on the political constituents of one or more policy makers.

However, the primary focus of most advocacy organizations' constituency development efforts is on one or two, sometimes overlapping, groups of citizens. One of those groups consists of citizens who are directly affected by the problems the advocacy organization seeks to solve. The second group consists of citizens who care about those problems and policy issues because of their concern for and solidarity with those who are affected; many also realize that all of society is harmed when any part is marginalized.

Some advocacy organizations are organized around an affected constituency. Many of those constituencies are local communities or general population groups that are marginalized because of economic status (poor, working-class employees in a certain industry and so forth) or discrimination (nondominant racial, ethnic, and religious groups, women, gays, lesbians, the disabled, etc.). On the other hand, an advocacy organization may also be organized around a constituency that is not marginalized or the subject of discrimination but is still affected by many policies and has a common set of needs and interests (for example, an association of organic farmers, teachers, or owners of socially responsible businesses).

These constituency-centered advocacy organizations are sometimes established by people from within the affected community and other times initiated by an outside community or labor organizer. Typically the organizations have formal membership, and the members choose leaders from among their ranks. In any case, constituents directly affected by a set of problems should have the right to and are in the best position to identify which problems or issues are of greatest concern to them at any particular time; their assessments should then determine which policies the advocacy organization will seek to influence. As a result, the accountability of these organizations to their constituency is often very high.

Other advocacy organizations are defined by the policy issue they pursue. In many of those cases, issue-centered organizations may find it difficult to connect with and be accountable to those who are directly affected. This is especially true for organizations that focus on policy issues at the international or national level or on issues that have an impact on the general population. Global climate change is an example of a policy issue that fits both categories. While some populations are more affected by climate change than others (for example, people with limited resources who live in areas highly prone to drought, flood, or rising sea water), it would still be nearly impossible for a climate change advocacy organization to reach out to them all, or even a significant portion of them, as potential constituents. When such organizations are unable to directly connect with the affected people and communities, they can sometimes do so indirectly via networking with other constituent-centered organizations that represent or work directly with them.

The second category of advocacy constituents, citizens not directly affected but motivated by a value-based concern for others and the common good, is often a major source of support and action for many advocacy organizations. This category overlaps with the first, since it is common for marginalized people to care deeply about problems that are not affecting them but are affecting others. On the other hand, people from privileged social classes and groups often have resources (funds, free time, personal networks, and so forth) that are important for some advocacy strategies and less accessible to some marginalized groups.

The ways to reach out to and engage this second group of constituents are more diverse and fluid. Often such constituents are managed as a list of individuals who are interested in receiving information about the issue and willing to take some action, from donating funds to signing petitions and participating in rallies. The Internet provides a fast-evolving set of tools for finding, educating, and mobilizing such individuals (e-mail to online action software, Facebook, YouTube, Twitter, Flickr, special apps, and so forth), including horizontal linkages between supporters and their social networks. By the time this book is published, it is likely new and more sophisticated tools will be available.

Some advocacy organizations whose primary constituency is people in the second category go beyond managing the relationships as individual connections. In some cases, they are membership organizations like the League of Women Voters or the Sierra Club, and their constituents are organized into chapters at levels ranging from local to national. In other cases, online communication is used to initiate face-to-face meetings and collective actions among individual supporters who live near each other. In yet other cases, an advocacy organization recruits potential leaders from among its individual supporters, provides special training related to the policy issues and leadership, and then supports leaders' efforts to build active groups in their communities, college campuses, and so forth.

Thus, while there are different types of constituents and multiple ways to connect to them, a constant is that effective advocacy organizations identify, motivate, and mobilize constituents to influence policy makers through coordinated actions.

Advocacy Networks and Coalitions

A second method for building people power involves making and strengthening connections among advocates, their organizations, allies, and other relevant actors. The work is often essential for generating enough power to overcome opposition and change policies, but it has other benefits or advantages as well. There are also limitations and costs or disadvantages.

The benefits, limitations, and costs of building networks and coalitions vary with the level of structure and corresponding investment required. The most informal and loosely structured set of relationships is most commonly referred to as a network. And, most commonly, the term *coalition* is used for an intentional and more formal set of relationships between organizations. VeneKlasen and Miller and Shultz describe networks and coalitions as end points on a continuum between least to most formal.[11] As shown in figure 8.1, they divide up the continuum at different points and use different terms for the type of relationship at each point. Here the distinction will be between networks and all the different forms of alliances and coalitions.

Networks
While a great deal of attention has been paid to networks of service delivery, social planning, and other types of organizations, in the field of advocacy, networks have received less attention than coalitions. That may be because they are composed of multiple relationships, primarily between

Figure 8.1 Typologies based on level of structure

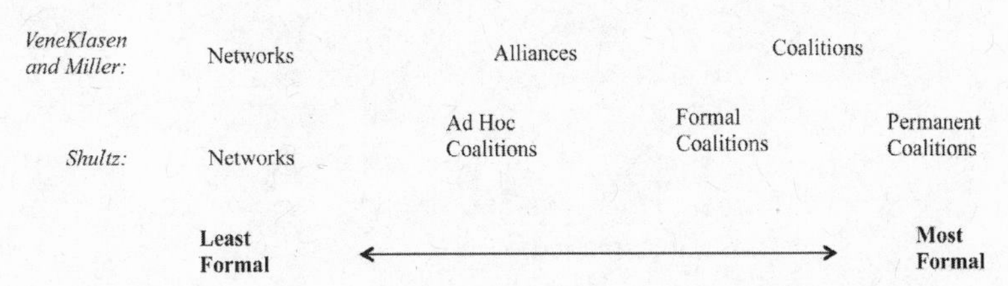

VeneKlasen and Miller:	Networks	Alliances	Coalitions
Shultz:	Networks	Ad Hoc Coalitions	Formal Coalitions	Permanent Coalitions

Least Formal ←————————————————→ **Most Formal**

individuals, and are thus far less visible than the more structured coalitions among organizations.[12] However, networks play essential roles in effective advocacy, including the formation of formal coalitions. Figure 8.2 is a simplified representation of a network that connects ten individuals (letters A–J), four of whom are advocates affiliated with three different advocacy organizations (1–3). In network language these people are called *nodes*. Nodes are connected by links or ties, represented by arrows.

Individual network relationships exist in organizations but outside the formal lines of authority. In this case, Advocates B and C in organization 2 have such a nonhierarchical, flat relationship. As is the case in many large organizations, their relationship might allow communication to occur and tasks to get done that might otherwise have gotten bogged down in institutional inertia.

Individual relationships often exist among people working with different organizations. The various relationships between advocates A, B, C, and D facilitate communication and information sharing among their organizations, thereby creating a loose organizational network. The flow of information can help each organization improve its own work and reduce duplication of effort. The flow of communication can also result in mutual learning and the development of younger or less experienced advocates through exposure to a wider range of others.

Figure 8.2 Typologies based on level of structure

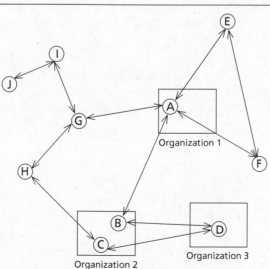

Individual networks that include people outside the advocates' organizations offer additional benefits. For example, advocate A has developed a relationship with E and F, who also have their own relationship; they might be journalists who are now interested in advocate A's issues. Advocate A is also in a position to link or broker a connection between advocate B and media people E and F if and when necessary.

Advocate A also has a relationship with G, who might be a staff member in the office of a relevant policy maker. Advocates C and staff member G both have relationships with H, who might be a researcher whose work is relevant to the advocates' policy issues.

Staff person G is in a position to link or broker a connection between the advocates and I, who might be the policy maker G works for, providing access for direct lobbying and the potential for one or more of the advocates to develop their own independent relationship with I. In turn, policy maker I is in a position to link them with J, who might be working for one of the advocates' opponents; depending on that person, the link may provide advocates with the opportunity to secure useful information or have low-profile discussions of a possible compromise.

As suggested in the preceding examples, networks offer many benefits, including information and resource sharing, reducing duplication of effort, mutual learning, exposure to diverse perspectives and experiences, and so forth. The primary limitation is that networks do not allow for the coordination and collective actions that are most often needed to influence powerful institutions. On the other hand, networks such as those that exist between organizations 1, 2, and 3 in the diagram offer a strong foundation for building more formal coalitions. Moreover, even after a coalition is formed, individual and organizational networks will continue to be one of the ways communication occurs and tasks get done outside any formal procedures the coalition may have created.

Coalitions

When administrators of organizations agree to work together, they gain most of the benefits of a network and many additional ones. But from the perspective of a member organization, they can also have greater costs. Benefits and costs tend to increase as coalitions become more formal or structured.

The main benefit of coalitions over networks is the ability to systematically pool resources and coordinate actions among multiple organizations to accomplish changes that no individual organization could achieve on its own. By working together, the advocates can

- broaden the base of support;
- increase the scale and influence of coordinated actions (from getting signatures on a petition to holding a march or rally);
- share information, knowledge, and contacts;
- bring together diverse ideas;
- connect strategies of organizations working at different policy levels (local, subnational, national, and global) or places;
- create a stronger public image;
- increase legitimacy and credibility;
- enhance the consistency and strength of the message;
- stimulate learning, especially between more and less experienced advocates;
- create space for leadership development;
- provide moral support when the challenges are great; and
- produce safety in numbers when there might be retaliation.

But there are also downsides. Coalitions require investment of finite time and energy and in many cases funds. In addition, they can

- divert those resources from other organizational priorities;
- produce resentment, tension, or conflict if the division of workload and resource investment is uneven;
- take longer to make decisions and generate action;
- require compromises among different members in terms of strategy;
- limit the visibility of organizational members; and
- pose risks for a member's credibility and legitimacy.

The more organized the coalition is in terms of membership responsibilities, planning, and decision-making systems and structures, the more effective it can be in realizing those benefits. The most formal (what Shultz refers to as "permanent"; see figure 8.1) coalitions incorporate, raise funds through membership dues and other sources, hire staff, and have the greatest capacity for thorough planning and implementation of strategies.

On the other hand, the most formal coalitions usually require the greatest investment of time and resources of their member organizations, so much so that it is possible to be more focused on coalition operations than on collective strategy. For this reason, Shultz suggests that coalitions be only as formal as is necessary to achieve the policy changes or other goals they were created for. The least formal coalitions (what

Shultz refers to as "ad hoc coalitions" and VeneKlasen and Miller call "alliances") still allow for resource pooling and coordinated actions, but require less investment and reduce the danger of organizational entropy (see figure 8.1).

Another useful dimension in a typology of coalitions is discussed by Rinku Sen in *Stir It Up: Lessons in Community Organizing and Advocacy*.[13] Sen's work draws on her experiences as an organizer on race, gender, and class issues in the United States. She has held leadership roles at the Center for Third World Organizing and is currently executive director of the Applied Research Center, which focuses on media, research, and activism for racial justice.

The additional dimension is the level of political alignment among the members of a coalition represented in figure 8.3. A coalition with low political alignment is composed of organizations that do not share core interests and may actually oppose each other on other policy issues. Sen describes these as "tactical coalitions" and argues that they are best suited for defeating a policy effort (an "oppositional agenda") that will harm the interests of all parties. A coalition with high political alignment is composed of organizations that share common values and goals. She describes these as "strategic coalitions" and argues that they are necessary for defining a "new agenda."[14]

Figure 8.3 Typologies based on structure and political alignment

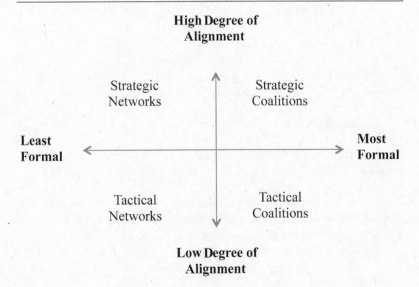

This dimension also affects benefits and costs, which is particularly true regarding "legitimacy and credibility." The higher the level of political alignment in a strategic coalition, the more likely it is that the coalition will enhance these as benefits. Likewise, the lower the level of alignment in a tactical coalition, the more likely it is to "pose threats to a member's legitimacy and credibility." On the other hand, the coalitions with the highest level of alignment may be less likely to "bring together diverse ideas."[15]

VeneKlasen and Miller offer seven tips on how to maximize the advantages and minimize the disadvantages of coalitions. A summary of their advice is presented in table 8.2.

Table 8.2 Tips for establishing a coalition

1. Be clear about the advocacy issue proposed as the focus of the coalition.
2. Develop membership criteria and mechanisms for including new members and sustainability.
3. Resolve what the coalition will and will NOT do.
4. If the group is large, select a steering committee.
5. Establish task forces to plan and coordinate different activities.
6. Assess progress periodically and make whatever changes are necessary.
7. Develop a code of conduct to ensure mutual respect and responsibility.

Source: Lisa VeneKlasen with Valerie Miller, *A New Weave of Power, Politics and People: The Action Guide for Advocacy and Citizen Participation* (Warwickshire, UK: Practical Action Publishers, 2007), 315–17. Printed with permission.

Notes

1. Marshall Ganz, "Why David Sometimes Wins: Strategic Capacity in Social Movements" in *Rethinking Social Movements: Structure, Meaning and Emotion,* ed. Jeff Goodwin and James M. Jasper (Lanham, MD: Rowman & Littlefield, 2004), 181.

2. For purposes of simplicity, an "unmet need" is considered one type of problem.

3. Jim Shultz, *The Democracy Owners' Manual: A Practical Guide to Changing the World* (New Brunswick, NJ: Rutgers University Press, 2002), 113.

4. Ganz, "Why David," 180.

5. For example, see Marshall Ganz, "Another Look at Farmworker Mobilization" in *The Social Movement Reader: Cases and Concepts,* ed. Jeff Goodwin and James M. Jasper (Malden, MA: Blackwell, 2009), 282–300.

6. Ganz, "Why David," 178.

7. Ganz, "Why David," 184.

8. Ganz, "Why David," 185.

9. Ganz, "Why David," 186.

10. Ganz, "Why David," 187.

11. Lisa VeneKlasen with Valerie Miller, *A New Weave of Power, Politics and People: The Action Guide for Advocacy and Citizen Participation* (Warwickshire, UK: Practical Action Publishers, 2007), 311; Shultz, *Democracy Owners' Manual,* 126.

12. Facebook, LinkedIn, and other web-based social media have increased general awareness of individual networks and in some cases may make parts of an advocates' network more visible. However, in many cases the value of such networks is that at least some of the relationships are not visible.

13. Rinku Sen, "United We Stand," chap. 7 in *Stir It Up: Lessons in Community Organizing and Advocacy* (San Francisco: Jossey-Bass, 2003).

14. Sen, "United We Stand," 136–137.

15. Sen, "United We Stand," 136–137.

CASE F

Conclusion
Safe Power Vermont: Phase Two

The learning exercise that culminated the first part of Case F asked you to make notes in response to five questions about strategy and coalition development. If you wish, you can now add to or modify your notes based on the discussion of strategy in chapter 8. Compare your notes with the the coalition's actual strategy to block continued operation of the Vermont Yankee reactor (see the following first two sections). The next section of the case discusses how that strategy evolved, the results of the vote that eventually took place in 2010 and its aftermath.[1]

Advocates: Coalition Structure

All involved agreed that the new coalition's form, its structure and leadership, should be determined by its function. The coalition would be only as formalized as necessary to effectively carry out its strategic activities. There was some initial disagreement about whether to actively recruit new members to have the largest number and perhaps the greatest diversity of members possible. In the end, the decision was to only invite other organizations if and when one of the current members had an established relationship with it, and the new member was prepared to invest person power or other resources in carrying out the strategy.

As a result, the Safe Power Vermont coalition initially grew to six members. In addition to the Citizens Awareness Network (CAN; including its increasingly active Vermont chapter), Nuclear Free Vermont (NFV) and Vermont Public Interest Research Group (VPIRG), three new members were identified from their networks. The Toxics Action Center (www.toxicsaction .org) has an office and a field organizer in five New England states; its executive director, Vermont organizer, and several other staff members shared

VPIRG's office space in Montpelier, the state capital. The Vermont Chapter of the national Sierra Club (http://vermont.sierraclub.org) has members in many parts of the state and politically savvy volunteer leadership. And the Vermont Yankee Decommissioning Alliance (www.vyda.org) was formed by antinuclear activists in central Vermont.

Later, Greenpeace USA sent a full-time organizer to Vermont to work on closing the reactor and joined the coalition. At about the same time, a group of long-term political activists who lived in the reactor's emergency evacuation zone decided to focus on the Vermont Yankee advocacy and founded the Safe and Green Campaign, which became an active coalition member. In 2010 the Conservation Law Foundation and the Vermont Businesses for Social Responsibility also joined.

In terms of Safe Power Vermont's organization, the coalition members usually met once a month, spoke by conference call each of the other weeks, and communicated heavily via an e-mail Listserv. Facilitation at meetings tended to rotate. Decisions were made more or less through consensus with no designated leader or spokesperson. The approach succeeded largely because the Toxics Action Center offered to have its Vermont organizer devote part of her staff time to coordinating and supporting the coalition's planning, meetings, and other activities.

Strategy: Plan

Each organizational member of the coalition was free to continue strategies and tactics that were consistent with its background and approach. The coalition meetings and communication channels provided a space for keeping members informed of any such plans.

However, as the Safe Power Vermont coalition, the members agreed on a highly focused strategy around a single goal: convince 76 or more of the 150 members of the house of representatives to vote against continued operation. (Remember that the advocates needed to win in only one chamber.)

A variety of factors influenced the decision to focus on the house and not the senate. For example, at the time, the senate membership was considered to be less progressive. However, the primary reason was that members of the Vermont house are more easily influenced by a small number of constituents in their relatively small districts. Senators have larger constituencies, and so convincing sixteen or more of the thirty members of that chamber would require more effort and resources, perhaps more than what the coalition could generate. And, in any case, each house district is part of a larger senate district, and thus the constituents of many of the targeted representatives would also be constituents of senators who might need to be targeted if the house strategy did not go as planned.

District Organizing

The core element of the Safe Power Vermont strategy was outreach to and education and mobilization of constituents of those house members whose support or opposition would be most likely to determine the final vote. The first step in that process was for the coalition members with the most contacts in the state capital to rate every representative on a 1 to 5 scale in terms of the coalition's position (1 = strongly supports; 2 = likely to support; 3 = unknown or on the fence; 4 = likely to oppose; 5 = strongly opposes). The initial ratings indicated a daunting challenge: to reach seventy-six votes, all strong supporters, nearly all the likely supporters, and the majority of unknowns or on-the-fence representatives would need to side with the coalition. One person familiar with Vermont politics guessed the chances of successfully influencing that many representatives was 3 to 5 percent.

Working with spreadsheets and a state map with color-coded districts, the coalition focused primarily on representatives who were rated in categories 2 and 3 on the scale and a handful in category 4. The prioritization was largely based on a calculation of which combination would be necessary to secure at least seventy-six votes, ideally with a comfortable margin for error or unexpected turns of events. Different coalition members were asked to volunteer to take primary responsibility for constituent work in each of the top priority districts. The number of districts any one member organization would work with was based on its resources. When possible, a decision about which specific districts a member would taken on was based on where the organization had done previous work or had significant contacts. When that was not possible, the assignments were largely divided geographically. Members of VPIRG and CAN, which had the greatest resources, volunteered for the majority of the districts; Toxics Action and the Sierra Club each took a significant number; NFV and the Vermont Yankee Decommissioning Alliance, which are grassroots associations, each took a far smaller number, primarily in the area of the state where each is based.

The initial strategy for each targeted district was diagramed in a presentation at a statewide environmental action conference (see figure F.1). The objective was to get a critical mass of citizens in each targeted district to call, write, and meet directly with their representative, as well as to write letters to the editor of local papers and organize events or other activities that would less directly convey the advocates' message to their representatives.

To achieve that objective, a list of potential activists was generated for each district, combining the names and information for the members or contacts from all Safe Power Vermont organizations. Those people then received e-mails and phone calls from the coalition member who had taken responsibility for their district. And when possible, the responsible organization organized a public forum or other open meeting to educate citizens and to identify yet other potential activists among those attending the event.

Figure F.1 District strategy plan

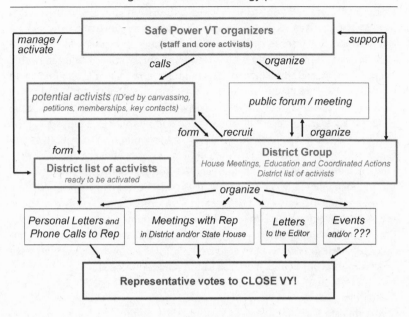

Whenever possible, the Save Power Vermont member would help potential activists to form a district group. Members of these groups would then take over contacting others in the district, hold house meetings, and do other activities to educate their neighbors and lobby their representative. In some cases, their first task was simply to confirm or adjust the coalition's assessment of their representative's level of support or opposition for extending the operation of Vermont Yankee. When it was not possible to organize a district group, the Safe Power Vermont organization would use the combined list to identify and, at key moments, mobilize people willing to take individual actions (for example, writing or calling their representative).

Influence the Mandated Studies and Public Engagement

Per the directive in Act 160, the Vermont Department of Public Service was responsible for arranging the studies and engagement process.[2] The coalition members believed that unbiased studies would support their arguments. On the other hand, the department was led by political appointees of the state's Republican governor, who was publicly in favor of extended operation as long as it is safe, and he fully trusted the US Nuclear Regulatory Commission to determine that. Thus the coalition's strategy included closely monitoring the department managers' decisions, pushing for studies to be as independent as possible and the public engagement to be as open as possible.

Parallel Legislation

During 2007 and every subsequent legislative session until a vote on Vermont Yankee's future was taken, the coalition's strategy included initiating and actively supporting a series of new bills before the Vermont legislature. These included several that would increase funding for efficiency and renewable energy, and thus address the concerns of many citizens and legislators about how to replace the electricity the reactor generates. Another bill addressed the fact that the decommissioning fund was inadequate, largely because the Entergy Nuclear Corporation had not been adding to it since purchasing the reactor in 2002. The bill helped highlight the corporation's profit motives and thus reduce the level of trust by the public and policy makers. Advocacy related to such bills had still other advantages for the coalition's strategy. Promoting efficiency and renewables helped Safe Power Vermont articulate a positive vision and message for Vermont's future, rather than only a negative message about closing the reactor. Moreover, supporting the bills forced the organizers to quickly develop, test, and refine the district-level infrastructure and keep their grassroots base activated until it was time for the major push related to the vote on the operation of the reactor post-2012.

Messaging

While the advocacy messages used to pass Act 160 focused on good governance and due diligence and not on arguments for or against Vermont Yankee, much less nuclear power, those messages were no longer useful for convincing the public and policy makers to oppose the Vermont Yankee reactor's operating for another 20 years. However, once again, the advocates were careful not to frame the debate as pro- or antinuclear power. If someone believed in the viability of a new generation of reactors, the advocates' response was: "But Vermont Yankee is one of the oldest in the country; no reactor would be approved today with its now outdated design. Think about how much has changed in terms of technology since it was built in 1972—computers, the Internet, and so forth." As one way to make the point, and old, beat-up car from 1972 made an appearance at various rallies, Fourth of July parade entries, and other events. Some of the earlier messages continued, for example, "We can't trust the NRC or the Entergy Corporation." On the other hand, the advocates worked hard to communicate a positive message of a nuclear-free Vermont that relies on increasing efficiency and the use of renewable energy sources. A corollary message was: "Vermont's citizens can make that happen; we can close the reactor; there are alternatives."

Opportunities Created by Vermont Yankee

Many involved in developing the Safe Power Vermont strategy believed that a victory would likely require surfacing new problems at the reactor or with its corporate owners. Lost fuel rods, a fire in a transformer building, cracks in the steam dryer discovered after the 20 percent power uprate, and other problems at the reactor had previously provided opportunities for advocates to make their case about the dangers of an aging, corporate-run reactor. The fact that in every one of those situations the NRC quickly announced there had been no threat to public safety provided opportunities for the advocates to make their case that the public cannot trust the federal regulators. While the new coalition's strategy could not predict what the new problems might be or when they might occur, the advocates understood the need to be prepared to take advantage of new opportunities.

Strategy: Implementation

The coalition did indeed do extensive district-level organizing. Beyond contacting potential activists from the combined lists for each district, CAN identified new supporters and potential activists through door-to-door canvassing and through efforts such as the solar rollers—volunteers who bicycled from town to town, meeting with citizens on the street, over meals hosted by local families, and various events. VPIRG (like most public interest research groups across the country) recruits and deploys a team of young canvassers to go door-to-door during the summer, distributing educational materials and asking for contributions to fund VPIRG's activities. For two consecutive summers, the educational materials focused on replacing Vermont Yankee with safe and green alternatives. One summer canvassers invited residents to sign a postcard to their representative; VPIRG collected them and staggered the mailing so that the representative received one or two every day. The second summer the canvassers carried cameras and invited members of the household, often with their children, to hold a sign (there were several to choose from) asking their representative to vote against Vermont Yankee; these were also collected and mailed in a similar fashion.

However, with a few exceptions, the strategy of organizing self-sustaining district groups proved too difficult to justify the level of effort. More commonly, the organizer from the Safe Power Vermont organization needed to play a more active role in generating communications and arranging for meetings between representative and constituents. A small portion of those meetings occurred during lobby days organized by environmental action organizations each year; citizens were invited for a brief orientation and then connected to the representatives.

Efforts to influence the Department of Public Service had mixed results. Its studies were contracted out to a consulting group, and the results were generally biased in favor of Vermont Yankee (for example, one study calculated the economic benefits to the state in terms of electricity rates, taxes, local purchasing, and such, but did not include an equally thorough calculation of costs). However, because the advocates insisted on a meeting with the lead consultant and were visibly monitoring the entire process, they likely prevented the results from being yet more biased. Moreover, the process helped prepare the advocates to provide policy makers with strong critiques and thus partially undermine the studies' credibility. In terms of public engagement, the advocates had an overwhelming presence at each event.

The strategy of parallel legislation proved useful. Several bills related to efficiency and renewable energy passed, though after amendments were more limited in scope than desired. A decommissioning bill was passed but was then vetoed by the Republican governor. When a vote on Vermont Yankee's future did not happen in 2008 or in 2009, the coalition and its allies in the legislature continued to put pressure on the Entergy Corporation through other bills. When a version of the decommissioning bill was reintroduced, passed again, and vetoed again, the legislature held a special session in an attempt to override the veto. While the effort fell a few votes short of the required two-thirds majority, it attracted additional media attention, was a topic of many letters to the editor and op-ed pieces, and generated another round of phone calls and visits from constituents, all of which helped undermine public confidence in the Entergy Corporation.

In 2008 the advocates strongly supported yet another bill, which called for a "thorough, independent, and public assessment of the reliability of the systems, structures, and components" of the Vermont Yankee reactor.[3] An important element of the bill was the creation of a public oversight committee with members appointed by the governor, the senate president pro tem, and the speaker of the house. The bill passed and was signed into law as Act 189. The importance of the legislation is discussed on page 177.

Parallel Efforts by Safe Power
Vermont Members and Other Advocates

As noted previously, coalition membership did not preclude members from their own actions to replace the reactor. For example, one of the most important such actions was a decision by CAN to push its fund-raising capacity to a new level and in early 2007 hire a full-time lobbyist. The person who joined CAN as its "people's lobbyist" provided the credibility and insider knowledge of a seventh-generation Vermonter who had previously served in the legislature as a Republican. He worked closely with the relevant staff in other coalition organizations to continually update Safe Power Vermont's ratings of House members and thus adjust their vote calculations and prioritization of which districts needed to be targeted. And his daily presence in the state house played a crucial role in the passage of parallel legislation.

Another important example of independent efforts by organizational members was VPIRG's decision to research and publish two important studies that demonstrated Vermont's ability to not only manage without the nuclear reactor but to benefit from its closing. The second study, "Repowering

Vermont," provided evidence to support the following argument: "Closing Vermont Yankee and moving forward with energy efficiency and local renewable energy would cost Vermonters 47–50% less, between 2012 and 2032, than relying on Vermont Yankee at predicted market prices. Replacing Vermont Yankee with local renewable energy resources would also add tens of millions of dollars to our state tax base and support the creation of hundreds if not thousands of new jobs."[4]

VPIRG also employed the most sophisticated constituent contact software for e-mail action alerts with links to online actions (petitions, e-mails to specific targets, etc.), and it independently supported two additional research projects focused on understanding public knowledge and opinion about Vermont Yankee, each of which made a significant contribution to the coalition's messaging.

The Safe and Green Campaign organized numerous rallies, marches, vigils, and other public actions, many in collaboration with CAN and other groups, including a 120-mile, midwinter walk from the evacuation zone to the state capital in January 2010. And, along with the Vermont Yankee Decommissioning Alliance, it supported a 2009 effort by yet another organization (Replace VY) to pass town meeting resolutions opposing Vermont Yankee in about forty towns across the state. It was an action that some coalition members considered too risky (years earlier NFV had to overcome Entergy's quarter-million-dollar public relations campaign to win resolution votes in towns near the reactor, but most of the 2009 targets were in the central and northern portions of the state and likely more vulnerable to a new corporate public relations campaign). However, Entergy did not attempt to influence the votes, and the resolution passed in at least thirty-three towns and was defeated in only one.

Elections

As anticipated, after the 2006 legislative session, senate president Peter Welch—the key internal ally in the passage of Act 160—stepped down and in November was elected to the US House of Representatives. At the same time the southern Vermont Senate district, which includes Vermont Yankee and the population most strongly opposed to the reactor, elected Peter Shumlin, a Democrat who had previously served in the state senate and been its president pro tem. When the new legislature convened he was selected by his party caucus to once again serve in that leadership role. Given the strong feelings among Shumlin's constituents, it was not surprising that he would also be a strong internal ally on issues of concern to the advocates. Shumlin played an important role in the passage of the energy, decommissioning, and reliability assessment bills and the veto override effort during the 2007–2008 sessions. He was reelected by a large majority in November 2008.

Events at Vermont Yankee and
Responses by the Entergy Corporation

The advocates did not have to wait long for a new opportunity and one with enormous visual impact. In August 2007 one of a series of very large cooling towers (for water from the reactor) collapsed. A dramatic photo showing the broken wood frame and water gushing from a large pipe was secured by one of the advocates and quickly distributed to the media. The event drew significant coverage in print, radio, and television throughout Vermont and the rest of New England. The NRC quickly announced there was no danger to public safety. While that was probably true, it was soon learned that NRC staff inspected the towers and had not detected any problems, creating another opportunity for the advocates to challenge the agency's credibility. More important, the photo of the collapsed tower became a powerful symbol (what is described as a *meme* in chapter 9) the advocates used extensively in their arguments about the vulnerability of the reactor's aging infrastructure.

Other smaller events continued to occur, including leaks in piping in the reactor buildings and problems with other equipment. The advocates contributed to the media coverage that each event received and added them to a long list of problems that they used in educational materials.

The Entergy Corporation helped the advocates once again when it announced a plan to spin off Vermont Yankee and six similar reactors into a new company. While the corporation's managers argued that the plan was to leverage investments, and the NRC approved the plan, advocates countered that it was actually an attempt to protect Entergy from the financial liabilities of the aging reactors and decommissioning costs. Even the initial name for the company—SpinCo (later changed to Enexus)—was helpful when making the argument about the corporation's motives. Policy makers in Vermont and the other affected states also questioned the viability of the new company. Entergy eventually dropped the plan but only after several years of negative publicity. The coalition's allies in the Vermont legislature reported that a growing number of their colleagues viewed Entergy as arrogant and dismissive of the state's values and institutions.

The Vote

A confluence of the advocates' evolving strategy and external events they had no control over created conditions in early 2010 that finally resulted in the vote on Vermont Yankee's continued operation—a vote that had been in the works since the passage of Act 160 four years earlier.

Act 189 mandated an assessment of the reactor's physical plant and management and established a public oversight panel. One of the panel members was to be appointed by the senate president, Peter Shumlin, who by then was a very public critic of Vermont Yankee and Entergy. He chose a nuclear engineer who had been a senior vice president in the industry before he was fired for reporting safety violations; he had subsequently created his own Vermont-based consulting firm that often provides expert witness and news analysis regarding nuclear power (see http://fairewinds.com/).

Advocates had long been aware that radioactive tritium, a by-product of nuclear reactors, had leaked into the ground at a number of power plants around the country. The Act 189 assessment and follow-up by the oversight panelist provided a formal opportunity to ask pointed questions about the presence of underground pipes at Vermont Yankee that could result in tritium leaks. The same questions were then asked in legislative hearings and other forums. Entergy officials consistently stated, at times under oath, that there were no such pipes.

However, Shumlin's appointee to the oversight panel secured information that led him to conclude the corporation's statements were not correct. By late 2009 Entergy officials were saying it was all a matter of miscommunication: there were buried pipes (which could leak radioactive substances into the ground), but they are technically different from underground pipes. Safe Power Vermont and other advocates said it was all a matter of intentional lies. The controversy was the subject of significant news coverage in and outside Vermont and allowed the advocates to make their strongest case yet for why Vermont should not trust a profit-driven, out-of-state, billion-dollar corporation.

In early January 2010 (in the middle of the Safe and Green Campaign's walk to the capital, which was already drawing media attention), Entergy was forced to reveal it had discovered tritium in one of its test wells. Entergy and the NRC assured the public and policy makers that the levels posed no danger to the public. But over the course of the ensuing weeks, tritium was found in other wells on the reactor site, some measuring one hundred times the federal limit. Hundreds of citizens joined the final day of the Safe and Green walk and flooded the state house chanting, "Leaks and lies."

As the situation worsened, including the discovery of other and more dangerous radioactive substances in the well water, Entergy officials sought to diffuse the problem by removing several key executives at the reactor and increased efforts by their public relations firms and lobbyists. At the same time, Shumlin was closely tracking the growing disillusionment of his fellow senators, including Republicans who had formerly supported Vermont Yankee. The Safe Power Vermont campaign quickly mobilized the constituents they had organized by house district to now call, write, and meet with their senators. In late February, when Shumlin was certain he had enough votes, he convened the senate to debate and defeat a bill that would allow Vermont Yankee to continue post-2012. An overwhelming majority of 26–4 voted to not allow continued operation. The senate's decision generated international media coverage and sent shock waves throughout the nuclear industry.

The Outcome

Once the bill to approve extension had been defeated in the senate, the house did not need to consider the matter, and its leadership chose not to. The senate's vote did not necessarily prevent the introduction and passage of another bill in 2011 that would provide permission, but Entergy and its lobbyists failed to gain support, despite a high-powered Vermont Yankee for Vermont (VY4VT) campaign that removed the focus from the corporation and highlighted local people Entergy called dedicated professionals and neighbors whose livelihoods depend on continued operation.

Entergy shifted its efforts to the court. The NRC's decision about continued operation had been delayed by numerous challenges by the New England Coalition and legal advocacy organizations, but the new license was finally approved in March 2011, the day after the nuclear disaster in Fukushima, Japan, began to unfold. Entergy immediately filed a lawsuit against the state of Vermont, arguing that Act 160 had denied it the right to a fair hearing before the Public Service Board and that the legislature had considered issues of safety (the exclusive responsibility of the NRC) when passing and implementing Act 160, Act 189, and other legislation.

Entergy spent over US$4.5 million on the legal team that represented it in the initial trial—more than ten times what the Vermont attorney general was able to invest—and won a ruling based on its lawyer's argument that the legislators who passed Act 160 did so out of concerns related to nuclear safety, and thus the law is an illegal preemption of the NRC. Many legal scholars believe the decision was inconsistent with the evidence. The state of Vermont has decided to appeal the ruling. And the judge did rule that Entergy must still secure a certificate of public good from the Vermont Public Service Board (PSB). However, during the appeals process (which may take years, since many observers expect it to eventually end up in the US Supreme Court) and until the PBS hearings are complete and a decision is issued, Vermont Yankee will continue to operate beyond the date it was to close in 2012.

In response, some advocacy efforts are now focused on supporting the state's legal appeal, opposing Entergy's filing with the PSB, and passing new legislation to protect Vermont from risks posed by the reactor. Perhaps the most active and certainly the most visible advocacy is being organized around protests and civil disobedience. CAN and the Safe and Green Campaign have provided leadership. Over one thousand people marched to Energy's local headquarters on the day the reactor should have shut down, and over 130 of the demonstrators chose to be arrested. At the same time, a handful of advocates were arrested at Entergy's corporate headquarters in Louisiana and its regional headquarters in New York. The advocates have pledged to continue the pressure for as long as it takes.

Thus it is not yet possible to know whether the many advocacy efforts will ultimately succeed in closing the Vermont Yankee reactor. On the other hand, there is little doubt that the advocacy was a major contributing force in passing landmark legislation and a senate vote that has reenergized the work of other advocates in other states across the country. The increased capacity of the different organizations and their networks and coalitions will allow the advocates to influence future policy decisions certainly with regard to issues such as decommissioning and storage of radioactive waste. And perhaps new policy options to close the reactor and create the safe and green energy future that the advocates seek are still to be found.

Notes

1. For a yet more in-depth description and analysis of the campaign, see Richard Watts, *Public Meltdown: The Story of the Vermont Yankee Nuclear Power Plant* (Amherst, MA: White River Press, 2012).

2. An Act Relating to a Certificate of Public Good for Extending the Operating License of a Nuclear Power Plant, 2006 Vt. Acts & Resolves No. 160, section 4(b), http://www.leg.state.vt.us/jfo/envy/ACT160.pdf.

3. An Act Relating to a Comprehensive Vertical Audit and Reliability Assessment of the Vermont Yankee Nuclear Facility, 2008, No. 189, Section 1(d), http://www.leg.state.vt.us/jfo/envy/ACT189.pdf.

4. James Moore, "Repowering Vermont: Replacing Vermont Yankee for a Clean Energy Future" (Montpelier: Vermont Public Interest Research and Education Fund, 2009), 4, http://www.vpirg.org/repowervt.

CASE G

Kids Are Priority One Coalition: Framing the Message

Kim Friedman, coauthor

This case focuses on an advocacy initiative to increase the access of early childhood education programs in Vermont to public education funding. It begins with an overview of the context, the Kids Are Priority One Coalition (KAP1), the policy issue, the political systems and actors, and the coalition's 2003–07 strategy. Their goal was for the Vermont legislature to pass a bill that would increase access to funds.

The case includes two KAP1 documents. "Using Public Education Funds to Support Early Care and Education: Talking Points," clarifies the group's policy position and provides an example of how it communicated that position to policy makers and the public (see appendix G.1 later in this chapter). The coalition was unable to convince the legislature to pass the bill in either 2005 or 2006. The second is an internal document, "Early Childhood Development: Getting Our Message Across Effectively," which presents new ideas for rethinking the coalition's approach to external communications (see appendix G.2).

The learning exercise invites you to use the information in the case, and especially the two documents, to prepare for a KAP1 staff meeting that will critique the "Talking Points" document and begin developing new materials for the next round of advocacy.

The conclusion, which follows chapter 9, provides an overview of what happened next. It includes fact sheet used during the 2007 legislative session, which reflects a reframing of KAP1's previous approach to talking about early childhood education based on the guidelines in "Getting Our Message Across."

Context

Throughout the United States, there is a long-standing policy debate about public funding for childcare and early childhood education prior to kindergarten.[1]

178

While nearly everyone agrees on the developmental importance of the initial years of a child's life, opposition to public programs includes social conservatives (who believe mothers should remain at home to nurture their own children) to fiscal conservatives (who argue government does not have enough resources to pay for such programs). As a result, most of public programs for early care and education that do exist, such as Head Start, were created as antipoverty and not education initiatives.

Vermont is one of the smallest and now one of the most politically progressive states in the country. Despite its size and thus limited tax base, Vermonters have consistently voted for generous funding for education.[2] However, there had never been a policy that facilitated the use of those funds for prekindergarten education; in fact, some Vermont towns have only relatively recently added kindergarten.

In 2002 Ray McNulty, an innovative state commissioner of education who had been appointed by Democratic governor Howard Dean, proposed a comprehensive early education policy. It included a recommendation to formalize and use a little-known provision in the state education funding law to increase access to high-quality early learning programs. For the policy to be implemented, the legislature had to pass a bill authorizing this use of the funds, which would then be signed by the governor. The final step became more difficult when Dean did not run for reelection (instead becoming a candidate in the 2004 Democratic Party primary for US president). In 2003 he was replaced by Jim Douglas, a fiscally conservative Republican, who then appointed a new commissioner who shared his conservative politics.

Advocates

KAP1 formed in 2000, and its members worked closely with McNulty. From 2002 onward they led the advocacy to make state funds available for early childhood education. According to its website, KAP1 is "Vermont's statewide early childhood coalition . . . [bringing] together organizations, businesses and individuals who are committed to ensuring that all Vermont's children get a good start. . . . To ensure that Vermont's children are healthy, nurtured and ready for success in school and life, we are working to:

- Improve the quality of early care and education programs;
- Make early childhood resources affordable for all families;
- Increase the availability of early care and education programs;
- Share costs of children's health, care and education costs more equitably among parents, government, and the private sector;
- Collect and report accurate information to help better anticipate future care, health and education needs of Vermont's children;
- Build a sound infrastructure that meets young children's needs."[3]

The coalition is led by six nonprofit organizations, including a community network of mothers, a policy center focused on children and youth, and various associations of professionals and service providers in the field of child care and early childhood education. Through several foundation grants, the coalition employs six part-time staff, one based at each of its six lead organizations. Working together in a horizontal system of accountability, each person has a specific role: lobbyist, organizing director, media consultant, parent organizer, policy specialist, and e-network coordinator. (Collectively, they represent the equivalent of 3.5 full-time staff.)

Again according to the website, through those staff and other coalition members' "constant public education, tireless grassroots organizing, skillful advocacy and ongoing leadership development activities, the Kids Are Priority One Coalition:

- Empowers people to speak out on behalf of children;
- Strengthens policies that make our early childhood system work better for children and families;
- Ensures that key decision-makers make children's health, care, and education a top priority."[4]

Policy

To resolve social problems caused or exacerbated by a lack of adequate, high-quality early childhood education (ECE) opportunities for all children, KAP1 members initially convened work groups around what they considered to be the three-legged stool of ECE: quality, affordability, and access.

After Commissioner McNulty's policy proposal was released, KAP1 members decided to focus their efforts on passing the legislation needed for codification and implementation of the policy. In 2003 the coalition worked with supportive members of the Vermont senate to introduce an initial bill. But progress was slow and limited. While the senate eventually voted in 2004 in favor of the bill, the House Education Committee would not take any action, and the bill died.

In 2005 the bill was reintroduced as Vermont Senate Bill 132 (S.132). Like the previous bill, S.132 would make it possible for local school boards to include three- and four-year-old prekindergarten children in their student count or average daily membership (ADM) and thus qualify for public education funding.

The coalition's policy analysis can be found in the "Talking Points" document it prepared for the 2005 legislative session (appendix G.1). The overall policy goal is clearly stated on the first page: "The Kids Are Priority One Campaign supports this use of public education funds to expand access—on a voluntary basis—to high quality early care and education (child care) programs in schools and community settings."

The document then provides facts in response to various concerns that had been raised about spending public funds for this purpose. On page 3, it concludes with, "There is a lot of misinformation circulating about this issue and S.132 in particular. Get the facts. Ask questions. Please consider all sides of the issue before forming an opinion!"

While the coalition's position is slightly muddled by its desire to respond to concerns expressed by one faction of its alliance[5]—and thus the reference to the possibility of changes or amendments to the bill—ultimately (after they "get the facts, ask questions . . . [and] consider all sides") the coalition wanted the legislators to pass S.132.

Politics

Targets

The advocates' primary target was Vermont's bicameral (senate and house of representatives) legislature. The 30 senators and 150 representatives are what is referred to as a citizen legislature. They are elected for two-year terms and receive only a modest stipend while the legislature is in session; each of their two sessions lasts only about five months (January through May in most years).

In the 2005–06 sessions of the legislature, the Democrats held the most seats, but even in alliance with a small number of very liberal Progressive Party legislators they did not have the two-thirds majority in both houses to override a gubernatorial veto of any bill.

Thus Republican Governor Douglas was also a primary target and, at least initially, an opponent given his public statements that he would veto S.132 if it required increased state education funding. The commissioner of education was an intermediate target, given his potential influence with the governor and to a lesser extent, the legislature.

The voluntary dimension of S.132 meant that were it to become law, each school district could decide whether to include preschool-aged children in its ADM count. In that case there would then be yet another target, or more accurately, many new targets: the local school boards and all the citizens in Vermont's 237 towns. At annual town meetings, a uniquely New England form of direct democracy that dates from the 1700s, citizens of each town gather not only to elect the members of their towns' school boards but also debate and approve their schools' budgets.

Supporters

In addition to like-minded members of the Vermont legislature who were active in the introduction of and internal advocacy for S.132, many other

Vermonters and local organizations shared KAP1's policy position. These included parents who need or want high-quality ECE and the providers of ECE services, some of whom are members of or otherwise affiliated with the six KAP1 organizations.

Opponents

The primary opposition was from fiscal conservatives, including Governor Douglas and many members of the Vermont legislature (some Democrats as well as Republicans) and the political organizations that shared their view. The primary organizational opponent was FreedomWorks, a national organization founded by a former Republican majority leader in the US House of Representatives. It "recruits, educates, trains and mobilizes millions of volunteer activists to fight for less government, lower taxes, and more freedom."[6] FreedomWorks opened a chapter in Vermont and helped organize what it called the No Universal Pre-K campaign (www.freedomworks.org/state/vermont).

Strategy

The "Talking Points" document was used for lobbying legislators and for building citizen support for the advocates' position, what the advocates referred to as their inside and outside strategies.

Early childhood education advocacy groups in many other states rely primarily on the inside strategy, using professional staff to do research and build long-term relationships with policy makers. KAP1 is relatively unique in that in addition to the more traditional tactics, it had an active outside strategy that focused on citizen organizing and mobilization concentrated in (but not limited to) the districts of the senators and representatives who were thought to be undecided on S.132.

The coalition also worked to strengthen alliances with other Vermont organizations concerned with child care and education (ranging from the Vermont Community Foundation's Child Care Fund of Vermont to the various associations of teachers and educational administrators) to negotiate a common understanding of how the ADM funds might be used.

The grassroots strategy involved outreach to and education of parents and other concerned citizens. Local activists in a legislative district then wrote letters, made calls, and often met with their legislators. They also generated a large number of letters to the editor in newspapers around the state.

An e-network kept the activists informed at every point in the legislative process. This made it possible to generate relatively large turnouts for the legislative hearings on the bill, with KAP1 supporters outnumbering opponents by a five-to-one margin at the pivotal hearings.

Outcome

Despite an effective strategy, KAP1 members were unable to convince the education committee in the house of representatives to pass the bill in either 2005 or 2006. On the other hand, they succeeded in achieving a potentially useful first step in that direction: a study committee that would consider the issues and report back with a recommendation. The bipartisan, bicameral Pre-K Education Study Committee was established at the end of the 2006 legislative session with a mandate to submit its report the following year.

Rethinking the Message

During 2006 KAP1 was selected to receive a one-year technical grant from the FrameWorks Institute, one of the country's pioneer research and capacity-building organizations on how public interest advocacy groups can more effectively communicate about policy issues (www.frameworksinstitute.org). Through a series of studies on different issues and collaboration with advocacy groups, the institute developed an approach it called Strategic Frame Analysis. The institute helps advocacy groups use this approach through training sessions, technical assistance, multimedia tools, and publications, the most comprehensive of which is the Framing Public Issues toolkit.[7]

Researchers at the institute had completed work on ways to strategically frame early childhood development when communicating with policy makers and the public. They proposed working with KAP1 to further develop and apply the findings of that research. And thus KAP1 staff became engaged in training workshops and ongoing consultations.

All who participated in the process were highly impressed by the potential power of paying more attention to how KAP1 frames its communications. To guide this work, Kim Friedman, KAP1's organizing director, developed a short overview of the key concepts and their relevance to the coalition's policy agenda: "Early Childhood Development: Getting Our Message Across Effectively" (see appendix G.2).[8]

LEARNING EXERCISE

It is late 2006 and you have joined the KAP1 staff. In fact you are about to attend a meeting on how to apply Strategic Frame Analysis during the upcoming legislative session. In preparation, all staff members have been asked to carefully reread the "Talking Points" document on S.132 and Kim Friedman's guidelines. To prepare for the meeting, you should make notes on how you would answer the following two questions:

- In what ways does "Talking Points" conform to or deviate from the guidelines about message framing in Kim's overview?
- Since it has been decided that a completely new document will be developed for the next round of advocacy to expand public funding, what are some specific ideas for that document's content and organization?

Notes

1. In most states, kindergarten is the first year of public school and children begin at age five.

2. While in the last few decades federal funding and regulations have had a growing impact on education, states are constitutionally responsible for all public education. In most states, responsibility for primary and secondary education has been that of local government. In Vermont most towns operate their own primary school (kindergarten through grade six or grade eight), either on their own or jointly with several other small towns and are part of a multitown district for secondary education (through grade twelve).

3. "Welcome to the Kids Are Priority One Coalition: Vermont's Future Prosperity, 2012, http://www.kidsarepriorityone.org.

4. "Welcome to the Kids Are Priority One Coalition."

5. For example, under "Concern #5 on page 3, "some family child care providers" object to the requirement of having a licensed teacher on site to be eligible for state funding, a cost well outside their limited budgets.

6. "About FreedomWorks," 2012, http://www.freedomworks.org/about/about freedomworks.

7. "Framing Public Issues," last modified June 2004, http://www.frameworks institute.org/assets/files/PDF/FramingPublicIssuesfinal.pdf.

8. This is the original document, developed for internal use, and thus provides only a general attribution to the FWI. Since it is now being used in this teaching case, the authors wish to more specifically acknowledge that the document is based solely on the institute's work, including its definition and eight elements of a frame, and to clarify that Lynne Davey is the institute's national field director.

Appendix G.1 Using Public Education Finds to Support Early Care and Education:
Talking Points

C/o Windham Child Care Association
130 Birge Street
Brattleboro, Vermont 05301

Tel. 802-348-9879
Fax. 802-348-7294
advocacy@windhamchildcare.org
www.kidsarepriorityone.org

Using Public Education Funds to Support Early Care and Education

TALKING POINTS

Overview

Since the late 1990s, public schools in Vermont have been allowed to use or "draw down" public education funds for early education purposes. To do this, a school district includes three and four year olds in their student count (called Average Daily Membership or ADM).

In many cases, schools have partnered with community-based early care and education (child care) programs to provide 10 hours per week of early education services to preschool-age children in those programs. Public schools have been using ADM funds for preschool for quite some time. Increased awareness has resulted in more school districts planning for expansion of preschool services, either on-site or in community-based child care programs.

The Kids Are Priority One Campaign supports this use of public education funds to expand access—on a voluntary basis—to high-quality early care and education (child care) programs in schools and community settings.

Key Points

- Using public education funds by adding preschool children to the student count is a way for school districts to draw down funds for eligible early care and education (child care) programs that serve three and four year olds.

- This is not a new program. A small number of schools and communities have been providing preschool in this way for almost ten years. The education funding law specifies the way in which schools can use these funds for preschool, and the legislature recently clarified this further.

- Using public education funds for preschool is a very effective use of public tax dollars: One dollar spent in a child's early years can save many more in the cost of remedial programs.

- Because education funding is based on spending per pupil, a school district can add students to its population without necessarily affecting its tax rate.

- Making preschool available to all three and four year olds (universal access) is different from making it mandatory to attend preschool. While public kindergarten has been available to all Vermont children for many years, children are still not required to start school until first grade.

Appendix G.1 Cont.

Addressing Concerns

Here are answers to some concerns that have been expressed about this growth in public financing for preschool.

Concern #1: Preschool programs in public schools will overtake private programs.

Fact: Child care providers, K-12 educators, parents and many others have been working on developing capacity for preschool throughout the state. A collaborative local planning process, which involves local child care providers, the regional Early Childhood Council, the regional child care resource and referral agency and local public schools, can identify whether a town needs and wants to establish a public preschool program. This planning process is included in the current bill pending in the Senate.

State policymakers have stated clearly and often that they do not want to make any policy decisions that put family child care providers or licensed centers out of business. They understand that child care is a critical component of a healthy economy; they know that there aren't enough regulated child care slots to meet current child care need, and they want to do everything possible to facilitate the development of more high-quality child care in a variety of settings.

Concern #2: If a public preschool program opens in your town, you might have to close your child care business due to decreased enrollment.

Fact: Experience in towns across Vermont suggest that parents will *not* necessarily move their child from a private child care program to the school's program, just because a town offers a public preschool program. Many families will always prefer to use family child care over center-based child care programs. Bottom line: *Parents* will continue to decide where their children spend their day—in registered family child care homes, licensed child care centers, or public preschool programs (all of which are eligible to access ADM funds if they meet the quality standards).

Concern #3: Policymakers in state government have started a universal preschool program in Vermont without consulting the early childhood community.

Fact: No one has decided to start a universal preschool program in the public schools. The decision to use ADM funds to support early education is being made on a town-by-town basis. Lawmakers simply approved use of ADM funds in this way.

Concern #4: The state Department of Education and the Agency of Human Services are not working together on this.

Fact: The state Department of Education and the Agency of Human Services developed joint guidelines for ADM partnerships between schools and community-based child care programs. There is an ongoing commitment to work to ensure consistency between early education standards set by both agencies.

Appendix G.1 Cont.

Concern #5: Some people don't like Senate Bill 132 (S.132), but we're stuck with it.

Fact: We have the power to influence legislation that comes out of Montpelier! We can talk to our legislators about making changes to S.132. For example, some family child care providers have expressed concern over having a licensed teacher on-site as an eligibility requirement for ADM funds. This is a concern that they should make known to policymakers. Legislators, child care businesses, parents and other community members can talk about early education. All involved can have a voice!

There is a lot of misinformation circulating about this issue and S.132 in particular. Get the facts. Ask questions. Please consider all sides of the issue before forming an opinion!

For more information, contact:
Barbara Postman, Kids Are Priority One Legislative Director
Vermont Children's Forum
bpostman@childrensforum.org or 229-6377
or
Kim Friedman, Kids Are Priority One Organizing Director
Windham Child Care Association
kfriedman@windhamchildcare.org or 348-9879

Kids Are Priority One is a statewide early childhood coalition of individuals, businesses and organizations committed to ensuring that every child in Vermont gets the best possible start in life.

www.kidsarepriorityone.org

November 2005

Appendix G.2 Early Childhood Development: Getting Our Message Across Effectively

Live the Promise

130 Birge Street
Brattleboro, Vermont 05301

Tel. 802-348-9879
Fax. 802-348-7294
info@kidsarepriorityone.org
www.kidsarepriorityone.org

Early Childhood Development:
Getting Our Message Across Effectively

These talking points were compiled by the Kids Are Priority One Coalition staff, based on materials provided by the FrameWorks Institute. FrameWorks has granted permission for us to use their language without concerns about attribution.

What Is A Frame?: "The way a story is told—its selective use of particular values, symbols, metaphors, and messengers—which, in turn, triggers the shared and durable cultural models that people use to make sense of their world" (from Power Point presentation by Lynn Davey, National Field Director)

To be effective, messages must be framed to:
➢ Define the community's responsibility and explain the role for public policy;
➢ Include the brain architecture simplifying model, which helps people understand child development;
➢ Incorporate the idea of plasticity so damage does not sound irrevocable;
➢ Define the economic consideration as prosperity and workforce development;
➢ Refer to values such as stewardship, future prosperity for society, or reciprocity, all of which allow people to respond both morally and rationally.

Eight Elements of the Frame
(Example: child development)

(1) Values
➢ Always begin with a Level One value (big ideas)
➢ In the case of the child development frame, the Level 1 values that resonate best are:
    o Future prosperity
    o Nurturance
    o Responsibility
    o Reciprocity (giving to children who give back to society later)
➢ These will help to avoid bringing up dominant frames, which don't get us to where we want to be:
    o the family bubble (bad parents)
    o early education (hurried child)
    o safety (physical focus)
    o self-made child (development is automatic)

Appendix G.2 Cont.

> ➢ Avoid starting a discussion with a Level Two (e.g. children's issues) or Level Three value (e.g. Child Care Subsidy Program, childhood immunizations, pre-k)

(2) Context: *Early childhood development* or *child development* are the best terms to use because they conjures up new frames that connote public responsibility and other Level One values to which people can relate.

(3) Simplifying Metaphors and Models
> ➢ In order to take responsibility, you have to be able to picture yourself as an actor in a system/scenario. Metaphors or a simplifying model bring big issues down to earth for people and enhance their engagement and responsibility.
> ➢ Most effective simplifying model for early childhood: "brain architecture"
> > o Example: "The early years of life matter because early experiences affect the architecture of the maturing brain. As it emerges, the quality of that architecture establishes either a sturdy or a fragile foundation for all of the development and behavior that follow—and getting things right the first time is easier than trying to fix them later."

(4) Stories
> ➢ When telling a story, link it to thematic frames (issues, trends, political/environmental, public, appeal to citizens, better policies, fix the condition) so the emphasis is on changing public policies rather than on changing individual behavior.

(5) Numbers (Social Math)
> ➢ "Uninterpreted numbers tell a story of random mayhem. Most people can't interpret size or meaning. Use fewer numbers and incorporate "social math" to embed frames in numbers."
> > o Example: Texas is the largest emitter of carbon dioxide in the USA. If Texas were a country, it would the 7th largest producer of carbon emissions in the world.

(6) Messengers: The right messengers make a difference. FrameWorks' research suggests that Kindergarten teachers and businesspeople are good messengers when talking about child development.

(7)Visuals: Use visuals that illustrate your simplifying metaphor/model.

(8) Tone
> ➢ Be reasonable.
> ➢ Avoid rhetoric.

2

Appendix G.2 Cont.

Structuring Our Discussions: Order Matters!

START WITH A *LEVEL ONE VALUE*:

"A sound investment in our society's future requires that all children have the opportunity to develop intellectually, socially and emotionally."

"Children are our future. They will inherit our institutions and steward our nation. We give to them now so that they can give back in the future."

MOVE TO *SCIENCE/MODEL*:

"But science tells us that many children's futures are undermined when stress damages the early brain architecture. That stress may result from family tensions over a lost job or a death in the family [or insert another specific example]. That stress makes babies' brains release a chemical that stunts cell growth."

"What science can now demonstrate is that the earliest stages of life require an environment…[see pg. 26]

BRIEFLY STATE *THE PROBLEM*: "Many young children in Vermont do not have access to affordable, high-quality child development services. This compromises future learning and the future workforce."

CONCLUDE WITH *SOLUTIONS*:

"When communities make family mental health services available so that early interventions can take place, they put in place a preventive system that catches children before they fall." (If you choose a different example in the "metaphor" section, you would probably want to use a different solution, such as early childhood education, access to health care, strong public and private environments that promote experiences that build health brain architecture.)

"Science shows that training, knowledge and skills of consistent caregivers are critical to the solid foundation…"

For more information, contact Kim Friedman, Organizing Director, Kids Are Priority One Coalition, at (802) 348-9879 or kfriedman@svcable.net.

Kids Are Priority One is Vermont's statewide early childhood coalition of individuals, organizations and businesses committed to ensuring that every child in Vermont gets a good start.

April 2008

3

9

Advocacy Communications
(Re)framing and Storytelling

As will be evident from the conclusion to the Kids Are Priority One Co-alition (KAP1) case, advocates have much to gain from the latest developments that link human cognition, information processing, and the construction of meaning to public policy and social change. Concepts such as framing, reframing, and storytelling are not new in the practice of advocacy. However, over the past decade various advocates, researchers, and think tanks have been refining (and in some cases redefining) those concepts. The decision to devote a separate case and chapter to the topic reflects the potential of those developments for powerfully enhancing advocacy communications within a larger advocacy strategy.

It is possible to draw at least four key insights from work discussed in this chapter:[1]

1. People think and make meaning through the creation or adoption and use of mental structures or organizing principles. Frames and stories are the most commonly used concepts and terms for understanding and describing those structures. However, there is considerable variation in the use of those and related concepts and terms (*messages, values, metaphors, memes,* and others) among those at the forefront of advocacy communications; in fact, many of those same people and organizations tend to be internally inconsistent in their own use of terms.[2] Thus, as always, advocates should be less concerned with terminology and more focused on the implications of communicating with audiences whose pre-established frames or stories will significantly shape whatever ideas or information they receive.

191

2. One of the most important implications for advocates is that frames or stories so strongly shape the cognition of experiences, ideas, and information that when a frame and facts are inconsistent, it is the facts and not the frame that is discarded. Thus the tendency of progressive advocates to try convincing audiences primarily through evidence and facts is only successful with people who already share their frames, that is, constituents, allies, and the like-minded.

3. The latter point is important because other and very important audiences, especially most policy makers, the major media, and most members of the public, will most often *not* share the advocates' frames. The sources discussed in the rest of this chapter suggest different reasons why that is the case in the United States: the *episodic framing* that dominates news media reports on policy issues, how conservative think tanks have systematically worked to establish *dominant frames* that are consistent with their values and political interests, or how corporate capitalism has used everything from advertising and public relations to history books in order to instill *control stories*. Whatever the reason, advocates must recognize and address the challenges of audiences whose frames limit their interest and ability to accept and understand the advocates' communications.

4. One of those challenges advocates face is that every time the dominant frame is evoked, even by attempting to negate it, that frame is reinforced. Thus, in all their communications, advocates must work to reframe how their audiences think about the relevant policy issues. That is, in all their communications, they must identify and evoke other frames that result in a better understanding of and support for the advocates' policy analysis.

But how can advocates analyze the dominant frames and stories relevant to their policy issues, and how can they effectively reframe the issue? Or in terms of the conceptual approach discussed at the end of the chapter, how can they win the *battle of the story*?

To answer those questions, I first summarize a paper by George Lakoff, one of the most well-known and influential proponents of rethinking advocacy communications. I then do the same regarding the analysis and methods of two organizations that are making important contributions to this work: the FrameWorks Institute (FWI) and, the *smart-*Meme Strategy & Training Project. Because of FWI's collaboration with

KAP1, Case G introduces FWI's approach, which it calls SFA. FWI has also done similar groundbreaking work on a wide range of other policy issues. *smart*Meme's approach, called Story Based Strategy, while overlapping with Lakoff and FWI, offers a distinct analysis and methodology that grows out of work in and with grassroots social movements.[3]

George Lakoff

Lakoff is a professor of cognitive linguistics at the University of California, Berkeley, widely recognized for his research and publications related to how Americans think about public policy; his work includes *Metaphors We Live By* and *Moral Politics: What Conservatives Know and What Liberals Don't*.[4] A political progressive, he has worked closely with activists and allied politicians to translate what he and others have learned about cognition into political action, including founding the Rockridge Institute, which published many research and strategy papers by Lakoff and colleagues, as well as the comprehensive *Thinking Points: Communicating Our American Values and Vision: A Progressive's Handbook*. Among the institute's publications is a short and very accessible paper that Lakoff wrote in 2007: "Simple Framing: An Introduction to Framing and Its Uses in Politics." The following summarizes many of its key points.[5]

Lakoff begins "Simple Framing" with an admonition he is particularly well known for: "Don't think of an elephant!" He then notes that despite the fact that the reader (or audience, more generally) is asked to not think of an elephant, the statement inevitably leads one to think about, even visualize, a large animal with a trunk and floppy ears. This illustrates four points: every word evokes a frame, words defined within a frame evoke the frame, negating a frame evokes the frame, and evoking the frame reinforces the frame. It is simply a matter of "neural circuitry." ("Every time a neural circuit is activated, it is strengthened.")

As he did in *Moral Politics*, Lakoff goes on to argue that a group of right wing conservatives in the United States learned those and related points about communication decades ago.[6] They poured resources into new think tanks responsible for researching and developing language that would frame public understanding of policy issues in ways consistent with their pro-capitalist, antigovernment agenda.

Frank Luntz is one of the leaders in the process of conservative political framing. He is perhaps best known by his advice to Republicans about what had always been called the estate tax, a well-established and relatively unquestioned requirement for the richest American families to pay a tax when large amounts of wealth are passed from generation to generation. Siding with the rich, Republicans opposed the tax. Based on framing research, Luntz advised conservatives to reframe the policy as the death tax. That one change is widely thought to have been critical in changing the general public's understanding of the tax. The majority of the public, very few of whom have even close to the amount of wealth that would have been taxed, came to identify with those being taxed (after all, everyone dies) and concluded that a death tax is unfair and inhumane. Their support helped Republicans repeal the tax.

In "Simple Framing," Lakoff discusses a later and broader language shift that Republicans were advised to adopt: tax relief. He points out that "on the day that George W. Bush took office, the words 'tax relief' started appearing in White House communiqués to the press and in official speeches and reports by conservatives." He then goes on to describe the cognitive frame evoked by the word *relief* and how it is an instance of a yet more general "rescue scenario." The components are

- a "blameless Afflicted Person who we identify with"—all taxpayers;
- an "Affliction" (or even a "crime")—taxes;
- a "Cause-of-pain" (or a "villain")—the proponents of taxes and, more generally, "big government";
- a "Reliever-of-pain" (or a "hero")—those who wish to at least lower if not repeal taxes.

According to Lakoff, the media soon began using the term. When liberal or progressive politicians were asked about their position on tax relief, even their criticism of the conservatives' policy evoked their frame. He concludes: "Every time the phrase tax relief is used and heard or read by millions of people, the more this view of taxation as an affliction and conservatives as heroes gets reinforced."

Lakoff advises liberals and progressives to learn from the conservatives' success and invest in the clarification and infusion of alternative frames, that is, to reframe the language of policy debate to reflect their values or morals and cue audiences to think in terms of their positions. He emphasizes that reframing is a long-term project. ("It takes time and a lot of repetition for frames to become entrenched in the very synapses of people's brains.")

At the core of reframing is structuring communications around "fundamental progressive values: empathy, responsibility, fairness, community, doing our fair share." More specifically, Lakoff describes a four-step procedure he and his colleagues used to reframe a specific policy issue: efforts in the state of Texas to cap the amount of punitive damages juries can award to plaintiffs in lawsuits, typically against large corporations found guilty of harming consumers or the community.

1. Pick out the relevant core values for this issue.
2. Write down how your position follows from these values.
3. Articulate the facts and their consequences within this moral framing.
4. Define us and them within this moral frame.

Lakoff suggests that the conservatives, who were the proponents of the policy, had already done this. Their values: "You alone are responsible for what happens to you. You shouldn't get what you haven't earned. You should be disciplined, prudent and orderly." They labeled their position as "tort reform," which cues a more general "corruption frame" further reinforced by language like frivolous lawsuits, greedy trial lawyers, and out of control (or runaway) juries.

Lakoff worked with progressives who opposed the policy to clarify their values: "We are empathetic; we care about people. Be responsible. Help, don't harm. Protect the powerless." Thus, to cue a more general "public protection frame," they adopted fundamentally different language to describe the legislation, including the corporate immunity act, corporate raid on responsibility, accountability crisis, closed courts, rewards greed and dishonesty, protects the guilty, and punishes the innocent.

Efforts to defeat caps on lawsuit awards in a state long dominated by conservatives have yet to succeed, but the progressives' framing was adopted by some of the major newspapers in Texas, and liberal and progressive members in the state legislature (while still a minority) "have now been given a powerful tool to express their values." And the much larger and longer struggle over whose frames will dominate political discourse and thinking marches on.

FrameWorks Institute

We now review in somewhat more detail the approach and methods of one of the best funded and most academic/professional of the organizations at the forefront of rethinking advocacy communications. Founded in 1999, FWI states its purpose as "to advance the nonprofit sector's communications capacity by identifying, translating and modeling relevant scholarly research for framing the public discourse about social problems."[7] Over the past decade it has done framing research on a very wide variety of those problems or policy issues, from early childhood development (including its work with KAP1 in Vermont) to child abuse, community health, education, domestic toxins, food systems, gender equity, global warming, immigration, race, and a rapidly growing list of other issues of concern to US advocates. FWI's website is a very rich resource for research reports, message memos, communication toolkits, and other materials that address different issue areas, as well as training materials and an online e-workshop on its general approach: Strategic Frame Analysis (SFA).[8]

According to the FWI website, "Strategic Frame Analysis is a proprietary approach to communications research and practice that pays attention to the public's deeply held worldviews and widely held assumptions." More specifically, "Strategic Frame Analysis™ offers policy advocates a way to work systematically through the challenges that are likely to confront the introduction of new legislation or social policies, to anticipate attitudinal barriers to support, and to develop research-based strategies to overcome public misunderstanding. This approach is strategic in that it not only deconstructs the dominant frames of reference that drive reasoning on public issues, but it also identifies those alternative frames most likely to stimulate public reconsideration and enumerates their elements (reframing)."[9]

This approach involves "multi-disciplinary, multi-method, iterative processes that emphasize empirical testing of potential frame effects." Figure 9.1 summarizes the eight methods FWI uses when doing a comprehensive analysis and testing of new frames.

The multiple methods involved in a comprehensive SFA obviously require highly trained researchers and other professionals, time, and money. While few advocacy organizations have such resources, those focused on policy issues that FWI or other communications research and development organizations have analyzed can use existing reports and recommendations in planning their communications.[10] For example, while KAP1 was fortunate to receive training and technical support as well as materials from FWI, all advocates concerned with early childhood education policy have online access to eleven papers that report findings from one or more of the eight SFA research and development methods,

Figure 9.1 FWI methods for SFA

(1) *Media Content Analysis.* Research examines a wide variety of media (television, radio, major newspapers, news magazines, and online news) to identify the leading frames within that coverage.

(2) *Cultural Models Interviews.* In-depth, one-on-one interviews based on methods from cultural anthropology and cognitive linguistics to understand "the way people think about a topic, the pattern of reasoning, the connections they make to other issues, and the devices they use to resist new information."

(3) *Peer Discourse Sessions.* Focus groups designed to (a) understand the "social context effects" of the findings from the previously discussed methods, (b) demonstrate how groups make sense of numeric and graphical "facts" used in the public discourse, (c) and experiment with alternative frame elements, most specifically values and metaphors.

(4) *Expert Interviews and Field Frame Analysis.* To better understand the issue from the perspective of policy experts and advocates, the research involves one-on-one expert interviews, attending professional meetings and the analysis of publicly available communications materials—with a focus on producing "a core story that lays out the central problems associated with the issue, the evidence or science base that supports these conclusions, as well as the policy and program solutions that expert knowledge and understandings suggests will help resolve the issue."

(5) *Mapping the Gap Conceptual Analysis.* The findings about how the public and experts understand or conceptualize the policy issues are compared with the objective of identifying gaps—where there is "incongruity" between the two. "These incongruous spaces then become our primary targets for reframing."

(6) *Simplifying Model Development.* "A simplifying model is a reframing tool that concretizes and clarifies technical concepts and processes through a familiar and easily understood metaphor. These metaphors capture the essence of a scientific concept or explain an important mechanism on an issue and have a high capacity for spreading easily through a population. . . . As a result, we actively develop simple and concrete metaphorical frame elements that help people to organize information on issues in new ways, to fill in understanding currently missing from the public's repertoire, and to shift attention away from the default patterns they already use to understand those issues."

(7) *National Experimental Surveys.* Representative and randomly assigned populations are asked to complete online surveys; some participants are exposed to simplifying models and other elements of the framed messages, while other "control groups" are not. The objective is to "ascertain any effects that emerge as a result of the way in which the issues were framed in the stimuli. Using this method, we can demonstrate the magnitude and extent to which exposure to particular frames affect the public's policy preferences."

(8) *Persistence Trials.* In conversational groups, pairs of individuals are asked to think about a simplifying model and then communicate about it and a target issue with others. "By measuring and comparing subjects' acceptance of and facility with different simplifying models and frame elements—as they try to explain and reason about an issue—FrameWorks is able to judge how effectively these elements are likely to be absorbed and used once introduced to the wider public."

Source: FrameWorks Institute, "Strategic Frame Analysis: Research Methods," www.frameworksinstitute.org/methods.html. Adapted by permission.

three message briefs, and a comprehensive message memo: "Talking Early Childhood Development and Exploring the Consequences of Frame Choices."[11]

Where such extensive resources have not been produced, SFA can still provide a perspective advocates can use to plan their communications. FWI's e-workshop, "Changing the Public Conversation on Social Problems: A Beginner's Guide to Strategic Frame Analysis," provides a useful resource. The remainder of this section is largely based on it.

Understanding Current Frames or Stories

First, advocates need to examine the dominant frames and stories their audiences bring to any communication. FWI describes the mass media as the primary shaper of the dominant frames in political and policy discourse. This assessment is reflected in the fact that content analysis of major news sources is the very first of the eight methods of an SFA. While FWI does not discuss the political-economic forces that largely control the mass media in the United States, the e-workshop and other materials focus on the fact that most news stories the public reads, hears, and (especially) sees about an issue are produced by mass media. They then examine the implications of the fact that partially due to their brevity, those stories most often use an episodic frame as opposed to a thematic frame.[12]

Episodic framing focuses on individual events or people with little or no context. Such stories work against one of the primary challenges of advocates, which is to get people to think their issue should be solved through public policy and not just individual action. In response, advocates need to "create communications that enable the public to understand social issues in a broader context, thereby moving Americans away from blaming individuals and toward systemic and community-based solutions to social problems."[13] That is, the task is to shift the framing in the media and public discourse more generally from episodic to thematic, as shown in table 9.1.

Reframing

To make that shift, advocates first need to develop alternative stories or frames. More specifically, these need to be constructed with the understanding that "every story, every frame has a set of component elements, all of which must work together to deliver an effective message to the public and policy makers. These elements are a kind of framework or checklist against which you can gauge whether you are building an effective public story. In other words, each element is a cue to the meaning of your story."[14]

Table 9.1 Different frames set up different policy solutions

Episodic Frame	Thematic Frame
Individuals	Issues
Events	Trends
Psychological	Political/environment
Private	Public
Appeal to consumers	Appeal to citizens
Better information	Better policies
Fix the person	**Fix the condition**

Source: FrameWorks Institute, "Changing the Public Conversation on Social Problems: A Beginner's Guide to Strategic Frame Analysis," http://sfa.frameworksinstitute.org/, slide 43. Reprinted by permission.

FWI's e-workshop notes six key elements of an effective story: big ideas or values, metaphors and simplifying models, messengers, visuals, tone, and solutions.[15] It gives the most attention to the first two. Elsewhere, FWI discusses an additional element: numbers and social math. All seven elements are described in the following section.

Element 1: Big ideas. These are the values or morals at the heart of Lakoff's discussion of reframing. In fact, Lakoff and FWI (in "Framing Public Issues" and other publications, though not in the e-workshop) present a similar three-level framework in which big ideas or values are viewed as the highest level of people's understanding of politics and policy issues.[16] These act as primes for the lower levels: issue types or areas and specific issues or policies. Each source illustrates the framework with several examples in table 9.2.

In its e-workshop, FWI describes the big ideas or values as the anchors of a story and recommends introducing them as early as possible in a communication. "When you begin the conversation with a VALUE, you are telling people what your issue is all about—in the largest possible sense. This gives people an opportunity to understand what is at stake, AND prevents them from defaulting to ideas that can derail your message."[17]

Element 2: Metaphors and simplifying models. The importance of this element is suggested by how the final three of the institute's eight methods of an SFA are largely dedicated to identifying and testing simplifying models in search of a "brief, metaphor-driven explanation that allows the lay public to understand a complex issue in a vivid, user-friendly way."[18] The fact that the final three methods (including national experimental surveys) are largely dedicated to simplifying models also suggests how

Table 9.2 Common concept, different terminology

	FrameWorks Institute	Lakoff
Level One	Big ideas: justice, community	Values: fairness and opportunity
Level Two	Issue-type: child care	Issue Area: civil rights
Level Three	Specific issues: income tax credits	Policy: affirmative action

this may be the most difficult element for advocates who cannot conduct and do not have access to such research and development.

For example, few advocates focused on global climate change might have been able to simply think through the limitations of the dominant model in use (greenhouse effect, which is scientifically accurate but limiting because most members of the public have had limited or no experiences with an actual greenhouse and, more important, it suggests something positive: places of growth and life). Nor would they have likely identified the metaphor that ultimately emerged from FWI's research: heat trapping blanket, that is, "global warming is caused by a man-made blanket of carbon dioxide that surrounds the earth and traps in heat."[19]

Element 3: Messengers. While not a new insight in advocacy, FWI has research data that confirms that the choice of messengers can enhance or detract from the message. They are "the physical symbol of the issue" and answer the question, "who says this is a problem I should pay attention to?"[20]

Element 4: Tone. A "reasonable tone activates a community approach and can-do attitude" while an "argumentative tone . . . makes audiences less likely to be open to new information and solutions-based thinking."

Element 5: Visuals. Images can support or work against the story and thus must not provide close-up images of individuals (episodic frame) but rather step back and show context (thematic frame). The first triggers sympathy at best; the latter triggers systems and the need for problem solving.

Element 6: Solutions. Progressive advocates tend to focus far more of their communications on the problem than on the solution, and when the latter is presented it is too often "highly rhetorical and abstract, in contrast to the vivid and concrete picture we paint of the problem. This leaves the public feeling that the problems are overwhelming and unsolvable—and they turn away with a sense of frustration and helplessness."[21] However, "FrameWorks research strongly suggests, contrary to popular convention, it is far more effective to announce a solution first and then back into a problem definition, rather than the other way around."[22]

Numbers and social math. Most advocacy communications include data to support the proposed policy solution. Communications by policy researchers often contain far too much data, especially too many numbers, than can be included in an advocacy story if it is to effectively communicate with policy makers and the public. FWI summarizes its advice in four points:

- Use numbers sparingly. When you use dramatic numbers, you may have the inadvertent effect of making the problem seem too big, too scary or too far away.
- Provide the meaning first, then the numbers. Use social math to reinforce the meaning.
- Use numbers strategically; not simply to establish the size of the problem but to convey the cost of ignoring it.
- Use the numbers to demonstrate efficacy, demonstrating cost-effectiveness.[23]

My students have found the concept of social math particularly helpful. Essentially it involves translating numbers, especially large numbers, into a context the audience can easily relate to. FWI provides several examples, one from an Oxfam America communication about conflict and underdevelopment: "Two years ago in Nigeria, an AK-47 could be had in exchange for two cows. Now the price is down to one cow. And in the Sudan, you can get an AK-47 for a chicken."[24]

*smart*Meme Strategy and Training Project

We now review the approach and methods of one of the most grassroots activist-oriented organizations at the forefront of rethinking advocacy communications. Founded in 2002 *smart*Meme operates as a national strategy center for progressive social movements, offering training workshops and strategic support for campaigns on the front lines. Its website (www.smartmeme.org) contains multiple resources for those interested in its approach: story-based strategy. These include various papers, a downloadable version of *Re:Imagining Change: How to Use Story-based Strategy to Win Campaigns, Build Movements, and Change the World,* a video of a presentation of the strategy at a national gathering of the Progressive Communicators' Network, and many other resources.[25]

This section draws primarily on *Re:Imagining Change,* what the authors describe as "an introduction to our methodology and a report-back from our first five years."[26] Some of the concepts, terms, and methods presented in the book are very similar to those of Lakoff and FWI. However, others are quite unique and provide advocates with important new insights and tools and case examples that illustrate them; for the most part, these grew out of *smart*Meme's deep involvement in the theories and activism of grassroots social change movements.

*smart*Meme's analysis uses the concept and terminology of stories or narratives to help advocacy communicators understand the mental structures and organizing principles that shape how their audiences process information and make meaning. "As humans, we are literally hardwired for narrative."[27] Therefore, "a sea of stories tells us who are, what to do, and what to believe. People use stories to process information we encounter from our families and upbringing, educational institutions, religious and cultural institutions, the media, our peers and community. We remember our lived experiences by converting them to narratives and integrating them into our personal and collective web of stories."[28]

According to *smart*Meme, effective stories consist of five key elements and ideally include a meme. A *meme* is "a unit of self-replicating cultural information (for example, idea, slogan, melody, ritual, symbol) that spreads virally from imagination to imagination and generation to generation." With regard to stories, a "meme operates as container, capsule or carrier."[29]

*smart*Meme's goal is to integrate material power analysis (which seeks to understand and change how wealth and politics create inequality and injustice) and traditional organizing with narrative power analysis (which seeks to understand and change the dominant stories that support or hide their real causes) and storytelling.

According to *smart*Meme, most advocates have focused almost exclusively on material power analysis and organizing at one or more of what they call physical points of intervention. These are point of production (for example, a factory), point of destruction (a logging road), point of consumption (a retail store), and point of decision (a corporate headquarters). In so doing, the advocates' communications have generally been focused on the arguments and evidence that support their positions. *smart*Meme calls this *battle of the story* and notes that it is effective in mobilizing those who already share their values and assumptions.

However, the stories most people use to process information and make meaning about politics and policy are currently based on assumptions that are inconsistent with and often the opposite of those of the advocates. Thus, at each of the physical points, as well as at one other, the point of assumption (the existing narrative), the challenge is to win the battle of the story. To do so, advocates must understand the current stories and where they come from, and then design and infuse counterstories into the culture.

Understanding Current Frames or Stories

Lakoff traces the dominant frames or stories to the work of conservative think tanks; FWI's publications focus primarily on the mass media as their source.[30] In contrast, *smart*Meme is more direct and comprehensive in its analysis of corporations and other political-economic institutions; it argues that these are the forces that created those think tanks and that control the media, as well as so many other dimensions of peoples' lives.

*smart*Meme's analysis incorporates Antonio Gramsci's writings about ideological hegemony. Gramsci analyzed how the powerful dominate the powerless not only through their control over economic and political institutions but also, when necessary, through direct coercion.[31] Even more effective, he argued, is the domination through the creation and reinforcement of cultural narratives (through media, but also schooling and other institutions) that assign blame for social problems to individuals (as suggested by FWI's discussion of episodic framing) or, more often, to the social classes and population groups who experience the problems. Hegemonic narratives are so deeply ingrained in the culture that they become "conventional wisdom" and create a "silent consensus of assumptions" that make "ideas that challenge the status quo almost unthinkable."[32]

*smart*Meme introduces the concept and term *control mythologies* to describe hegemonic narratives, that is, a "web of stories, symbols and ideas that define the dominant culture . . . , [including] stories that assume the system is unchangeable or limit our imagination of social change." An example is the Thanksgiving myth in US history.[33]

*smart*Meme also introduces related concepts and terms for understanding dominant stories. Special attention is given to the role of advertising and public relations in creating designer stories as a means for corporations to infuse individualism and consumerism into the dominant or popular culture values.[34]

Branding plays an important role in designer stories and control mythologies more generally. It "operates like a magical process where a thing—usually an inanimate product, but sometimes an idea, candidate or political agenda—is endowed with specific narrative and emotional qualities." In this way, it "is the sum total of the stories that are told about the branded entity and encompasses images, impressions, gut feelings and associations."[35] An example is the way Marlboro cigarettes are made to appeal to men through the image and mythology of the cowboy.

Brands are one type of designer meme. When a brand or other form of a meme is used as "a container for control myths or replicates oppressive stories and spreads them through popular culture, *smart*Meme calls it a *control meme*."[36] Among *smart*Meme's examples are phrases Lakoff traces to conservative think tanks, including death tax. Several other examples most likely have a similar origin, like family values, liberal media, war on terror, and clean coal. But *smart*Meme also notes other control memes were infused deeply into US culture centuries before think tanks existed, such as "Columbus discovered America" and "manifest destiny."

In some ways, these examples are simply different (though more detailed and I think more powerful) language for what Lakoff calls a frame, at least in his example of *tax relief.* Recall from page 194 that he describes the phrase as words that evoke larger relief and rescue frames. Using *smart*Meme's concepts and terminology, *tax relief* is a control meme that acts as a container to spread the story of sympathetic characters (the victims of taxes, that is, all Americans) trapped in a conflict between bad guys (tax-and-spend liberals, itself a control meme) and good guys (conservatives who are trying to cut taxes). The imagery associated with tax relief is an expression of conservative values (for example, freedom). A positive outcome (tax cuts) is foreshadowed. The story is believable as long as the audience does not question certain assumptions; for example, big government (another control meme) is not efficient; the private sector is.

Reframing: Winning the Battle of the Story

Once advocates understand the control stories, they need tools to create and spread counterstories consistent with their values and analyses. *smart*Meme recommends developing a "framing narrative" as "an internal, working document that can help your group develop messaging strategy and tactics as you conduct your campaign." The process of doing so "often requires considerable creativity, experimentation and collective commitment. The most important thing to remember is that all of the elements of the story should reinforce each other to connect seamlessly into a coherent story. As you brainstorm images, develop slogans, and hone your messaging, you must adhere to a common narrative logic: a coherent, cumulative narrative arc that produces cognitive consonance (as opposed to cognitive dissonance) in the minds of your audience. In other words, the story has to make sense! The message should be self-evident."[37] The story must then be told and retold, consistently and with discipline.

*smart*Meme provides a Battle of the Story worksheet, which is shown in figure 9.2.[38] The worksheet has one column for deconstructing the

Figure 9.2 Battle of the Story

BATTLE OF THE STORY WORKSHEET

This exercise is intended to help grassroots activists create more compelling narratives to communicate their campaigns. The Battle of the Story is a framework for applying a "narrative power analysis" to an issue—whether it's the story that specific power holders are telling about the issue or just the accepted status quo perception that we are campaigning to change. The worksheet asks you to apply four different elements of story (conflict, characters, imagery/show don't tell and foreshadowing) to both the power holder's story and then our story as grassroots activists. Tell each story on its own terms, not the "truth" but rather the story. The bottom row is the place to step out of the story and analyze it by identifying the assumptions that allow each of the stories to operate. For our stories these assumptions may be our core values but many times the assumptions of our opponent's story are contradictions and weaknesses that we can use to challenge their story's framing by exposing hidden agendas or contrasting alternate visions of the future. At the completion of this chart you should be able to revisit each story and beginning developing some frames and core messages that will help you win the Battle of the Story!

ELEMENTS OF STORY	OPPOSITION OR STATUS QUO STORY (THEM)	ADVOCATES / CHANGE AGENTS (US)
Conflict How is the problem being framed? Who or what is the conflict between? Are there good guys and the bad guys? What's at stake?		
Characters Who are the specific victims? Who are the messengers that tell the story? Do they get to speak for themselves or is someone speaking on their behalf?		
Imagery/show don't tell What powerful images does the story provide? Are there relevant metaphors, symbols or specific examples that embody the story?		
Foreshadowing How does each story show us the future? What is the vision that the story offers of how things will be if the conflict resolves successfully?		
Assumptions What are the unstated assumptions? What does someone have to believe to accept the story as true? What values are reflected in the story?		

elements of the dominant status quo story of the political or policy issue as told by the power holders and a second column for the elements that become part of the advocates' counterstory. *Re:Imagining Change* also provides advice and more great examples for making the new story effective.

Conflict. Using the example of the edges of a television screen, Reinsborough and Canning argue that conflict and indeed the whole story need a frame that helps the audience understand what is and what is not part of the story. What is the problem? Whom is the conflict between? They provide a powerful example: two photos from the US war in Iraq of a group of Iraqis pulling down a statue of Saddam Hussein that stood at one end of a relatively large city square. The first is a relatively close-up photo that shows little more than the statue and those pulling it down. The second was taken from much farther back and exposes the fact that the surrounding streets were empty with the exception of thirteen US military tanks. The framing of the first photo, broadcast widely in the United States by CNN and then by other major media, suggests that the conflict is between the evil Hussein and the Iraqi people who are ecstatic about having been liberated. The second suggests something quite different: the US military is in control of the event, if it did not also stage it. While taken by a Reuters photographer and broadcast around the world, the second photo was not picked up by the US media. The authors point out that "in order to change the story and change our understanding of the story's power dynamics, we often have to expand the frame or reframe."[39] Depending on the story, advocates can do this through what *smart*Meme calls *framing actions* (such as a huge banner flown at the start of the 1999 World Trade Organization meeting in Seattle that had two arrows pointing in opposite directions, one with the word "DEMOCRACY" and the other with "WTO") and *reframing actions* (a new logo that incorporates the yellow ribbon that has become the symbol of supporting US troops into the design of the universal peace symbol, adding the words "Bring them home now!").

Characters. "Every social change story has lots of characters; deciding which characters should be the focus is a significant organizing and strategy question." To make the decision, advocates should ask: "Who is impacted? Who are the victims? Villains? Heroes?" And then ask: "Which characters do we sympathize with or relate to? These characters have the power to personalize the story and deepen the audience's connection"; for example, members of Military Families Speak Out, who have family members serving in the military and question the war, using the peace sign with the yellow ribbon logo.[40]

Imagery. Use images but also "metaphor, visualization, and the five senses to illustrate what is important in the story as if we were painting a picture with our words." An example is illustrating a story about cosmetic corporations that refuse to test most of their products for human safety (villains) with an advertisement showing a young girl (sympathetic victim) putting on her mother's lipstick, with the tag line: "Putting on makeup shouldn't be like playing with matches."[41]

Foreshadowing. This involves "offering vision, posing a solution to the problem, and constantly referencing the future. How will the conflict come to a resolution? . . . What does a better world look, feel and taste like?"[42] The authors' example is offering the plausible possibility of removing dams from a major river in California, thereby helping to restore the salmon population and the culture of local Native Americans.

Assumptions. This involves identifying your organization's or alliance's "own underlying assumptions. These assumptions are the shared values (for example, 'equity') and core beliefs (for example, 'All people deserve equal access to opportunity')." The advocates should then "synthesize these elements into . . . an overarching narrative [that] should be both compelling to [their] target audience(s), and challenge the key underlying assumptions that are preventing the dominant narrative from changing."[43]

Memes. Many "successful campaigns rely on a few 'sticky' memes to spread their story and build support amongst a wider audience."[44] Among the authors' examples of advocacy memes are phrases such as *conflict diamonds, sweatshop-free,* and *living wage.* Another example is the meme "Billionaires for Bush (or Gore)," a street theater tactic initiated during the 2000 presidential election. Now mutated to apply to many other issues, for example, "Billionaires for Wealthcare (Not Healthcare)," the meme is the tactic: advocates dress up like the ultrarich and in various public forums articulate the true self-interested motives of the elite.

*smart*Meme's overall approach is cogently summarized in Reinsborough and Canning's "Story-based Strategy Campaign Model" (see figure 9.3) and offers a fitting summation for this chapter.[45]

Notes

1. Most phrases or terms that are italicized are from the work of either Lakoff, FrameWorks Institute, or *smart*Meme and will be defined and fully credited in the relevant sections.

2. As an example of the fluid use of this terminology, see note 12.

3. George Lakoff, "Simple Framing: An Introduction to Framing and Its Uses in Politics," http://www.cognitivepolicyworks.com/resource-center/planning-

Figure 9.3 *smartMeme's* Story-Based Strategy Campaign model

*smart*Meme's Story-based Strategy Campaign model   www.smartmeme.org

Strategy Development

Narrative Power Analysis

Battle of the Story (deconstructive)
- What are the stories we need to change? (Status quo assumptions and/or from a specific institution?)
- Use narrative power analysis to deconstruct with elements of story
- Identify underlying assumptions
- Are there larger mythologies of the dominant culture that must be challenged?

TOOLS: battle of the story

Battle of the Story (constructive)
- Use narrative power analysis to apply elements of story and construct our story
- How does our story target underlying assumptions in the dominant story?
- What are our shared assumptions?

TOOLS: battle of the story

Identifying Targets and Audiences
- Targeting Institutions: What institutions are operating?
- Targeting Decision Makers: Who can give us what we want?
- Audiences: Who are we talking to and what do we want them to do?
- What do we know/need to know about our audiences? What are their filters/assumptions? What is our spectrum of allies I focus groups

TOOLS: power map I influence map I spectrum of allies I focus groups

Design: Campaign Narrative & Action Logic
- Synthesize campaign narrative
- Memes: How do we encapsulate our story?
- Visualization: What are the venues, networks, cultural currents, media environments and/or spectacles where our meme could catch on?
- Action Design: Tactics? Scenarios?
- R & D: Creativity experimentation, testing
- Group preparation for action

TOOLS: what's in a meme? I tactic star

Visioning & Campaign Goal Setting
- What do we really want?
- What are the incremental steps to get there?

SOCIAL MOVEMENT BUILDING

Ongoing Practices
- Building networks & alliances
- Leadership development
- Skill & capacity building
- Monitoring narratives & re/assessment
- Self & community care
- Celebration!
- Innovation!

Evaluation
Is there evidence that:
- Our memes are spreading?
- Target has moved? Framing has shifted? Organizing goals met? new leadership, membership, alliances, moral, etc.?

PRACTICES: reflection writing I paired/small group listening I group debriefing I self & community care I celebration

Intervention
- Identify physical points
- Identify points of assumption
- Intervention tied to goals organizing, persuasion, pressure on target, etc) and appropriate for group capacity
- Interventions launch/repeat core memes

TOOLS: points of intervention I nonviolent direct action toolbox I strategic communications & new media toolbox

Results?
- Victory?
- Story has changed?
- Goals met?

Shared problem/ issue identified

Constituency Organizes
- Research
- Power analysis
- Outreach & Education
- Organizing

Action

Reflection

tools/frame-analysis-framing-tutorials/simple-framing/; FrameWorks Institute, "Strategic Frame Analysis," 2012, http://frameworksinstitute.org/sfa.html; *smart*Meme, "Story Based Strategy: Storytelling as Social Change," 2012, www.smartmeme.org/article.php?id=283.

4. George Lakoff and Mark Johnson, *Metaphors We Live By* (Chicago: University of Chicago Press, 1980); George Lakoff, *Moral Politics: How Liberals and Conservatives Think* (Chicago: University of Chicago Press, 2002).

5. Rockridge Institute closed in 2008, five years after it was founded. However, a group of the institute's fellows subsequently formed Cognitive Policy Works (http://www.cognitivepolicyworks.com) and as part of their work provide access to an archive of the institute's electronic publications; George Lakoff, *Thinking Points: Communicating Our American Values and Vision: A Progressive's Handbook* (New York: Farrar, Straus and Giroux, 2006), http://www.cognitivepolicyworks.com/resource-center/thinking-points/. The web page also has links to a series of articles that expand the content of each of the chapters in *Thinking Points;* Lakoff, "Simple Framing." All the following quotations in this section are from "Simple Framing."

6. George Lakoff, *Moral Politics: How Liberals and Conservatives Think* (University of Chicago Press, 2002).

7. FWI, "Mission of the FrameWorks Institute, 2012, http://frameworksinstitute.org/mission.html.

8. Includes a very comprehensive Framing 101: "Framing Public Issues," last modified June 2004, http://www.frameworksinstitute.org/assets/files/PDF/FramingPublicIssuesfinal.pdf; FWI, "Changing the Public Conversation on Social Problems: A Beginner's Guide to Strategic Frame Analysis," 2012, http://sfa.frameworksinstitute.org/.

9. See http://frameworksinstitute.org/sfa.html.

10. For example, see Cultural Logic, http://www.culturallogic.com.

11. See http://frameworksinstitute.org/ecd.html.

12. FWI, "Changing the Public Conversation." The e-workshop suggests that TV news is the most powerful of the media in shaping how political issues are framed and offers a bit of data to support the brevity and episodic nature of TV news reports, including that the average length of local TV news stories in the United States is thirty seconds (slide 37) and a study that analyzed ten thousand local and national TV news stories on international events and issues in 1999 found that only eight-four provided thematic framing (slide 44).

13. FWI, "Changing the Public Conversation," slide 24.

14. FWI, "Changing the Public Conversation," slide 48.

15. Beginning at this point in the e-workshop, *frame* and *story* and even *message* are used somewhat interchangeably. Since story is used most frequently, I consistently use that term for the remainder of this section. However, in other publications, including FWI's "Framing Public Issues," a frame is defined as the combination of most of these same elements (that is, metaphors or simplifying

models, messengers, visuals, and tone) as well as context and numbers (pp. 16–32). Moreover, the same work describes big ideas or values as a high-level frame that acts as primes for and map their reasoning onto lower-level frames such as an issue type or area and specific issues or policies (p. 5). To make matters yet more confusing, the same work states that all communication is storytelling and that effective stories must have the following elements in place: frames, messengers (an element of a frame?), evidence, cause and effect (p. 5).

16. Jason Patent and George Lakoff, "Conceptual Values: Bringing it Home to Values," www.cognitivepolicyworks.com/resource-center/planning-tools/frame-analysis-framing-tutorials/conceptual-levels-bringing-it-home-to-values/; Frameworks Institute, "Framing Public Issues," 5.

17. FWI, "Changing the Public Conversation," slide 53.

18. FWI, "Changing the Public Conversation," slide 57.

19. FWI, "Changing the Public Conversation," slide 60.

20. FWI, "Changing the Public Conversation," slide 63.

21. FWI, "Changing the Public Conversation," slide 72.

22. FWI, "Changing the Public Conversation," slide 74.

23. FWI, "Framing Public Issues," 21.

24. FWI, "Framing Public Issues," 20 (comment attributed to Marie Griesbraber of Oxfam America).

25. Patrick Reinsborough and Doyle Canning, *Re:Imagining Change: How to Use Story-based Strategy to Win Campaigns, Build Movements, and Change the World* (Oakland, CA: PM Press, 2010). While it is possible to download a full-color or black-and-white version of the book, I encourage readers to purchase it or make a donation of equivalent value via the website.

26. Reinsborough and Canning, *Re:Imagining Change*, 18.

27. Ibid., 17.

28. Ibid., 18.

29. Reinsborough and Canning, *Re:Imagining Change*, 122. At another point in the book, the authors point to "personal mannerism" and "political jargon" as two other examples of memes.

30. The fact that neither writes directly about these larger systems of power should not lead to the conclusion that they are unaware or uncritical of the systems.

31. See, for example, Antonio Gramsci, *The Antonio Gramsci Reader: Selected Writings, 1916–1935,* ed. David Forgacs (London: Lawrence and Wishart, 1999).

32. Reinsborough and Canning, *Re:Imagining Change*, 20, 22.

33. Reinsborough and Canning, *Re:Imagining Change*, 120.

34. While almost no one would question the fact that advertising is pervasive, Reinsborough and Canning include a statistic that provides dramatic evidence of just how pervasive it is: in 2004 the average US American child age two to eleven saw 25,600 television advertisements, and that year the average adult saw over twice that number, 52,600.

35. Reinsborough and Canning, *Re:Imagining Change,* 31–32.

36. Reinsborough and Canning, *Re:Imagining Change,* 36

37. Reinsborough and Canning, *Re:Imagining Change,* 60–61.

38. The worksheet can be downloaded from www.smartmeme.org/downloads/sMbattleofthestoryworksheet.pdf.

39. Reinsborough and Canning, *Re:Imagining Change,* 50.

40. Reinsborough and Canning, *Re:Imagining Change,* 53.

41. Reinsborough and Canning, *Re:Imagining Change,* 56.

42. Reinsborough and Canning, *Re:Imagining Change,* 57.

43. Reinsborough and Canning, *Re:Imagining Change,* 60.

44. Reinsborough and Canning, *Re:Imagining Change,* 63.

45. Ibid., 15. Also available from www.smartmeme.org/downloads/smartMeme.SBS.chart.pdf.

CASE G

Conclusion
Kids Are Priority One: Framing

The learning exercise that culminated the first part of Case G asked you to answer two questions.

- In what ways does the "Talking Points" document conform to or deviate from the guidelines about message framing in Kim Friedman's overview?
- Since it has been decided that a completely new document will be developed for the next round of advocacy to expand public funding, what are some specific ideas for that document's content and organization?

Compare your notes with the following description of what occurred. Give special attention to the degree to which the Kids Are Priority One Coalition's new document incorporated your ideas.

Implementing a New Frame

In preparation for the 2007 session of the Vermont legislature, Kim and her colleagues recognized the need to replace their 2005 "Talking Points" in light of what they had learned from the FrameWorks Institute. They realized the old document broke many if not most of the rules of good framing. For example, it began with a discussion of level-three policy issues: information about draw down funds, average daily membership, hours per week of services that some districts are offering, and so forth. More than half of the document was formulated as responses to concerns. That content might have been useful for an internal communication to prepare advocates to anticipate and respond to those concerns. But here it created a negative or defensive tone, perhaps even reinforcing fears. Even more of a problem than what was included is what was not. For example, there are no references to level-one values, such as future prosperity, nurturance, responsibility, or reciprocity, and no use of a simplifying metaphor or model.

The new document was a 2007 Legislative Priorities Fact Sheet titled "Ensuring a Healthy Future for Vermont's Children: The Importance of a Good Start." The document restates the coalition's primary policy goal as "continued use of public education funds for high-quality early education programs" (see appendix G.3). It also provides new clarity about the need for a system of standards to ensure consistent quality, a requirement for community planning, and ensured support for existing programs that meet those standards.

However, those policy solutions no longer appear at the beginning of the document. The new order and content reflect many of the guidelines in "Getting Our Message Across Effectively." For example, it begins with a level-one value presented in the title and the opening sentence: "Vermont is a place that cares for its children." This is followed by a simplifying model or metaphor: brain architecture and development. A brief problem statement then leads into the solutions. The tone is positive. Underlining is used to emphasize words and phrases such as *voluntary, families must have options, augment, not replace, encourage and facilitate partnerships,* and *community planning.* It concludes with a very effective paragraph (so much so that it might have been moved to the beginning) about "Vermont's ingenuity," "can-do attitude," and "planning today for our prosperity tomorrow."

The guidelines were also used for all the coalition's other communications. Where appropriate, it used recommendations not directly incorporated into the 2007 fact sheet, such as care in choosing the right messengers and telling stories that linked to their thematic frame. In preparation for meetings with legislators and other audiences, coalition members diligently reviewed and rehearsed how they would apply relevant guidelines.

While the coalition staff felt that the most important change in their strategy was this reframing of their message, there were other new elements. For example, they had helped convince the legislature to establish a short-term committee to study and report on pre-K education; once it was launched, the advocates focused on influencing what was included in the study and the committee's policy recommendations.

The coalition also strengthened its inside-outside strategy for the 2007 legislative session. For example, members built up their regional teams to do more targeted lobbying, and they enhanced their media work capacity so they could quickly address the concerns of specific legislators through letters to the editors of local newspapers.

Outcome

In June 2007 the multiyear effort of the coalition, its supporters, and allies paid off. They overcame the opposition. The new framing was especially effective in influencing Republican legislators. One of the legislators who had been originally opposed to the bill become one of its primary proponents. And with bipartisan support, the legislature passed what is now Act 62.[1] The vote in the house was an overwhelming margin of 99 to 45.

According to the KAP1 website, the "law solidifies the practice of using public education funds to support high-quality early education. School districts can contract with community-based early education programs, or they can establish on-site pre-k programs. Before starting an on-site program, school districts must undertake a community needs assessment."[2]

As with many new laws, the next step was to develop rules or regulations for its implementation. In the case of Act 62, two state agencies, the Department of Education and the Department of Children and Families, were responsible for managing the rule-making process. And KAP1, its supporters, and allies were prepared to engage in that process, well aware of the new political terrain they were working in. In the coalition's words: "When legislation as sweeping as Act 62 is enacted, there inevitably are growing pains associated with its implementation. This is especially true when two different systems—the public education system and the early care and education system (both its private and public components)—intersect in new ways as they do with Act 62. Ironing out issues as they arise becomes more difficult when state agencies responsible for implementation are short-staffed."[3]

The advocates mobilized broad community input into the rule-making process and prepared a document that identified challenges and proposed solutions. To ensure ongoing input, KAP1 joined an advisory group to work with the commissioners of the two state departments and their staff.

Notes

1. See http://www.leg.state.vt.us/docs/legdoc.cfm?URL=/docs/2008/actsACT 062.HTM.

2. "Pre-Kindergarten Education: 2012 Legislative Session," 2012, http://www. kidsarepriorityone.org/prekindergarten-education.html.

3. "Pre-Kindergarten Education: 2012 Legislative Session."

Appendix G.3 2007 Legislative Priorities *Fact Sheet:* Pre-K

L-*ive the Promise*

130 Birge Street
Brattleboro, Vermont 05301

Tel. 802-348-9879
Fax. 802-348-7294
info@kidsarepriorityone.org
www.kidsarepriorityone.org

2007 Legislative Priorities
Fact Sheet:
Pre-K

Ensuring a Healthy Future for Vermont's Children
The Importance of a Good Start

Vermont is a place that cares for its children. As we look for ways to prepare them for the future, science has something to add to the discussion. It tells us that a child's early years are crucial because early experiences shape the developing architecture of a young, maturing brain. As it emerges, the quality of that architecture establishes either a sturdy or a fragile foundation for all of the development and behavior that follows.

Nurturing interactions with adults build a strong foundation for future growth and development. When relationships are supportive, responsive and predictable, they increase the odds of desirable outcomes. When communities make high-quality early education available, where their young citizens gain additional opportunities to have positive relationships with adults, they are putting in place a system that can help lay the right foundation. For example, well-trained caregivers and early childhood educators can build positive, caring relationships with children that literally wire the brain for later learning. In addition, skill builds on skill so getting things right the first time is easier than trying to fix them later.

The demand for high-quality early care and education programs (including preschool) far outstrips Vermont's capacity to meet that demand, and existing options are limited. As a result, many children end up in mediocre or sub-standard arrangements that do little to contribute to healthy brain architecture. Cuts in federal funding, reduced or level funding at the state level, and few employer-sponsored initiatives contribute to the conditions that plague Vermont's child development services: low salaries, inadequate benefits, insufficient start-up funds, limited access to affordable higher education, and outdated child care subsidy reimbursement rates. These factors explain why overall capacity in regulated child care/preschool can only meet 50%-60% of estimated need (Vermont Child Care Advisory Board, 2006 Legislative Report).

One solution lies in a state policy that has already been successful for our children. It allows local communities, on a voluntary basis, to use public education dollars to provide high-quality pre-k programs, thus expanding options for Vermont families.

- Approximately 60% of communities statewide currently offer some publicly-funded pre-school programs, with many others moving in this direction.
- 25% of 3- and 4-year old children in the state are already in such programs.
- Public education dollars provide much-needed funding to early education programs to help make them affordable for parents.

Appendix G.3 Cont.

The Kids Are Priority One Coalition supports this forward thinking policy. Join us in calling on the legislature to*:*
- Support continued use of public education funds for high-quality early education programs;
- Set standards that ensure consistency across the state;
- Require community planning to ensure public education funds support qualified *existing* quality early childhood development programs.

We offer the following **guidelines** as policymakers at the state and local level clarify the use of public education funds by counting preschool children in a school district's Average Daily Membership (ADM):

➢ Children's participation in any early education program funded by public education funds must remain voluntary.

➢ Families must have options in terms of where they decide to enroll their children. This makes a mixed delivery system (public/private, center-based/family-based, etc.) even more important.

➢ Public education funds should be combined with those from other state sources, federal monies and parents' fees to augment, not replace, the resources available for early care and education services. Top priorities should include increasing access among all children to high-quality services and improving the quality of early care and education programs by increasing compensation of early childhood educators.

➢ Public education funds should be used to support qualified, existing early care and education programs, thereby improving the availability, quality and affordability of early care and education.

➢ Laws/regulations should encourage and facilitate partnerships between public school districts and qualified child care centers and family child care homes.

➢ Laws/regulations should require and provide resources for a community planning and needs assessment process that moves communities towards equal access to high-quality early care and education for all children.

➢ School districts should be permitted to establish agreements with other school districts and/or community-based early care and education programs if parents need to use services outside the school district.

➢ Since the use of public education funds requires high-quality standards, resources should be provided to individuals, programs and communities to enable them to reach those standards.

Let's use Vermont ingenuity to find new, creative ways to meet the needs of all young children in Vermont. With a "can-do" attitude and responsible planning today for our prosperity tomorrow, we can meet the challenge of providing and funding adequate early childhood development services.

For more information, contact Barbara Postman, Kids Are Priority One Legislative Director, Voices for Vermont's Children, (802) 229-6377, bpostman@voicesforvtkids.org.

Kids Are Priority One is Vermont's a statewide early childhood coalition
of individuals, businesses and organizations committed to ensuring that every child in Vermont gets a
good start.

January 2007

CASE H

Oxfam America Climate Change Campaign: Monitoring, Evaluation, and Learning

Gabrielle Watson, coauthor

This is the second case study of Oxfam America's campaign for an international climate change agreement that is a fair and safe deal for poor countries and communities.

Case E, which precedes chapter 7, introduced Oxfam America as the advocates, and the context, policy analysis, and goals of its Climate Change Campaign (CCC). The exercise for that case asked you to help map the relevant political institutions and actors and later described the campaign team's actual analysis.

It is assumed you have read all of Case E. Building on that information, the first part of this case describes the campaign's strategy for the year leading up to the 2009 United Nations Climate Change Summit in Copenhagen and an innovate approach of embedding a key member of Oxfam's Learning, Evaluation, and Accountability Department (LEAD) in the campaign team. This enhanced the campaign's capacity to concurrently plan and implement its strategy and its monitoring, evaluation, and learning (MEL) processes.

The learning exercise asks you to help think through a MEL plan for the 2009 phase of the campaign. The conclusion of the case that follows chapter 10 allows you to compare your ideas with the actual MEL plan and to learn how it evolved as the campaign was under way. The conclusion also includes a brief overview of the campaign's outcomes, Oxfam's assessment of its efforts, and a few of the lessons it has begun to apply in its next major campaign.

Strategy

Oxfam's Climate Change Campaign (CCC) strategy was driven by its policy goals and by the political realities of its immediate and ultimate targets: the

US government and the United Nations Framework Convention on Climate Change (UNFCCC) Conference of the Parties (COP) in Copenhagen. The strategy was also shaped by Oxfam's macroassessment of the campaign's larger historical, economic, and political context and its more specific assessment of possible allies and opponents. These were described in the first case.

As with all Oxfam campaigns, the CCC strategy was expected to be adaptive and evolving. At key moments, the strategy was reviewed, clarified, and refined in response to changes in the external environment (including new opportunities or obstacles that result from some of those changes) and to new knowledge and insights gained through the campaign's implementation. One such moment was at the start of 2009, at the same point that Oxfam's LEAD unit assigned one of its MEL staff to participate as a full member of the CCC team.

Oxfam's campaign strategic framework emphasizes that a clear theory of change (ToC) is essential for planning and monitoring and evaluating advocacy campaigns. Thus, one of the first tasks of the new MEL member of the team was to facilitate a step-back session to review progress to date and to clarify the CCC's ToC. In different internal documents, it was represented as a general diagram (see figure H.1) and a more detailed chart (appendix H.1).

The chart version of the ToC in appendix H.1 provides a fairly complete description of the Oxfam's strategy. It is best understood by reading from

Figure H.1 CCC theory of change

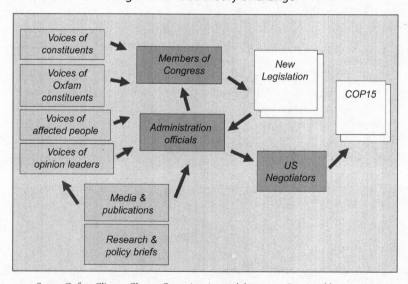

Source: Oxfam Climate Change Campaign, internal document. Reprinted by permission.

right to left, beginning in the seventh column, "Ultimate Outcomes." The theory was that a fair and safe global deal, will happen only if the advocates can achieve the second outcome in that same column: US climate negotiators commit to the position that the United States and other developed countries should go "first, farthest and fastest" and that there should be adequate support for adaptation financing for developing countries.

Oxfam's ToC was that US negotiators will fully commit if two other outcomes are achieved. One is the third item in the ultimate outcomes column: US policy (legislation) is adopted with domestic and international commitments to funding adaptation, funding clean technology, adequate emissions targets, equitable solutions, and green jobs for economically depressed areas of the United States.

The other requisite outcome is the first item in the next column to the left, "Intermediate Outcomes": that the US administration (president and relevant members of the Cabinet) has taken "a positive stand."

The theory was that those outcomes will happen if all the other outcomes in the sixth column are achieved.

US policy (legislation) that supports the necessary commitments will happen if key deciders in the House and Senate, working with the administration, push through the necessary bills before the COP meeting in Copenhagen.

Those deciders will push the bills if champions in the House and Senate write the bills so that they contain the necessary language or provisions.

The US administration would take a positive stand if key administrative officials, working with key deciders in Congress, put forward strong climate policy proposals.

The theory was that these outcomes will happen if the six lower-level intermediate outcomes in the fifth column are achieved. Those intermediate outcomes will happen if the five outputs in the fourth column are achieved, and those outputs will happen if the advocates successfully use the inputs and the combination of activities listed in the first, second, and third columns.

Those activities constitute the core of the CCC's strategy and can be clustered as follows:

1. Continue research to document impacts of climate change and refine policy arguments. The CCC plan was to expand on the evidence and arguments in the Oxfam International policy paper, adding and refining them for a US audience that includes the general public, Oxfam's own supporters and allies, and especially policy makers.[1] The campaign had two policy researchers dedicated to this task. Oxfam's publications unit would provide expert support.

2. Engage and strengthen poor countries and communities. Soon after Oxfam was founded in the early 1970s, staff made two choices that have guided their work since that time. One was to provide development support through long-term partnerships with local nongovernmental organizations

and community organizations. Thus the CCC plan included helping partners in three countries (Cambodia, Ethiopia, and Peru) to increase national awareness of and influence their governments' policies and plans related to climate change and adaptation. Working through its regional offices, Oxfam could provide funding and could collaborate with the partners to ensure the poorest and most vulnerable communities have a meaningful voice when policies and plans are being formulated, and that as a result, their needs are prioritized in those decisions.

Moreover, according to the plan, those processes would identify effective spokespeople from the affected communities, who in turn would be invited to speak at events and to policy makers in the United States. The process would also build the capacity of countries' delegations to UN climate change conventions (involving government and nongovernmental organization members) to be more effective in pressuring the United States and other industrial countries, partially because they would have demonstrated their own commitments to change and have replicable models for adaptation processes.

3. Further strengthen and mobilize Oxfam's US support base. The other defining choice Oxfam's staff made in the early 1970s was not to accept funding from the US government but instead to develop broad-based, grassroots support for its work: its partnerships for development in the global South and its advocacy focused on the US government, World Bank, World Trade Organization, and other multigovernmental bodies. The CCC could plan to inform and engage many of the thousands of individuals who donate money or volunteers with fund-raising and consciousness-raising events (such as hunger banquets on college campuses and in communities), primarily through e-mail and web-based tools. One element of the CCC plan was to make those tools more dynamic and expand Oxfam's use of new media or social networking.

Through recent advocacy campaigns, Oxfam had built up new infrastructure for grassroots mobilization. Four field organizers were stationed around the country. The lead organizer had set up Oxfam Action Corps groups of advocacy volunteers, each with leaders who had been trained through national workshops. There are currently groups in fourteen cities across the country, and the field organizers support the work of those in their regions. In addition, for each of the previous six years, Oxfam's CHANGE leadership development program had selected about fifty college students to attend a summer workshop. Once back at their campuses they served as leaders, mobilizing support for Oxfam's advocacy and often initiating an ongoing Oxfam club. The CCC plan involved using all those resources, especially the organizers and volunteers from the districts of legislators the campaign would be targeting.

In its first year, the CCC launched a new group of supporters called Sisters on the Planet (SoP). Members were recruited by highlighting the fact that women and children are disproportionately harmed by the effects of climate change. While the effort reached out to women as well as men at the grass roots, there was also a concerted effort to involve women at the "grass tops": leaders of national organizations and state governments, celebrities, and others who were identified as SoP Ambassadors. The CCC plan for 2009 was to use the current ambassadors to help recruit others, including some women members of Congress, and to engage them all in events and targeted lobbying. One key event was a national meeting in Washington, DC, and a day of lobbying timed around International Women's Day.

4. Strengthen current alliances and build new ones. As described in Case E, Oxfam identified eight types or groups of key influencers they might collaborate with in pushing for adaptation funding and other pro-poor climate policies. The CCC plan assigned key staff to build on existing relationships or develop new relationships with each group.

The plan was to use several different approaches. One of the main methods of building relationships with environmental organizations was to join one of the largest climate change advocacy coalitions in the country. One of Oxfam's objectives was "to put human impact/adaptation onto [the coalition's] platform" and thus expand the base of support for their policy goals. "We gain more influence by being involved and can cultivate relationships with other groups we need as allies."[2] The coalition was also seen as a means to gather and share information about the policy makers and to engage in some of the crucial legislative districts without having to invest large amounts of its resources.

With businesses, the CCC plan was to work with a new coalition of progressive businesses. Oxfam was able to educate its members and included human impact/adaptation as a core element of its policy position.

With other international development organizations, Oxfam already had long-standing alliances from previous campaigns and advocacy focused on international aid, debt, and trade policies. Thus the CCC plan was to provide leadership in a relatively new Climate and Development Network.

With the other key influencers, women and women's organizations, faith-based groups, Hispanic and Latino organizations, the CCC plan was to use funded allies, a relatively new approach that had emerged from its recent campaign focused on the international food assistance and other elements of the US Farm Bill. Oxfam would provide small grants to organizations that had the interest and potential to influence key members of Congress, but lacked resources for that purpose. For example, the CCC plan included funding a national women's organization to carry out outreach, education, and lobbying work in key legislative districts. Some of the other funded allies were focused on influencing a single member of Congress, in some cases with the hope of converting that legislator into a "champion" for Oxfam's policy position.

With US domestic organizations focused on adaptation and green jobs in their own communities, the CCC plan was to work through Oxfam's regional office that supports pro-poor development programs in the Southeast. It developed numerous partnerships, and one or more of those organizations might be supported as a funded ally.

With national security experts and organizations, the CCC plan was to learn more about the different options and build relationships based on that assessment.

5. Achieve massive earned media coverage. Oxfam has its own media relations office, and one of its staff members was dedicated to the CCC. The plan was to promote press coverage when key policy documents were released, various events (such as policy dialogues) were held, when representatives from poor communities in the Global South visited, during testimony before Congress, and so forth. In addition, the plan was to have at least one major stunt that would draw media attention.

6. Effectively lobby legislators in their districts and on the Hill. The CCC team included staff dedicated to government relations, responsible for rigorously tracking the formulation and progress of climate change legislation in Congress and identifying key legislators and staff members who would support their position or who needed to be influenced.

Depending on the situation, the CCC would draw upon Oxfam's own supporters and allies to put pressure on legislators in their districts and in DC. Field organizers, Action Corps groups, change leaders, members of funded allies such as the League of Women Voters, and others would help amplify the voices of constituent and other grassroots citizens. Their support for a fair and safe deal would be the focus of local events, resolutions, petitions, media, and so on. SoP Ambassadors and other grass-top supporters, as well as CCC staff, would meet with the legislators and their aides in the Capitol.

As an extension of the latter, key CCC staff would build relationships with the congressional staff responsible for drafting and redrafting legislation as it moved through the process from formulation to enactment. The objective would be for the relationships to be close and trusted enough to insert CCC policy language into the bills.

LEARNING EXERCISE

You are still a member of the CCC team. The political map of key policy makers and actors was completed, and the team has now clarified its ToC and made a plan for achieving the various outputs and outcomes the theory indicates are necessary to achieve a safe and fair deal in Copenhagen. You have now been asked to prepare for a follow-up meeting.

The MEL member of the team will facilitate. As preparation, you and the other campaign team members are to do the following:

1. Based on your ToC, make a list of five to ten elements (outputs or outcomes) of the campaign you think might be most important or useful to monitor and evaluate during 2009.
2. For at least two of those elements, try to identify (a) one or more indicators that would allow you to judge whether the campaign has achieved or made meaningful progress toward that output or outcome; and (b) the types of evidence or data you might use to assess progress or achievement.

Make a set of notes now or after reading chapter 10. The conclusion of the case follows the chapter and will allow you to compare your ideas with the actual plan and gain insights into how such a plan evolves along with the campaign.

Notes

1. Kate Raworth, "Adapting to Climate Change: What's Needed in Poor Countries, and Who Should Pay" (Oxfam Briefing Paper 104, Oxford, UK: Oxfam International, 2007).
2. Internal campaign document.

Appendix H.1 Oxfam America Climate Change Campaign theory of change "logical framework"

Inputs	Activities	Activities	Outputs	Intermediate Outcomes	Intermediate Outcomes	Ultimate Outcomes
	Carry-out research that helps move towards our campaign goals	Sharp synthesis of research to shape policies		**International Moments** and international figures (e.g., ambassadors, foreign ministries, etc.) put pressure on Congress & Administration through media and direct pressure		**Fair & Safe Global Deal**
	Develop messaging guide	Amplify voices in strategic districts (local resolutions, sign-on letters, local media, member events)	Hard-hitting messaging around CC as a humanitarian crisis with high costs today real opportunities for US global leadership and economic development becomes part of public debate.	**US Administration** takes positive stand in climate negotiations		
Oxfam Staff	Collect and produce human impact stories from the regions	Allies representing different voices (Latino, Black, Women, Enviro, Health, Faith) cultivate champions and pressure fence sitters in Congress		**Developing Country Governments & Vulnerable People** speak out slowly, supported by Oxfam in-region and in the US		**US Climate Negotiators Commit:** • US & developed countries go First, Fastest, Farthest • Adaptation $
	Polling and message testing to refine our messages for our constituents and target segments			1,000's of **Key Voices** in the US (Faith, African American, Latino, Women, Health, Security, Enviro's, Gulf Coast, Development NGOs) demonstrate broad support on equitable and fair adaptation to legislators in-district and in DC	**Key Administration Officials** develop and put forward strong climate policy proposals	
Alliances	Support southern delegations and southern voices at international events	Coordinated Field & Hill lobby of key targets	Sisters on the Planet Ambassadors are willing and able to wield influence on key targets are recruited			
Constituents	Cultivate and secure Sisters on the Planet Ambassadors & Celebrities	Develop policy positions on adaptation funding, technology transfer, insurance, and reduced deforestation	Key targets reached and influenced to be champions	Massive **Earned Media** exposure that gets us into the climate change discourse		**US Policy Says:** Domestic & International: • $ for adaptation • $ for clean tech • Adequate emissions targets • Equitable solutions • Green jobs for economically depressed areas of U.S.
	Engage with allies to bring the message of human costs and the need for climate adaptation at home and abroad	Actively scan for legislative opportunities to address our issues	Draft legislative language provided for Congressional staff to forward proposals	A broad spectrum of **US Companies** to advocate for strong adaptation policy in Congress & Administration	**Key deciders** in House and Senate push through strong climate bill & national climate legislation addressing adaptation by Fall of 2009	
Money	In-District engagement with Congressional target via allies, SOPs, Field Organizers, media, Action Corps, Change Leaders, constituents, etc.	Oxfam and allies elevate voices of impacted communities	Vulnerable communities are more directly engaged in policy debate at national and international level			
Regional Partners	Policy symposiums to educate new and potential allies to join campaign efforts	Oxfam uses celebrities and a highly dynamic website and new media to engage new supporters & mobilize constituents		**Public Discourse** on climate change increasingly reflects Oxfam's analysis & proposals & a significant SHIFT in the terms of debate to focus on the human impacts of CC	Senate & House **Champions** put forward language co-sponsor strong climate legislation	
	Rigorous tracking of legislation: up-to-date target information					

Management, Planning & Tracking Activities & Outputs | **Influence & Results (MEL)**

10

Advocacy Evaluation and Learning

MONITORING, EVALUATION, AND LEARNING (MEL) WERE INTRODUCED IN CHAPTER 3 as processes that are crucial to successful advocacy.[1] They are relevant at multiple points in an advocacy campaign or initiative. At the beginning, attention to MEL processes can:

- help clarify and focus a campaign's overall plan, including its long- and shorter-term goals and methods.

During the advocacy, MEL processes can:

- stimulate ongoing assessment of and adjustments in the plan, and generate data to inform decisions.

At key moments during and following the advocacy, MEL processes can:

- provide data that are essential to making judgments about the level of success;
- encourage accountability to the larger organization, supporters (including funding sources), and the communities or populations most directly affected by the policy issue; and
- initiate and facilitate reflection and the synthesis of knowledge that can improve future advocacy.

Despite all of those benefits, the fast pace and scarce resources typical of advocacy campaigns and organizations often result in limited or no attention to MEL. Oxfam America is among the minority of advocacy organizations that are making a significant investment in these processes, which is one reason its Climate Change Campaign is this chapter's case. However, whatever the level of investment in advocacy MEL, efforts to monitor and evaluate advocacy confront the fact that politics and policy change are highly complex processes. As Paul O'Brian, Oxfam America's vice president for policy and campaigns, put it in a foundation report:

> Too many NGOs [nongovernmental organizations] treat policy change as a Newtonian science. Weaned on "logical frameworks," they seek to identify and measure the linear causes that will lead to specific policy effects. The reality is that policy change is better understood through the new sciences. Policy change rarely happens simply because NGO A applies force B to [get] outcome C. Policy change happens when critical masses form to create tipping points that dissipate opposition, shift momentum, and coincide with political climate change. And so monitoring and evaluating is increasingly trying to comprehend and measure issues that are more about politics than logic—relationships, alliance cohesion, nimbleness, timing, momentum, ideological resistance, resource implications—concepts often hard for NGOs to swallow with our humanitarian ("apolitical") roots.[2]

Given the fast pace and limited resources of advocacy campaigns and the complex reality of politics and policy change, it may not be surprising that monitoring and evaluation experts have given limited attention to advocacy campaigns. Fortunately, that is changing. A reasonable body of literature now exists that provides relevant concepts, methods, and tools for advocates to draw upon. Much of it is accessible online.[3]

One of the most useful contributions to this emerging literature by one of the leaders in the field of innovative MEL practice is A *User's Guide to Advocacy Evaluation Planning* by Julia Coffman.[4] According to Coffman, while "advocacy has long been considered 'too hard to measure,' . . . the main barrier preventing more organizations from using evaluation is lack of familiarity with how to think about and design evaluations of advocacy efforts."[5] The guide addresses this barrier by providing a set of steps, concepts, and tools for designing an evaluation. These are summarized in the following section, "Best Practice Guidelines for Evaluation Design," along with examples that are discussed again in the section "The Role of Advocates" on page 235.

On the other hand, in another important contribution to the emerging literature, "The Elusive Craft of Evaluating Advocacy," authors Steven

Teles and Mark Schmitt argue that the main barrier to advocacy evaluation is not lack of design guidelines but rather the complex nature of politics and policy change.[6] They offer numerous insights into that complexity and several unconventional and insightful recommendations about what should be evaluated and who should do it. The section "Why Evaluation Designs Are Not Always Best Practice" beginning on page 232 summarizes some of their key ideas and arguments.

"The Role of Advocates" section offers ideas about how advocacy organization staff might think about and approach their MEL processes, drawing on ideas from the previously cited works. One of the key ideas is to give increased attention to learning, the L dimension of MEL.

The final section of the chapter, and indeed the book, "Using Multiple Maps" (page 239), returns to one of the major ideas discussed in chapter 2 and repeated throughout: advocates should know and be able to use multiple maps or frameworks for observing, thinking, and acting that include evaluating and learning. The evaluation framework described in chapter 3 is reintroduced because it illuminates types of outcomes most others omit or obscure.

Best Practice Guidelines for Evaluation Design

Coffman's user's guide offers a clear, comprehensive and yet concise set of steps and corresponding concepts and tools for planning an evaluation.[7] It grew out of her work as a senior consultant with the Harvard Family Research Project and later as director of the Center for Evaluation Innovation, which specializes in "areas that are hard to measure, like advocacy, communications and systems change" (www.evaluationinnovation.org). She founded the American Evaluation Association's interest group on advocacy and policy change and is a widely recognized leader in this emerging field of evaluation practice.

The guide recommends four steps for developing an evaluation plan, which are cogently presented in the downloadable "Advocacy Evaluation Planning Worksheet."[8]

Step one: Focus. This includes deciding who will use the evaluation, the advocates themselves, their partners, their funders, or others. It also includes deciding how it will be used, either as strategic learning (to inform a campaign as it evolves and to generate knowledge relevant for future advocacy) or accountability (to the organization, funders, and the public). Finally, focusing involves identifying the questions the users want answered.

Step two: Map. This involves developing a visual map, theory of change, or logic model that illustrates how a chain of advocacy activities results in the desired change. One of the most useful aspects of the *User's Guide* is the composite logic model, which attempts to identify most of the possible elements of a map. See figure 10.1 (the model is the second section of the worksheet).

At the top of the model are impacts, divided into two types of long-term change the advocates seek to achieve: improved services and systems and positive social and physical conditions.[9] According to the model, those impacts require the advocates to achieve one or more of seven possible policy goals. These offer a more detailed and quite useful way of dividing up the four stages of the policy making cycle described in chapter 7.

According to the model, the advocates' policy goal(s) will be achieved through some combination of interim outcomes, which are clustered in the lower right portion of the model as changes in advocacy capacity and changes related to policy. And those outcomes will be achieved through some combination of activities/tactics, which are clustered in the lower left portion of the model as either types of communications and outreach or as types of politics and policy.

The guide includes a definition for each activity/tactic, interim outcome, policy change, and impact. According to Coffman, "Rather than start the mapping process with a blank piece of paper, the model offers a menu of possible strategy elements to choose from." The planners can "literally trace or highlight a 'pathway' through the model."[10]

Step three: Prioritize. Advocacy organizations rarely have enough evaluation resources to address each element in their pathway. Thus it is important to ask questions such as, What do the evaluation's users (most) want to know? What is the advocacy effort's unique contribution?

Step four: Design. This involves identifying "measures" (also called "metrics," "indicators," or "benchmarks") which, when captured and tracked over time, will signal whether advocacy strategy elements have been successfully implemented or achieved."[11] The guide includes suggested measures for each activity/tactic, interim outcome, policy change, and impact and discusses different methods for collecting and analyzing data necessary to measure those changes.

In general, activities/tactics have *measures of effort* and count *what and how much* each produces. "Although these measures capture what was done, they do little to explain how well it was done or how well it worked. . . . Because they count tangible products, people or events, [they

Figure 10.1 Advocacy Evalution Planning Worksheet

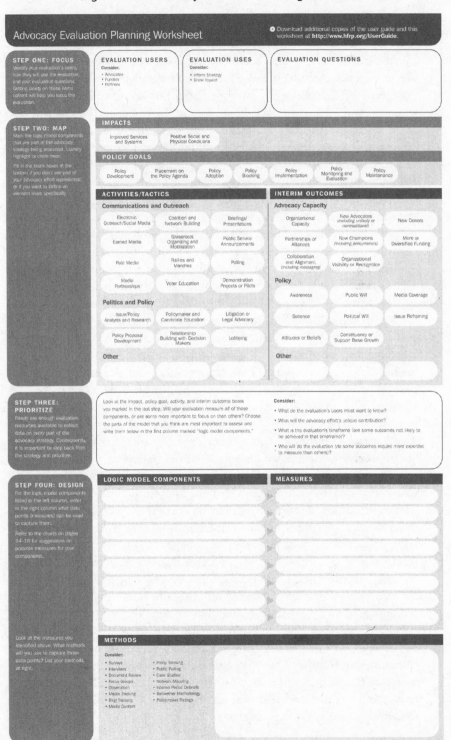

Advocacy Evaluation Planning Worksheet

⊙ Download additional copies of the user guide and this worksheet at http://www.hfrp.org/UserGuide.

STEP ONE: FOCUS
Identify your evaluation's users, how they will use the evaluation, and your evaluation questions. Getting clarity on these items upfront will help you focus the evaluation.

EVALUATION USERS
Consider:
- Advocates
- Funders
- Partners

EVALUATION USES
Consider:
- Inform Strategy
- Show Impact

EVALUATION QUESTIONS

STEP TWO: MAP
Mark the logic model components that are part of the advocacy strategy being evaluated. Usually highlight or circle them.

Fill in the blank boxes at the bottom if you don't see part of your advocacy effort represented, or if you want to define an element more specifically.

IMPACTS
- Improved Services and Systems
- Positive Social and Physical Conditions

POLICY GOALS
- Policy Development
- Placement on the Policy Agenda
- Policy Adoption
- Policy Blocking
- Policy Implementation
- Policy Monitoring and Evaluation
- Policy Maintenance

ACTIVITIES/TACTICS

Communications and Outreach
- Electronic Outreach/Social Media
- Coalition and Network Building
- Briefings/Presentations
- Earned Media
- Grassroots Organizing and Mobilization
- Public Service Announcements
- Paid Media
- Rallies and Marches
- Polling
- Media Partnerships
- Voter Education
- Demonstration Projects or Pilots

Politics and Policy
- Issue/Policy Analysis and Research
- Policymaker and Candidate Education
- Litigation or Legal Advocacy
- Policy Proposal Development
- Relationship Building with Decision Makers
- Lobbying

Other

INTERIM OUTCOMES

Advocacy Capacity
- Organizational Capacity
- New Advocates (including unlikely or nontraditional)
- New Donors
- Partnerships or Alliances
- New Champions (including policymakers)
- More or Diversified Funding
- Collaboration and Alignment (including messaging)
- Organizational Visibility or Recognition

Policy
- Awareness
- Public Will
- Media Coverage
- Salience
- Political Will
- Issue Reframing
- Attitudes or Beliefs
- Constituency or Support Base Growth

Other

STEP THREE: PRIORITIZE
Rarely are enough evaluation resources available to collect data on every part of the advocacy strategy. Consequently, it is important to step back from the strategy and prioritize.

Look at the impact, policy goal, activity, and interim outcome boxes you marked in the last step. Will your evaluation measure all of those components, or are some more important to focus on than others? Choose the parts of the model that you think are most important to assess and write them below in the first column marked "logic model components."

Consider:
- What do the evaluation's users most want to know?
- What will the advocacy effort's unique contribution?
- What is the evaluation's timeframe (are some outcomes not likely to be achieved in that timeframe)?
- Who will do the evaluation (do some outcomes require more expertise to measure than others)?

STEP FOUR: DESIGN
For the logic model components listed in the left column, enter in the right column what data points (measures) can be used to capture them.

Refer to the charts on pages 14–16 for suggestions on possible measures for your components.

LOGIC MODEL COMPONENTS

MEASURES

Look at the measures you identified above. What methods will you use to capture those data points? List your methods at right.

METHODS

Consider:
- Surveys
- Interviews
- Document Review
- Focus Groups
- Observation
- Media Tracking
- Blog Tracking
- Media Content
- Policy Tracking
- Public Polling
- Case Studies
- Network Mapping
- Bellwether Methodology
- Policymaker Ratings

are] the easiest of all evaluation measure to identify and track." For example, the guide's suggested measures for "coalition and network building" are "number of coalition members ... constituency types represented in the coalition (e.g., business, nonprofit) [and] number of coalition meetings held and attendance."[12]

In contrast, interim outcomes have measures of effect that "demonstrate changes that happen—usually within target audiences—as a result of advocacy efforts." For example, the guide suggests that a number of the policy outcomes be measured in terms of the percentage of audience members whose knowledge or behavior is consistent with what the advocates seek to achieve. Awareness is the percentage with "knowledge of an issue." Salience is the percentage for "saying an issue is important to them." Attitudes and beliefs is the percentage with "favorable attitudes." And public will is the percentage "willing to take action on behalf of a specific issue." The guide suggests an additional measure that can be used for two of those outcomes: "activity for portions of the website with advocacy-related information" for awareness and "attendance at advocacy events (e.g., public forums, marches, rallies)" for public will.[13]

Suggested measures of progress toward or achievement of policy goals are relatively straightforward. For example, successful placement (of the desired policy) on the policy agenda can be measured by "policies formally introduced (bills, ballot measures, regulations, administrative policies)." The guide suggests two indicators for success with regard to policy maintenance—"funding levels sustained for policies or programs," and "eligibility levels maintained for policies or programs."[14]

The guide suggests that the measures for impact depend on the specific policy goal. But it does provide some examples of possible measures. There are four for improved services or systems: "more programs offered; easier access to programs and services; higher quality services; [and] more affordable services." The five examples for the other long-term impact, positive social and physical conditions, reflect five different policy goals: "reduced greenhouse gas emissions, improved kindergarten readiness; reduced teen driving accidents; reduced dropout rates; [and] increased percentage of minority students attending college."[15]

The final section of the guide focuses on methods. "Some choices will be obvious, as some measures can be collected using only one method. Other measures may be captured using several possible methods, and each may carry a different price tag or level of effort. It may be necessary to further prioritize the list of measures based on the number and types of methods required to capture them."[16]

The guide lists a series of common methods, including surveys, interviews, focus groups, document review, and observation. Polling random samples of advocacy stakeholders about their knowledge, attitudes and behaviors, and case studies of individual advocacy strategies and results, are also listed in this category. The guide then describes six other less common methods used for advocacy evaluation. They are media tracking, policy tracking, network mapping, and "several new methods that have been developed specifically for advocacy evaluation, including bellwether methodology, policymaker ratings, and intense-period debriefs."

For example, bellwether methodology was developed to track political will. Bellwethers are influential and well informed about the politics surrounding a broad range of policy issues that include the advocates' priority issues. They may be policy makers (or key aides), journalists, researchers, experienced advocates, or others who "are knowledgeable and innovative thought leaders whose opinions about policy issues carry substantial weight and predictive value in the policy arena."[17] The method involves selective sampling to ensure a range of different types of bellwethers, none of whom is specifically engaged with the advocates' issue. They are then interviewed using a set of questions that first elicit an unprompted list of the issues they think are at the top of the policy agenda; this allows the evaluator to determine if and how highly the bellwethers rank the focus of the advocacy. The interview then explores the bellwethers' familiarity with and opinions about that focus.

A second example of an advocacy-specific method is the intense period debriefing. The process captures data that are in the heads of the advocates themselves, in a way that recognizes and respects the fact they often have little time to "pause for interviews and reflection." A debriefing is a focus group discussion convened after a period of high-intensity activity, such as the months preceding the passage or defeat of one of the advocates' policy goals. The process involves "participation from key groups and individuals engaged in different levels of 'spheres of influence' surrounding decision makers, . . . providing ways for individuals in the 'inner circle' of those spheres [to] tell the story of what happened behind the scenes."[18]

As a whole, the guide offers a solid orientation to advocacy evaluation and a useful set of concepts, tools, and methods that advocacy organizations and campaigns can easily use as they develop their MEL plan. Some of the specific benefits, as well as a potential limitation, are discussed later in the chapter.

Why Evaluation Designs Are Not Always Best Practice

"The Elusive Craft of Evaluating Advocacy" offers a strong critique of what Teles and Schmitt characterize as "a growing industry"[19] of organizations and experts who are refining old approaches and developing new ones to advocacy evaluation. Teles is a political scientist and professor of public policy at the University of Maryland and a fellow of the New America Foundation. Schmitt is a senior research fellow at the New America Foundation; his prior experience includes serving as policy director for former US senator Bill Bradley. Thus their analysis draws on extensive qualitative research about and practice in the field of policy change.

According to Teles and Schmitt, the "form of evaluation based on assessing the theory of change underlying an initiative" and other "sophisticated tools [is] almost wholly unhelpful." The reason for this harsh assessment is

> because advocacy, even when carefully nonpartisan and based in research, is inherently political, and it's the nature of politics that events evolve rapidly and in a nonlinear fashion, so an effort that doesn't seem to be working might suddenly bear fruit, or one that seemed to be on track can suddenly lose momentum. Because of these peculiar features of politics, few if any best practices can be identified through the sophisticated methods that have been developed to evaluate the delivery of services. Advocacy evaluation should be seen, therefore, as a form of trained judgment—a craft requiring judgment and tacit knowledge—rather than as a scientific method. To be a skilled advocacy evaluator requires a deep knowledge of and feel for the politics of the issues, strong networks of trust among the key players, an ability to assess organizational quality, and a sense for the right time horizon against which to measure accomplishments. In particular, evaluators must recognize the complex, foggy chains of causality in politics, which make evaluating particular projects—as opposed to entire fields or organizations—almost impossible.[20]

The article continues with a series of insightful points about those "peculiar features of politics," and thus about the nature of advocacy. Three of the points are captured in the following:

> The American political system is profoundly wired for stasis, and competition for limited agenda space is fierce. In an overwhelming

percentage of cases, organizations fail to get substantial traction on their agendas for change.[21]

Items often wind up on the political agenda by random and chaotic routes that may have little to do with advocacy campaigns. If it is hard to know whether advocacy played any part in a policy outcome, it is harder still to know whether any particular organization or strategy made the difference.[22]

Because issues spill over from one domain to another (issues of poverty affect health and education), particular issues are almost impossible to disentangle from general ideas and broader governing philosophies. Consequently, the fortunes of issue-specific mobilization may be due to actions conducted within that domain, but they may be reinforced by mobilization in another domain entirely, by generic, ideological activity, or by more neutral scholarly research (Ibid., 42).[23]

They offer many more such points. For example, even when it is possible to identify an important contribution by one or more advocacy organizations, it is unwise to assume that the strategies or tactics that worked for that effort will be equally useful in the future. Conditions change. Effective advocacy often results in the mobilization of opposing forces. A disruptive innovation—such as online petitions—loses its impact as more organizations adopt the approach. There can also be long periods when there is little visible (read measurable) action on a policy issue, but quiet ongoing efforts by advocates make it possible to respond if and when the situation changes.

It is important to pay attention to the value an advocacy organization provides indirectly to others and the benefits it receives from the actions of others. Identification and analysis of such interactions requires a unit of analysis that is larger than a specific advocacy campaign or effort.

For those and similar reasons, Teles and Schmitt make what they refer to as a "radical recommendation": evaluate the advocates, not the advocacy. "We believe that the proper focus for evaluation is the long-term adaptability, strategic capacity, and ultimately influence of organizations themselves."[24] They define strategic capacity as "the ability to read the shifting environment of politics for subtle signals of change, to understand the opposition, and to adapt deftly."[25]

The authors suggest that one way to evaluate the advocates is to evaluate their relationships within policy change networks, more specifically through an examination of "network centrality" or of which actors play vital roles in issue networks. While there are challenges to gathering such data, "members of policy networks generally do develop reasonably accurate assessments of which of their peers they listen to and trust, who does good work, and who policymakers take seriously. The real art of [network assessment] is *assessing influence.*"[26]

Teles and Schmitt make yet another provocative point: it is "the evaluator, rather than the formal qualities of the evaluation, that matters."[27] The type of evaluator they recommend has a skill set that is many ways analogous to those of two other professional groups. One is the

foreign intelligence analyst. She consumes official government reports and statistics, which she knows provide a picture of the world with significant gaps. She talks to insiders, some of whom she trusts, and others whose information she has learned to take with a grain of salt. In many cases, she learns as much from what she knows are lies as from the truth. It is the web of all of these imperfect sources of information, instead of a single measure, that helps the analyst figure out what is actually happening. And it is the quality and experience of the analyst—her tacit knowledge—that allows her to create an authoritative picture.[28]

The second professional group is

applied anthropologists. They study a particular culture, in a particular place, that works differently in practice than it does on paper. Cultures are often characterized by a "hidden structure" that is largely invisible to outsiders and sometimes poorly understood even by insiders. Many cultures actually develop a lack of transparency precisely to prevent comprehension by outsiders. Discovering how a culture works requires one to create networks of informants and use research methods such as participant observation. This requires trust, which may take years to develop.[29]

The article, including all of the recommendations, is addressed to foundations and other funding organizations committed to policy change. More specifically, the focus is on how those funders should evaluate their entire portfolio of grants to advocacy organizations. Some may be obvious from the preceding, such as identify and support advocates with strategic capacity and network centrality. Others may be less obvious, such as "involve multiple unlikely bets in ways that are more likely to succeed" and "take chances on big efforts to change policy and public assumptions, rather than retreating to the safer space of incremental change."[30]

At the same time, the article's perspective and significant insights can be very helpful as advocacy organizations and campaigns develop their own MEL plans. Some of those benefits are discussed in the following section.

The Role of Advocates

The previous sections provide different perspectives about evaluation design, but both focused on the role of evaluators. This section explores ways to think about and approach monitoring, evaluation, and learning from the perspective of the advocates and their organizations. It supplements the MEL overview in chapter 3, drawing heavily on ideas and language from the two very different readings summarized in the previous sections.

Teles and Schmitt's brief article makes three key contributions to this discussion. First and foremost, their discussion of the complex reality of politics and policy change identifies the essential starting point for all advocacy evaluations. Advocates must ensure that their MEL processes are in fact grounded in a highly contextualized understanding of policy change, one that takes into consideration the multiple and nuanced points in the article. Evaluation findings will have limited value or even be misleading if they fail to address this context.

Second, Teles and Schmitt make a persuasive case for focusing evaluation on advocacy organizations rather than on advocacy processes, and particularly an organization's strategic capacity and network centrality. Advocates should ensure their MEL processes examine the long-term growth of their own capacity and networks as an outcome that transcends any single campaign or effort and is thus of equal or greater importance than examining change in policies.

Third, they also make a persuasive case for approaching evaluation as more of a craft than as a technical or purely rational process, and thus for finding evaluators who have a unique set of competencies. Advocates should carefully consider who leads their MEL processes and how to find and develop the requisite competencies in their own organizations and networks.

Coffman's *User's Guide* makes many contributions. The specific steps, concepts, and tools provided are immediately practical as advocates plan their MEL processes. Given the reality of limited resources, the guide provides important advice about prioritizing and focusing advocates' MEL effort on only a subset of their activities/tactics and interim outcomes that are most relevant to a specific campaign and about selecting data collection methods based on available resources.

Coffman's composite logic model has multiple uses for planning MEL processes, but also for planning the campaign itself. The model provides a specific structure that advocates, often with different backgrounds and orientations, can use to collectively clarify and refine an initial theory of change. It forces them to identify a path of activities/tactics and interim outcomes they think are most likely to achieve their policy goals and which goals are most likely to achieve the desired impact. Without going through some collective thinking process, different advocates may work at cross purposes or may not even agree on where to begin. Moreover, if some or all of that initial strategy proves unsuccessful, the logic model can be used to quickly identify alternative paths and parallel changes in advocates' MEL plan.[31]

Among the categories and indicators in the composite logic model are some that specifically address the elements raised by Teles and Schmitt: strategic capacity and network centrality or influence. The model includes eight interim outcomes and corresponding measures in the category of advocacy capacity, including an organization's ability to adapt to new obstacles, opportunities, and other shifts in political and policy conditions. Three of the outcomes are specifically related to an organization's roles in networks (partnerships and alliances, collaboration and alignment, and the engagement of new advocates in an advocacy campaign). At a minimum, the list of outcomes and possible measures or indicators offer a strong starting point as the advocates begin planning their MEL processes. Moreover, network mapping is one of the new methods described in Coffman's guide.

Coffman's overview of emerging methods for collecting evaluation data is another very useful portion of the guide, especially since many advocates generate data useful for planning their strategies even if they are not also incorporated in their MEL plans. For example, if a bellwether methodology is used during the planning stage of a campaign, it can produce insights into the level and nature of public will that can help advocates determine the approach and amount of effort necessary to increase awareness and knowledge.

On the other hand, many of the guide's benefits can be lost if it is not read and implemented with a strong appreciation of and allowance for the complexities of politics and policy change.

Coffman appreciates that complexity. For example, the guide indicates that evaluators should be modest in their objectives; they should "concentrate on determining if a *credible and defensible case* can be made that the advocates contributed to policy outcomes and goals instead of attempting to prove that the advocates definitively caused them."[32] However, that point does not go far enough. As Teles and Schmitt note, very effective advocates, especially in the time frame of a specific campaign, fail more often than they succeed in achieving the desired policy outcomes. And, when an outcome is achieved, it may have been due to factors totally unrelated to the advocates' efforts or contribution.

Coffman's guide would be stronger if it more directly and extensively addressed the challenges of complexity. As is, it is certainly possible for its steps, elements, indicators, and methods to be read and implemented using the more linear thinking of mainstream evaluation. Activities/tactics cause interim outcomes that cause policy changes that cause impact. In O'Brien's words, quoted at the beginning of this chapter, traditional evaluators who have been "weaned on logical frameworks" will find the challenges of advocacy evaluation "hard to swallow" (if they even recognize the challenges in the first place).[33] Using the guide with such limited understanding of politics and policy change is what Teles and Schmitt would quite correctly call "wholly unhelpful."[34]

The guide's benefits will be most fully realized if as much attention is given to who is doing the evaluation as is to *how* it is done. According to Teles and Schmitt, "There is a natural temptation to formalize this process in order to create at least the appearance of objective criteria, but it is far better to acknowledge that tacit knowledge and subjective judgment are what really underlie good advocacy evaluation, and to find evaluators who can exercise that judgment well."[35] However, it may not be so easy to find (and pay for) such evaluators. Foundations may have the resources to do so. If an advocacy organization can do the same, it should. But most will not be able to.

On the other hand, nearly all advocacy organizations can access experienced advocates (from within their own organization or from others) who have the perspective and analytical skills to provide the same type of trained judgment and can provide various levels of leadership for evaluation processes.[36]

Moreover, staff of all organizations can approach MEL in a way that helps all advocates develop those same competencies. To do so, staff need to increase the attention they give to the L dimension of MEL. Unfortunately, the M and E dimensions often take up most if not all of the attention and resources, even though the amount, consistency, and quality of learning among the advocates is perhaps the single most important determinant of an advocacy organization's strategic capacity.

Whenever possible, organizations should attempt to integrate the M and E and L dimensions of MEL. The intense period debriefing evaluation method described in Coffman's guide can provide an example of how that can be done and includes the advantages of having an experienced advocate lead (or colead) the process.

The debriefing method begins with the understanding that important data already exists in the heads of the advocates. That data is captured through one or more focus groups. Without any effort to do so, focus group discussions can result in some cross-learning among participants. But if the objective is to capture data and facilitate learning, then slight but intentional changes in process can increase attention to the latter without a significant reduction in the former. The choices about whom to bring together in which focus groups is one way to enhance cross-learning.

One advantage of this type of learning is that it can be applied almost immediately in the context of an ongoing campaign. Data analysis and reporting of findings from a debriefing process will often be too slow to inform pressing decisions.

On the other hand, intense period debriefing data analysis and reporting, if well done, can be invaluable for informing longer-term decisions and shaping future campaigns. But to do so the analysis must be accurate and meaningful. It requires interpretation and synthesis of different input, sometimes conflicting, from different advocates. An experienced advocate is generally more likely than a mainstream evaluator to understand the overall context of the advocacy campaign, to discern which sources to trust, and to identity which input is most significant.

The involvement of an experienced advocate as a debriefing leader offers additional learning benefits. That person's experiences are a source of knowledge and perspective useful for the data analysis. The experienced advocate can also be a source of new learning for advocates if space is created for sharing some of the most relevant experiences and lessons during the group discussions or in the report. If the advocate/evaluator is from another organization, the process might also lead to new or more trusted partnerships or networks. Moreover, the evaluation process and findings will almost always generate significant new learning for advocates/evaluators, which can then inform their own future work.

Other evaluation data collection and analysis methods (especially those that are similar to the intense period debriefing in that the data they reveal is in fact knowledge already in the heads of the advocates) provide learning opportunities for those directly involved and for experienced advocates in the role of evaluator.

Methods for evaluating activities/tactics, if they focus on what Coffman describes as "measures of effort" that "count what and how much," are often of limited value and a lost opportunity for learning. However, other methods directly engage the advocates and examine an activity in light of the context and similar experiences in other campaigns or organizations. In some cases, such as the activity of producing a policy paper, counting does not even make sense. Are three poorly researched papers better than one done well? In this example, reviews by and dialogue with experienced advocates and policy researchers might generate a more helpful assessment and new learning.

Organizations can also increase attention to the learning dimension of MEL by naming and encouraging, in some cases formalizing, the learning that occurs naturally through reflection on experience, informal conversation with colleagues, reading, and so forth. Organizations can also support formal learning opportunities, such as participation in professional conferences and seminars, or initiate new ones. For example, several advocacy organizations might meet for a day, each present a case study of one of their campaigns, and then identify lessons (common or unique) that can inform future work.

In a mutually reinforcing process, increased attention to learning expands the number and quality of advocates who have the trained judgment necessary to effectively evaluate their own and others' work in the context of complex politics and policy change. They will be able to read and implement Coffman's guide (and similar work) in ways that realize the full potential of its many benefits. And, in turn, when those advocates lead an evaluation process, they will be prepared to do so in ways that result in further learning for all involved.

Using Multiple Maps

Evaluation and learning will be improved if advocates develop or enhance their knowledge of and ability to use multiple conceptual maps or frameworks for understanding advocacy. As discussed in chapter 2, all such maps or frameworks illuminate some dimensions of the complex real world of advocacy campaigns and initiatives. And all omit or obscure some dimensions. As long as advocates know when and how to use different frameworks, they can use them as tools for observing, thinking, and acting.

That chapter summarized four conceptual maps: advocacy's road map from the *Democracy Owner's Manual,* advocacy process and strategy development map from *The Advocacy Sourcebook,* advocacy planning moments from *A New Weave of Power, People and Politics,* and my advocacy circles map.[37] While the first three were introduced as tools for planning advocacy campaigns or initiatives, all four can also inform and guide evaluation and learning processes.

For example, the advocacy circles will illuminate or focus MEL attention on different arenas of advocacy work: context (political and economic forces, conditions and historical moment); advocates (capacity and resources); policy (research and analysis of the problems, causes, and policy solutions or goals); politics (the policy makers, allies, opponents, and their interactions); and the strategies (or methods and tactics used to develop capacity and influence different phases of the policy agenda setting, formulation, and implementation cycle). The circles will also focus attention on how changes in any one or more of those arenas influence the others. For those reasons, the circles map is particularly useful for case studies that evaluate an overall campaign.

Coffman's composite logic model is also a conceptual map or framework, similar in scope to the four in chapter 2. While introduced as a tool for advocacy evaluation, she notes how it is also used to inform and guide campaign planning. Like the other frameworks, it illuminates some dimensions of advocacy and omits or obscures others. The model illuminates by identifying, categorizing, and relating a relatively comprehensive number of actions and outcomes, some combinations of which are used in all advocacy efforts. Many of the benefits of Coffman's guide, discussed previously, can be attributed to the quality of the composite logic model as a general map or framework for understanding advocacy. Advocates and advocacy evaluators will do well to include it in their conceptual toolbox.

The advocates' conceptual toolbox will be stronger if it also includes Covey and Miller's advocacy evaluation framework described in chapter 3, partially because it illuminates some advocacy outcomes that are obscure if not absent in Coffman's model.[38] In contrast to their more general "advocacy process and strategy development" map, the evaluation framework is specifically focused on identifying which outcomes of an advocacy effort are important to assess. It identifies three: changes in policy, civil society, and governance.

The first outcome, changes in policy, is the focus of most advocacy evaluations. As we have seen, this is the focus of the composite logic model. (As already noted, Coffman's differentiation between seven different types of policy goals is useful for assessing the whole range of these outcomes.)

The second outcome, changes in civil society or in the capacity of advocates and their networks, does not receive equivalent focus in most evaluations. When addressed it is typically viewed, as in the composite logic model, as an interim outcome that it is important because it is a means to achieve policy change. But Covey and Miller treat change in civil society as a long-term outcome that is as important as change in policy. This reflects an understanding of the complexity of politics and policy change similar to that of Teles and Schmitt, which led those authors to recommend that *the* primary focus of advocacy evaluations should be the strategic capacity and network centrality of advocacy organizations.

Covey and Miller recognize it is possible for an advocacy campaign or initiative to produce positive progress toward changes in policy and civil society. But they also recognize that some situations require tradeoffs between the two outcomes. For example, members of a strategic coalition may need to decide if they will accept a positive but compromised change in policy at the cost of losing key members who oppose that decision. More generally, Covey and Miller's attention to this outcome reflects their understanding that meaningful policy change must be part of a larger process of social change. That requires overcoming incredible power inequalities, which must involve ongoing and long-term increases in the capacity of social justice–oriented advocates and their networks.

The third outcome in Covey and Miller's framework, change in governance or increased political space, is not a specific focus in most advocacy evaluations; it is not highlighted in Coffman's model or by Teles and Schmitt. When the advocates' goal is some specific change in the processes of policy making, policy implementation, or governance more generally, progress toward this third outcome may be addressed as it would be with most any other policy change goal. However, the value of this framework is how it illuminates or focuses attention on whether change in governance is an indirect outcome of an advocacy effort focused on another policy issue. For example, the efforts to block the open pit mine in Tambogrande may have indirectly resulted in an opening for citizens to require open hearings before any mining concession is approved in Peru. But it is also possible that an indirect outcome of an advocacy effort might be negative and reduce political space for advocacy and citizen engagement in the future; an evaluation should track that as well.

One of the best applications of Covey and Miller's framework is in *Advocacy for Social Justice: A Global Action and Reflection Guide.*[39] Part three includes case studies of campaigns by Oxfam America partner organizations or Oxfam staff and their allies in Ecuador, Guatemala, Senegal, Cambodia, the United States, and an international policy campaign. Each case is a retrospective assessment of a specific campaign, most of which were written by advocates who were directly involved.

In a chapter that compares and draws general lessons from the six cases, Gabrielle Watson used the framework to analyze outcomes (impacts).[40] To do so, she synthesized a table that includes an expanded definition of policy, governance, and civil society change (differentiating instrumental and structural forms for each) and lists advocacy strategies and broad indicators of success that correspond with the three different types of outcomes. Table 10.1 includes Watson's definitions, and in light of the focus of this chapter, her indicators or measures of success.

Using the framework, Watson identified relevant change in all three dimensions for all six cases. More generally, her chapter captures many insightful lessons that emerge from comparative case analysis, for example, about situations when triangulation using external forces to leverage change or a good cop, bad cop strategy are effective. It is thus a good resource for expanding one's knowledge of different cases and advocacy approaches.

In terms of our discussion of MEL processes, Watson's chapter demonstrates the value of a framework that focuses on changes in civil society and governance as well as policy. Taken together, the cases and summary chapter also demonstrate the level of insights that can be gained by engaging advocates directly in the evaluation and learning.

In the same way that rigorous attention to conceptual frameworks and concrete practice produced significant insights for Watson and her colleagues, I hope the chapters and cases in this book offer similar benefits to each reader. If so, I am confident that the result will be more effective practice of policy advocacy for social and economic justice, environmental sustainability, and peace.

Table 10.1 Impact analysis for social justice advocacy

Dimension of Advocacy Impact	Policy	Governance	Civil Society
Instrumental	Policies, laws, programs, or practices that lead to other policy, governance, or civil society gains	Access to decision-making processes that facilitates policy gains or civil society gains	Increasing the ability of civil society organizations to articulate and fight for their interests with powerful actors and hold government and the private sector accountable
Structural	Specific policies, laws, programs, and practices that have direct benefit for excluded groups, when implemented	Opening and consolidating channels of participation, voice, and power for civil society to engage in decision-making processes affecting their lives	Creating internal cultures, practices, and structures consistent with their social justice ideals, and holding representative structures accountable.
Indicators of Success	Policy, law, precedent, and so on, instituted and implemented	• Democratic space expanded • New channels for participation • Freedom of action, engagement • Position, credibility, and power of campaign participants strengthened	• Strong grassroots organizations and NGOs with representative and accountable structures • Ability to articulate rights (political, civil, social, and economic) and formulate proposals to assert these rights • Increased awareness of members and other sectors of civil society and public about issues at stake

Source: Adapted from Gabrielle Watson, "Comparative Lessons for Social Justice Advocacy Case Studies," in *Advocacy for Social Justice*, ed. David Cohen, Rosa de la Vega, and Gabrielle Watson (Bloomfield, CT: Kumarian Press, 2001), 238.

Notes

1. I use the MEL acronym throughout this chapter. However, while I realize there are some important distinctions between the monitoring (M) and evaluation (E) elements, they are treated as one process and sometimes often simply called evaluation.

2. The point that NGOs with humanitarian roots find this hard to swallow is yet another challenge. It is also related to the fact (as discussed in chapter 5) that organizations that began by providing services to individuals and communities, including but in no way limited to humanitarian relief, often have internal resistance to adding advocacy to their mission.

3. A good collection of the online materials is available through the Innovation Network's Point K Learning Center at http://www.innonet.org.

4. Julia Coffman, *A User's Guide to Advocacy Evaluation Planning* (Cambridge, MA: Harvard Family Research Project, 2009), http://www.hfrp.org/UserGuide.

5. Coffman, *User's Guide*, 3.

6. Steven Teles and Mark Schmitt, "The Elusive Craft of Evaluating Advocacy," *Stanford Social Innovation Review* (Summer 2011): 39–43, http://www.ssireview.org/images/digital_edition/2011SU_Feature_TelesSchmitt.pdf.

7. Coffman, *User's Guide*.

8. "Advocacy Evaluation Planning Worksheet," http://www.hfrp.org/var/hfrp/storage/fckeditor/File/file/Supporting%20files%20for%20publications/UserGuideAdvocacyEvaluationPlanningWorksheet.pdf.

9. It is worth noting that the two types of impacts are often interconnected. Better conditions may be the result of improved services or systems.

10. Coffman, *User's Guide*, 6.

11. Coffman, *User's Guide*, 13.

12. Coffman, *User's Guide*, 14.

13. Coffman, *User's Guide*, 16.

14. Coffman, *User's Guide*, 14.

15. Coffman, *User's Guide*, 14.

16. Coffman, *User's Guide*, 14, 17.

17. Coffman, *User's Guide*, 18–19.

18. Stuart Bagnell, "Necessity Leads to Innovative Evaluation Approach and Practice," *Evaluation Exchange* 13, no. 1 (2007): 10–11, quoted in Coffman, *User's Guide*, 20. Bagnell is one of the developers of this method.

19. Teles and Schmitt, "Elusive Craft," 39.

20. Teles and Schmitt, "Elusive Craft," 39.

21. Teles and Schmitt, "Elusive Craft," 21.

22. Teles and Schmitt, "Elusive Craft," 40.

23. Teles and Schmitt, "Elusive Craft," 42.

24. Teles and Schmitt, "Elusive Craft," 42.

25. Teles and Schmitt, "Elusive Craft," 41.

26. Teles and Schmitt, "Elusive Craft," 43.

27. Teles and Schmitt, "Elusive Craft," 43.

28. Teles and Schmitt, "Elusive Craft," 43.

29. Teles and Schmitt, "Elusive Craft," 43.

30. Teles and Schmitt, "Elusive Craft," 40.

31. Coffman, *User's Guide,* 7. These points are a bit buried in one of a series of "tip" boxes that are spread throughout the guide. Coffman might have done more to emphasize that advocates and evaluators should expect the initial theory of change to evolve.

32. Coffman, *User's Guide,* 5; italics in the original.

33. A logical framework, or log frame, is a tool for program planning, management, monitoring, and evaluation. It is used extensively by international development aid agencies and organizations.

34. Teles and Schmitt, "Elusive Craft," 39.

35. Teles and Schmitt, "Elusive Craft," 43.

36. Even when an advocacy organizations can find (and pay for) an external evaluator who has the qualifications Teles and Schmitt describe, it can stimulate learning by forming a MEL team that includes her and one or more experienced advocates. The team approach is essential if the external evaluator has a more mainstream background and lacks the trained judgment for understanding the complexities of politics, policy change, and advocacy; as long as the external evaluator is willing to adopt a mutual learning peer approach, one or more experienced advocates can help fill that gap.

37. Jim Shultz, *The Democracy Owner's Manual: A Practical Guide to Changing the World* (New Brunswick, NJ: Rutgers University Press, 2002); Jane Covey and Valerie Miller, *Advocacy Sourcebook: Frameworks for Planning, Action and Reflection* (Boston: Institute for Development Research, 1997); Lisa VeneKlasen with Valerie Miller, *A New Weave of Power, Politics and People: The Action Guide for Advocacy and Citizen Participation* (Warwickshire, UK: Practical Action Publishers, 2007).

38. Covey and Miller, *Advocacy Sourcebook.*

39. David Cohen, Rosa de la Vega, and Gabrielle Watson, *Advocacy for Social Justice: A Global Action and Reflection Guide* (Bloomfield, CT: Kumarian Press, 2001).

40. Gabrielle Watson, "Comparative Lessons for Social Justice Advocacy Case Studies," in ed. Cohen et al., *Advocacy for Social Justice,* 217–40.

CASE H

Conclusion
Oxfam America:
Monitoring, Evaluation, and Learning

The learning exercise that culminated the first part of Case H asked you to make a list of which elements (outputs and outcomes) of the campaign you think might be most useful to monitor and evaluate during 2009. For each item on your list, you were asked to identify one or more indicators and corresponding evidence that might be used to assess meaningful progress or achievement of at least two of those outputs or outcomes.

The following portion of the case will allow you to compare your notes with what the monitoring, evaluation, and learning (MEL) staff member and the rest of the Climate Change Campaign (CCC) team planned and then learn how those efforts evolved during 2009.

The MEL Plan

After helping to clarify and refine the campaign's theory of change (ToC), the MEL staff member brought together the other CCC team members, including those in policy research, government relations, organizing, alliance building, media relations, web and new media, and publications, to code-sign an initial MEL plan for 2009. The result was described in an internal document: "Evidence of Access and Influence: Real-Time Influence and Tracking Plan."

The plan identified nine key elements of the campaign that would be monitored and evaluated. The first three elements corresponded with the major outcomes, which, according to the ToC, would be necessary to ensure that the US negotiators in Copenhagen are fully committed to and help achieve a safe and fair deal. Thus, MEL efforts were to focus on changes or developments regarding

- policy adoption,
- Congress (positions and actions of key deciders and champions in the House and Senate), and
- the administration (positions and actions of key officials).

The other six elements were related to key outputs, which, according to the ToC, were necessary to achieve the outcomes. MEL efforts were to focus on changes in the degree to which the following occurred

- public discourse that included adaptation dimensions of climate change policy
- US businesses/companies addressed the costs of not addressing these issues
- thousands of key voices (faith based, African American, Latino/Latina, women, health, security, environmentalists, Gulf Coast, development nongovernmental organizations [NGOs]) were mobilized in congressional districts and in Washington, DC, offices
- developing country governments and vulnerable people spoke out strongly on the issue
- targeted groups engaged in key international moments (such as the UN General Assembly in September 2009, three months prior to the United Nations Framework Convention on Climate Change Conference of the Parties)

For each element, the plan identified indicators of progress or success (key influence benchmarks), evidence, and methods for collecting and analyzing the evidence (tracking approach). Table H.1 is an example of what the document included for one of the outcomes (Congress), and table H.2 is for one of the activities (education and alliance building with US companies).

An annex to the plan focused attention on the campaign's work with six different groups of key influencers. Table H.3 is the table developed for monitoring and evaluating this work, with the actual plan for one group of the influencers.

The plan also indentified a set of elements that do not appear in the ToC. Those elements focused on assessing the campaign's internal objective to be "strategically prepared for multiple scenarios and [have] adequate decision-making processes and structures." Those elements were

- scenario preparedness,
- campaign planning,
- use of evidence in campaign implementation, and
- cross-team coordination and synergies.

Table H.1 Evidence of access and influence example: Congress

Key Element	Key Influence Benchmarks	Evidence	Tracking Approach
Congress: Key deciders in House and Senate push through strong climate bill and national legislation addressing adaptation by fall 2009 House and Senate champions put forward language and cosponsor strong climate legislation	Key legislative decision-makers (Speaker of the House, Senate Majority Leader, etc.) push forward legislative proposals that include Oxfam's policy asks Key Champions specifically incorporate, cite or reference Oxfam's policy arguments and positions, evidence, reports and/ or the interests of individuals, groups and organizations which Oxfam has brought forward in their private statements, public speeches and testimony Key Champions propose and cosponsor legislation Key Blockers are neutralized or persuaded Champions are willing to do something for us publicly and/or behind the scenes	Policy statements by key decisionmakers Legislative actions taken to move bills forward Positions of Champions regarding our policy ask and eventual bills that contain them Votes overall	*Evidence File:* Statements and legislative action *Congressional contacts management system:* Position shifts over time *Final Vote Tallies* *Analysis:* Inclusion of our policy proposals

Source: Oxfam America Climate Change Campaign, internal document. Used with permission.

For each of those four elements the plan identified specific, measurable, achievable, realistic, and timely (SMART) intermediate objectives and indicators. Table H.4 on page 252 is what the document included for the first element.

Advocacy and MEL in Action

The MEL plan provided a high level of clarity regarding which elements of the campaign were important to monitor and evaluate and which indicators and evidence would be appropriate for each. However, one reason for embedding the MEL staff member in the campaign team was the expectation that any plan could only be a starting point. Oxfam staff understood that as with most complex campaigns, their strategy would need to respond to factors and forces that were unknown or even unknowable during the planning

Table H.2 Evidence of access and influence example: US companies

Key Element	Key Influence Benchmarks	Evidence	Tracking Approach
A broad spectrum of US companies believe they can't afford NOT to address the human impacts of climate change and advocate for strong adaptation policy in Congress	Progressive businesses speak out on climate to key audiences & targets through lobby visits, public statements, etc. Members of [a new business coalition] and other leading businesses call for domestic and international adaptation with Members of Congress Unusual and strong array of companies sign on & publicly support Oxfam's policy positions	Sign-ons to Business Statement supporting Oxfam's policy positions (number and weightiness of sign-ons) Participation of influential & newsworthy businesses at Oxfam & other influential events	*Evidence File:* Public statements and actions by companies Sign-ons & participation in key events Companies lobbying with our messages *Analysis:* Influence and prestige of the companies speaking out; whether they are an effective counterbalance to anti-climate change action corporate lobby; evidence their statements and positions are being paid attention to by Congress & the administration.

Source: Oxfam America Climate Change Campaign, internal document. Used with permission.

process. Thus an effective campaign would have to be fast paced and able to respond to rapid shifts in opportunities and obstacles.

The MEL effort would need to correspond with that reality. The plan to monitor and evaluate internal scenario preparedness specifically addressed the team's capacity to respond strategically when there is a rapid shift. Overall, the MEL approach sought to engage the whole team in action learning, which to the maximum extent possible would inform key strategic decisions. At the same time, it was understood that the pace of a campaign would often limit the ability of team members to stop (or just slow down) to focus on MEL, much less to collect and record new types of evidence and document outcomes.

Table H.3 Evidence of access and influence (example): Key influencers

Influencers	Objectives	Approach	Indicators of influence
Sisters on the Planet Ambassadors	"Court" strategically positioned members of Congress (MoCs) to engage in Climate Change fight.	International Women's Day gathering of Ambassadors	SOP Ambassadors are speaking directly to MoCs on the issue of adaptation
	Focus on . . . key committees as defined by Policy team.	Use of SOP Video with off-line OA constituents	Messages from SOP are resonating and being picked up by media, MoCs, other influentials
	Project the message that we need comprehensive response—both causes and the consequences on poorest communities & women	Develop research and policy positions on gender and climate change	
	Create OA campaign visibility among MoCs and staffers as the debate accelerates.		

Source: Oxfam America Climate Change Campaign, internal document. Used with permission.

One MEL approach, given the demands on the campaign team's time and attention, was to use data that were already being collected and used as part of the advocacy process itself. For example, Oxfam had invested in a congressional contact management system to facilitate consistent communications with representatives and senators. The system is designed to record each time a staff member, key supporter, or group of Oxfam activists meets with or contacts a member of Congress. Those records should include any information gathered about the members' positions and actions related to Oxfam's policy priorities including climate change adaptation. Advocates can review the relevant records prior to any new communication. The MEL effort could compile and analyze data in those records as one means of assessing the campaign's access and influence.

Many elements of the MEL plan were approached as real-time tests that would determine what really works in practice. For example, the congressional contact system did provide some useful information, but it required a lot of an intern's time to access, and those data were limited by the fact that busy, over-stretched advocates found it difficult to make entries on a consistent basis. Overall, the campaign's MEL staff members frequently compared the experience to "building a plane while flying it."

Work With the House of Representatives

When congressional leadership decided to first move climate change legislation through the House and then the Senate, Oxfam's initial advocacy unfolded in the same order and thus so did the MEL efforts.

The advocates employed the full range of strategies described in the first portion of this case: continue research to document impacts of climate change on the most vulnerable and to refine their policy arguments, engage and strengthen the effectiveness of poor countries and communities in climate change advocacy, further strengthen and mobilize Oxfam's US support base, strengthen current alliances and build new ones, achieve massive earned media coverage, and effectively lobby legislators in their districts and on the Hill.

The House advocacy included a number of key events, and the MEL effort sought to identify outcomes and lessons in a time frame that could inform the campaign's next steps. For example, timed with International Women's Day in March 2009 and while climate change legislation was still being formulated in the House, campaign staffers brought eight of their most influential Sisters on the Planet Ambassadors to Washington, DC. After a series of briefings, the ambassadors spent a day lobbying with selected representatives. The ambassadors submitted reports on their meetings, and soon after, two debriefing sessions took place with staff on the campaign team and other Oxfam units, as well as several additional interviews. The information was captured in a short report that focused on key achievements and lessons for future lobbying days.

Another MEL effort related to access and influence with the House took the form of two case studies, which documented and assessed the specific methods, including collaboration with two different allies, which were used to influence four of the key representatives.

Ultimately, the House did pass a climate change bill in June of 2009, HR 2454: American Clean Energy and Security Act (also known as the Waxman-Markey bill). MEL efforts helped identify Oxfam's contribution and lessons. These included a step-back session with the whole campaign team, facilitated by the MEL staff. The participants discussed and documented the degree to which the campaign had gained access to and influenced key representatives, including House leadership, committee chairs, and others whom they hoped would have an important influence on their colleagues' votes. Reports by the staff most directly involved in this aspect of the campaign provided yet more details.

The combination of methods documented very clear evidence of effective access and influence, for example, drafting and securing signatures of representatives for sign-on letters to House colleagues and leadership, drafting a resolution that was passed by House vote, and working directly with the staff of committee chairs in composing the language of the final legislation. While the level of adaptation funding in the bill was much less than

Table H.4 Evidence related to internal objectives (example):
Scenario Preparedness

Elements	SMART Intermediate Objectives	Indicators	Indicators of influence
Scenario preparedness	Campaign team has clear "bottom line" criteria for adequate progress towards a fair and equitable deal and what a trigger point would be for a decision to walk away from engagement, and shift to aggressive public action. Campaign team has a clear and rapid-response process for deciding to walk away, and managing the resource implications for this.	Team meets quickly and makes evidence-based decisions based on solid, up-to-date intelligence on negotiation progress	SOP Ambassadors are speaking directly to MoCs on the issue of adaptation. Messages from SOP are resonating and being picked up by media, MoCs, other influentials.

Source: Oxfam America Climate Change Campaign, internal document. Used with permission.

Oxfam had sought, there may have been far less or no funding if it were not for Oxfam's influence.

Work With the Senate and Administration

Because of a variety of political factors, the Senate took up the legislation later than anticipated; only a few months before US negotiators would be going to Copenhagen. The pace of advocacy became even more demanding. The MEL staff facilitated another step-back review that clarified power assumptions and clarified strategy. But, overall, there was little time to process the information and learning from the House vote or to fully monitor and evaluate Oxfam's access and influence in the Senate.

MEL efforts included after-event debriefings of some key activities that occurred during this time period. They included a media stunt in New York City that coincided with the September meetings of the UN General Assembly and a second lobby day for Sisters on the Planet Ambassadors.

Some of the same political factors that delayed the Senate's work on climate change legislation ultimately resulted in the Senate's failure to pass the needed legislation. Two primary factors were far beyond the control of Oxfam or of all the advocates combined. Congress and the Obama administration had inherited and were forced to devote much of their attention and political capital to addressing the worst financial crisis, recession, and unemployment in decades. What remained was largely consumed by the administration's effort to pass the most comprehensive health care reform in decades, despite significant opposition from the Republicans and especially the new right-wing Tea Party movement that was escalating in the latter part of 2009.

Advocacy Outcome

Those factors blocked the two outcomes, which according to the campaign's ToC (see appendix H.1), would be necessary to achieve a fair and safe global deal in Copenhagen. "Key administration officials" did not "develop and put forward strong climate policy proposals" and "key deciders" in Congress did not "push through a strong climate bill." Even the bill that passed the House was not as strong as would have been necessary. Thus US negotiators could not commit the United States (and pressure other rich countries to commit themselves) to such a deal. The year 2009 ended in disappointment.

Evaluating the Campaign and the MEL Effort

On the policy front, Oxfam had not achieved the fair and safe deal that was its "ultimate outcome" goal. As the Obama administration took office at the start of 2009, that goal had appeared to be realistic. The new president had pledged to address climate change during his election campaign and had strong public support. The Democrats controlled the House and Senate. But, as discussed earlier, the political context changed over the course of the year in ways that were stronger than the massive effort of hundreds of advocacy organizations, of which Oxfam was just one.

However the campaign's MEL effort allowed campaign staff to assess progress toward intermediate outcomes and outputs. The most comprehensive documentation and analysis were reports by the various members of the campaign team, which were prepared for a January 2010 meeting to assess the year's effort and outcomes. Most of the reports followed the format suggested by the MEL member of the team: "headline achievements, evidence, key success factors, limiting factors, and learnings."

Particularly important were the self-reports by those most directly involved in the inside advocacy with congressional committees and staff. They provided clear evidence that as had been the case with the House, Oxfam had achieved a high level of access and influence with the Senate, including the inclusion of Oxfam's recommended language, in one place verbatim, in the Senate bill, and a request for Oxfam to provide a quote in a Senate press release announcing the passage of the bill in one of the key committees.

Other self-reports provided evidence that indicated significant progress in most of the other elements of Oxfam's strategy, including growth in its local support base, especially in some states and legislative districts; new or stronger relationships with some important groups, organizations, and coalitions; new or more nuanced insights into methods for influencing members of Congress; and new or more established access to and credibility with key members of Congress and their legislative staff.

The MEL effort allowed Oxfam to know and to be able to credibly demonstrate that progress had been made in building Oxfam's capacity to pursue its long-term goal of ending global poverty.

Moreover, members of the CCC team felt that the expanded role of MEL during 2009 played an important role in the campaign. The collective process used to develop the MEL plan resulted in a sense of ownership (rather than the very typical situation where MEL activities are seen more as an imposition or even a threat). A number of team members described the result as a shift in their organizational culture. In the words of one member, the process "forced us to reflect and refine our strategy." Another staff member described it as providing "increased discipline." The team regularly asked, What's working? What's not? How does this relate to the ToC?

While only some of the MEL effort was integrated enough into the advocacy process that it could inform real-time decisions, all of it generated learning that could be applied to future campaigns.

An internal report about the 2009 campaign listed a number of lessons, two of which were

- Beware of overambitious targets. This is a perennial pitfall of many campaigns. Calibrate your ambitions by vetting your campaign strategy with trusted peers. Cost out options. This will help us get better over time at having a sense of value for money. Set "doable" and "reach" goals.
- Pay attention to both short-term versus long-term objectives. Some strategies serve both, some don't so much. Be explicit about which investments serve short-term but not long-term goals, or serve long-term but not short-term goals. Be aware of these choices and make investments strategically.

These and other lessons from the CCC have indeed informed the design of the Oxfam's next major advocacy effort. Launched in 2011, the GROW campaign "aims to build a better food system: one that sustainably feeds a growing population (estimated to reach nine billion by 2050) and empowers poor people to earn a living, feed their families, and thrive."[1]

Note

1. "Grow: Food, Justice, Planet," 2011, http://www.oxfamamerica.org/campaigns/food-justice.

About the Author
and Coauthors

Author

Jeff Unsicker is a professor at the SIT Graduate Institute in Vermont, where he teaches courses in policy analysis and advocacy and chairs the MA in Sustainable Development program. At SIT, he has also been a dean, interim president, cofounder of a global partnership for NGO leadership and management education based in Bangladesh, and co-director of Leadership for Social Justice Institutes for the Ford Foundation's international fellowship program. Jeff was previously coordinator of education and leadership development programs for a coalition of 50 community organizations in San Diego, professor of international development at a progressive liberal arts college near San Francisco, research associate at the University of Dar es Salaam in Tanzania, and Fulbright lecturer at the University of Botswana. He has also consulted for the advocacy units of various NGOs, including BRAC, Oxfam America, and CARE and held different leadership and strategy roles in the coalition of anti-nuclear, environmental, and public interest organizations committed to replacing Vermont's nuclear power reactor with safe and green alternatives. Jeff completed his BA in learning and social change at the University of California, San Diego and his MA and PhD in international development education at Stanford University.

Coauthors

Kim Friedman has dedicated the past two decades to early childhood advocacy, community organizing, social action research, and public engagement work in Connecticut and Vermont. Kim's affiliation with Windham Child Care Association began in 1999 when she joined the staff as its Public Engagement Coordinator. That position grew into her role as Coalition Coordinator and then Campaign Director of the Kids Are Priority One Coalition. Kim has a MA in Third World Development from Antioch University, a BA in French from Vassar College, and senior organizer training from Midwest Academy.

Sheepa Hafiza is director of the Advocacy for Social Change and the Gender Justice and Diversity units in BRAC. She has held other leadership roles within BRAC (including director of Training and of Human Resources) and CARE Bangladesh. She completed a BA at the University of Dhaka, a received a postgraduate diploma in NGO Leadership and Management through the Global Partnership (formed by BRAC, SIT, and ORAP in Zimbabwe), and a MA from the Program in Intercultural Service, Leadership and Management at the SIT Graduate Institute.

Nikoi Kote-Nikoi is the founder and codirector of Centre for Policy Priorities in his native Ghana and a professor of Sustainable Development at the SIT Graduate Institute in Vermont, where he teaches courses in economics, globalization, the history and theory of development practice, and policy analysis and advocacy. He has also been a visiting professor at the University of Copenhagen. The case is based on work Nikoi did as a policy analyst and director of research at the Institute of Economic Affairs in Accra. He is the author of *Beyond the New Orthodoxy: Africa's Debt and Development Crisis in Retrospect* (Avebury 1996). Nikoi completed a BA in Economics and Philosophy at Vassar College and MA and PhD degrees in Economics from the University of Massachusetts.

Rosa Maria Olortegui works with community and educational organizations in Boston, focusing on capacity building, innovative outreach strategies, planning and monitoring systems and multilingual justice. She is a native of Peru and worked for several Peruvian NGOs, including during the period of the case study, 1999–2003. She completed her master's degree in the Program in Intercultural Service, Leadership and Management at the SIT Graduate Institute. The case study is based on her capstone paper, "*Tambo Grande Vale Mas Que Oro*/Tambo Grande Is Worth More Than Gold" (2006).

Gabrielle Watson is Manager for Campaign Evaluation and Learning within Oxfam's Policy and Campaigns Division. She is the coauthor (with David Cohen and Rosa de la Vega) of *Advocacy for Social Justice: A Global Action and Reflection Guide* (Kumarian 2001) and (with Jude Rand) of *Rights-Based Approaches: Learning Project* (Oxfam 2008). Gabrielle completed a MA in City Planning from the Massachusetts Institute of Technology.

Index

Also available from Kumarian Press

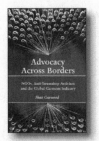

Advocacy for Social Justice
David Cohen, Rosa de la Vega, Gabrielle Watson

"Let's cut to the chase. This is a great book. If you are new to advocacy or you need a basic reference for your library, buy it. It would also be an excellent text for college-level international- or community-development students." — *Mary Boland, President,* Friends of the District

"An incredible guidebook that is packed with practical experiences, ideas and information for all activists, trainers, and development specialists. The authors have drawn on over 60 years of practical experience to provide the reader with the concepts and strategies necessary to support and strengthen advocacy. This book is well conceived and well organized, which makes it user friendly for all of us involved in the field of advocacy. It is a milestone."
—*M. Gloam Samdani Fakir, PhD,*
Global Partnership Program in Leadership and Management

Advocacy Across Borders
Shae Garwood

"In precise, meticulous prose and with an encyclopedic sweep of knowledge of the social movement, political economy and globalization literature Shae Garwood succeeds in bringing a measured observation of the antisweatshop movement and the challenges faced by it and by the workers for whose benefit it advocates. Garwood's work is a rare blend that commands the academic literature but has a 'feel' for the ways in which social movement activists and leaders attempt to construct solutions under constraint. The work adds the particular insights of movements-as-networks and the ways in which movement frames evolve over time. This is a book I can teach to my students; but it is also a book from which I, and we all, can learn."
— *Robert J.S. Ross, PhD,* Professor of Sociology, Clark University

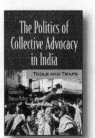

The Politics of Collective Advocacy in India
Nandini Deo and Duncan McDuie-Ra

"This is a long needed, finely researched, and admirably presented work of scholarship on civil society movements, advocacy networks, and social activism in India. Drawing from a variety of left and right movements—including Hindu Nationalist and women's movements, pro- and anti-dam movements, the book highlights the key determinants of social movement outcomes. It is required reading not just for scholars and researchers, but also those with any interest in the changing, emergent, future Indian society."
— *Arun Agrawal,* Professor and Associate Dean for Research,
School of Natural Resources & Environment, University of Michigan

Visit Kumarian Press at **www.kpbooks.com** or call **toll-free**
800.232.0223 for a complete catalog.

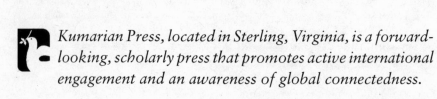 *Kumarian Press, located in Sterling, Virginia, is a forward-looking, scholarly press that promotes active international engagement and an awareness of global connectedness.*